The Hatherleigh Guide

to

Marriage and Family Therapy

The Hatherleigh Guides series

The Hatherleigh Guide

to

Marriage and Family Therapy

 Hatherleigh Press • New York

Gary Holmes, PhD, CRC
Emporia State University (Emporia, KS)

John Homlish, PhD
The Menninger Clinic (Topeka, KS)

Sharon E. Robinson Kurpius, PhD
Arizona State University (Tempe, AZ)

Marilyn J. Lahiff, RN, CRRN, CIRS, CCM
Private practice (Englewood, FL)

Chow S. Lam, PhD
Illinois Institute of Chicago (Chicago, IL)

Paul Leung, PhD, CRC
University of Illinois at Urbana-Champaign (Champaign, IL)

Carl Malmquist, MD
University of Minnesota (Minneapolis, MN)

Robert J. McAllister, PhD
Taylor Manor Hospital (Ellicott City, MD)

Richard A. McCormick, PhD
Cleveland VA Medical Center-Brecksville Division (Cleveland, OH)

Thomas Miller, PhD, ABPP
University of Kentucky College of Medicine (Lexington, KY)

Jane E. Myers, PhD, CRC, NCC, NCGC, LPC
University of North Carolina-Greensboro (Greensboro, NC)

Don A. Olson, PhD
Rehabilitation Institute of Chicago (Chicago, IL)

William Pollack, PhD
McLean Hospital (Belmont, MA)

Keith M. Robinson, MD
University of Pennsylvania (Philadelphia, PA)

Susan R. Sabelli, CRC, LRC
Assumption College (Worcester, MA)

Gerald R. Schneck, PhD, CRC-SAC, NCC
Mankato State University (Mankato, MN)

George Silberschatz, PhD
University of California-San Fransisco (San Fransisco, CA)

David W. Smart, PhD
Brigham Young University (Provo, UT)

Julie F. Smart, PhD, CRC, NCC
Utah State University (Logan, UT)

Joseph Stano, PhD, CRC, LRC, NCC
Springfield College (Springfield, MA)

Anthony Storr, FRCP
Green College (Oxford, England)

Hans Strupp, PhD
Vanderbilt University (Nashville, TN)

Retta C. Trautman, CCMHC, LPCC
Private practice (Toledo, OH)

Patricia Vohs, RN, CRRN, CRC, CIRS, CCM
Private practice (Warminster, PA)

William J. Weikel, PhD, CCMHC, NCC
Morehead State University (Morehead, KY)

Nona Leigh Wilson, PhD
South Dakota State University (Brookings, SD)

2531

92/57

The Hatherleigh Guide to Marriage and Family Therapy

Project Editor: Joya Lonsdale
Assistant Editors: Stacy Powell, Lori Soloman
Indexer: Angela Washington-Blair, PhD
Cover Designer: Gary Szczecina
Cover photo: Christopher Flach, PhD

Compiled under the auspices of the editorial boards of *Directions in Mental Health Counseling, Directions in Clinical Psychology,* and *Directions in Rehabilitation Counseling.*

Library of Congress Cataloging-in-Publication Data

The Hatherleigh guide to marriage and family therapy — 1st ed.
      p. cm. — (The Hatherleigh Guides ; 6)
      Includes bibliographical references and index.
      ISBN 1-886330-47-6 (alk. paper)
      1. Family psychotherapy. 2. Marital psychotherapy. I. Series: Hatherleigh
  guides to mental health practice series ; v. 6.
RC456.H38 1995 vol. 6
[RC488.5]
616.89 s — dc20
[616.89' 156]   96-21524
                                             CIP

First Edition: July 1996

10 9 8 7 6 5 4 3 2 1

About the photograph and the photographer

Versailles, 1995
A single father leads his children across uneven, shaky cobblestones, out of the shadows of divorce, toward the new beginning of a sunny, open clearing.

Christopher Flach, PhD, is a psychologist in private practice in southern California. An avid photographer for more than 20 years, his favorite subjects include people and nature. He has studied photography with Ansel Adams, and his work has been on display in public galleries and in private collections.

Table of Contents

Illustrations

Introduction

Marriage and family therapies have moved to the forefront of treatment modalities in recent years, taking their place alongside individual and group approaches. Why is this? In the 1950s, therapists began to appreciate the impact that the social context, including other family members, has on the identified patient. Treating a person individually and returning him or her to a family or living situation that might be fostering the problem, without attempting to modify the living situation, began to be viewed as ineffective in many cases. Methods were developed for including key family members — be they parents, siblings, or spouses — in the therapeutic process. However, the birth of marriage and family therapies was not an easy one. The systemic approach was seen as a challenge to more traditional modalities and turf wars ensued.

Forty years into the family therapy movement, the animosities have cooled. There is greater acceptance of the need for a variety of approaches to work with a vast array of client populations. By accepting that family members may be part of both the presenting problem and a solution to it, increased opportunities for intervention are created. At the same time, insurance companies are advocating for short-term, less expensive treatment. The mandate for new, quicker approaches grows. Therapy can progress more rapidly when there are more options for bringing about change. Family and marital therapies offer such possibilities.

With the effectiveness of marriage and family therapy confirmed in a number of recent studies,[1] therapists must be armed with up-to-date, practical information on this growing field. *The Hatherleigh Guide to Marriage and Family Therapy* provides mental health professionals with such information.

Although unflinching in their emphasis on the family and the couple, the authors do not exclude the adjunctive role of individual and group treatments.

This book provides a comprehensive approach to treating numerous diverse populations. The opening chapter by Dennis Bagarozzi is an appropriate beginning, with its emphasis on diagnosis. Bagarozzi skillfully demonstrates how various diagnostic instruments can aid us in understanding individual and family dynamics.

The chapters that follow address family and couple interventions, beginning with families affected by divorce and remarriage. Paul Ciborowski's chapter examines the needs children of divorcing couples have for treatment, particularly during the first 3 years after the separation. Children of divorce pass through specific emotional stages in response to the trauma of divorce; Ciborowski offers interventions for the therapist to consider at each one. My chapter discusses treatment prospects for one of the fastest growing divorce populations: single fathers with custody. These men lack role models and must have their experiences normalized. They often have to be taught how to cope with their children's feelings, how to negotiate the court system, and how to delegate household chores to the children. Florence Kaslow presents important information on treating the remarriage family. She emphasizes the necessity of completely healing from a divorce before considering a new marriage because the "ghosts" of a previous marriage can bind the newly forming one. If the client receives effective therapy during or after the divorce and allows ample time for the healing to occur, then the emotional, "psychic" divorce will be accomplished and the client will be more capable of investing emotionally in a new relationship.

The important role that family treatment can play with adolescent substance abuse is emphasized in William Quinn's chapter. He describes drug use as an attempt at separation from the parents; considering the whole family in the treatment context is the most important first step in combating the abuse. Gillian Walker discusses treatment implications for the devastating impact of HIV/AIDS on inner-city families. She highlights the broad array of issues that are addressed in family therapy, ranging from helping with feelings of shame, guilt, and fear, to building support systems and coping with the reaction of others.

Paula Bernstein and Leslie Gavin discuss therapy for the family after the death of a child. Strains after such a loss are inevitable and often require therapeutic intervention so the family can move on. Juanita Garcia and Jordan Kosberg focus on the other end of the spectrum, family care for the elderly. The increase in life expectancy and the changes in women's involvement in the workforce require potential caregivers to rethink the time they are able to commit to long-term care of the elderly. Strategies for interventions with family members are included.

The final four chapters focus on couples work, with the first two examining issues related to sexuality. Linda Dykes Talmadge and William Talmadge, in their discussion of low sexual desire, argue that treatment has been driven by techniques and has ignored the emotional component that often underpins this dysfunction. They take a holistic approach to relationships, contending that three "patients" — that is, the two partners and the marriage itself — must be treated so that the relationship as a whole can be healed. In their chapter on hyposexual desire, Gilles Trudel, Marc Ravart, and Sylvie Austin take a different approach by advocating for a cognitive-behavioral perspective. They suggest that therapists, in assessing clients with sexual desire disorders, should evaluate the clients' thinking styles; negative thoughts; and cognitive distortions they have about themselves, their partners, their relationships, and their own sexuality. Trudel and colleagues emphasize the quality of the sexual relationship as well as the quality of the couple's intimacy.

Paul Mullen presents his work on the clinical management of jealousy. He divides jealousy into two groups, normal and pathologic, and explains how to treat each type in individual and conjoint therapy. It is important to distinguish between the two. Those harboring pathologic jealousy have a great potential for becoming violent.

The final chapter, by Paula Schneider, addresses sexism in marital relationships. Gender identification imposes rigidity into the relationship in ways that couples struggling with intimacy are often unaware of. The key is to help couples struggle toward mutuality; that is, to help the man and the woman determine what they wish to do, feel, or represent to each other with a high level of concern and mutual respect. In order to obtain mutuality, it is necessary to balance individual self-interests with a commitment to nurturing the relationship.

This book provides beginning and advanced practitioners with a comprehensive guide to marriage and family therapy issues, strategies, and techniques — all of which are indispensable for treating the problems that frequently arise in daily practice. The balance between nuts-and-bolts, hands-on approaches and solid theory creates a compendium of vital information that will benefit therapists working in a variety of settings.

Geoffrey L. Greif, DSW
Baltimore, MD

Dr. Geoffrey L. Greif is Professor, School of Social Work, University of Maryland at Baltimore.

1.   For a recent review of these studies, see Pinsoff, W. M., & Wynne, L. C. (1995). The efficacy of marital and family therapy: An empirical overview, conclusions, and recommendations. *Journal of Marital and Family Therapy, 21,* 585-613.

1

Family Diagnostic Testing: A Neglected Area of Expertise for the Family Psychologist

Dennis A. Bagarozzi, PhD

Dr. Bagarozzi is Director, Human Resource Consultants; and a Licensed Psychologist and Marriage and Family Therapist who holds a private practice in Atlanta, GA and Athens, GA.

KEY POINTS

- The selection of appropriate tests, questionnaires, instruments, observation procedures, and interviewing formats to accurately assess marital and family dynamics is an essential part of the therapeutic process.

- Family diagnostic testing is used to provide specific information about a family problem constellation or dynamic. It should be used in conjunction with personality measures and assessments that highlight interpersonal dynamics and personal functioning.

- The author demonstrates various family diagnostic testing instruments by using the Smith family system. Among the instruments examined are the Family Environment Scale, Dyadic Adjustment Scale, and Spousal Inventory of Desired Changes and Relationship Barriers.

- Other diagnostic tools are presented, including behavioral task assignments, circular questioning, self-report questionnaires, and observational methods.

- A family diagnostic profile based on the test results is usually forwarded to the referring therapist. The theoretical orientation of the therapist and practical considerations will determine which scales and tests are used.

INTRODUCTION

The selection of appropriate tests, questionnaires, instruments, observation procedures, and interviewing formats for the purpose of accurate marital and family assessment is an essential part of the therapeutic process. Unfortunately, the selection of reliable and valid assessment instruments and procedures has, until recently, received little attention in the field (Bagarozzi, 1985). Too frequently, tests and procedures developed specifically for the diagnosis and assessment of individual personality traits or characteristics, intrapsychic processes, and personal functioning are used instead of reliable, valid instruments and interviewing procedures created specifically for marital and family assessment and evaluation. Personality measures and assessments designed to highlight intrapersonal dynamics and personal functioning can be used to complement measures of marital dynamics and family processes (Bagarozzi, 1985). However, they cannot and should not be used in place of reliable, valid instruments designed for the marital unit or family system.

Appropriate measures and procedures for assessing marital or family functioning can be selected in two ways. First, the therapist can choose from a number of instruments that are reliable and valid measures of some important theoretical construct or group of related constructs and are consistent with the practitioner's theoretical/clinical orientation. Theory essentially dictates which instruments or procedures the therapist selects.

For some therapists, however, theoretical purity may be of minor importance; these practitioners frequently focus on problems or issues. They tend to use instruments or interview formats that allow them to assess marital/family functioning as it relates to a particular presenting problem or constellation of problems. Practical considerations, therefore, offer a second way to guide instrument selection.

In my consulting practice, couples and families are frequently referred by therapists who request marital or family diagnostic testing. In most instances, the referring therapist asks for specific information about a particular family problem constellation or family dynamic. In a few instances, I have been asked to make assessments according to a particular school or theory of family functioning. However, this is the exception rather than the rule because therapists who adhere rigidly to only one theoretical view or epistemologic orientation usually prefer to do their own evaluations. For the most part, the instruments and procedures I use in family diagnostic testing are selected because they are helpful in shedding new light on the presenting problems and the attendant family dynamics. After testing has been completed, a family diagnostic profile report is written and forwarded to the referring therapist. Usually, some treatment suggestions are given in the final report.

I have selected the Smith family system (Mr. Smith, Mrs. Smith, and their children Michael and Ellen) to use as a basis for exploring the various testing instruments. An example of the Smith's family diagnostic profile report is presented in Table 1.1.

FINDINGS, INTERPRETATIONS, AND INTERVENTION RECOMMENDATIONS FOR THE SMITH FAMILY

Adjustment Scales:

The self-report measures of marital quality, adjustment, and satisfaction were similar for both Mr. and Mrs. Smith. (Please refer to Appendix 1A for detailed descriptions of each self-report questionnaire.) Both spouses perceive their marriage as severely distressed and in need of repair. Mr. Smith's score on the Locke-Wallace Marital Adjustment Test (Locke & Wallace, 1959) was 69, and Mrs. Smith's score on this measure was 65; both scores fall within the maladjusted range. Similarly, scores for both spouses on the Kansas Marital Adjustment Scale (Schumm et al., 1983) show them to be very dissatisfied with each other, their marriage, and their relationship in general. The four dimensions assessed by the Dyadic Adjust-

Table 1.1
FAMILY PROFILE REPORT

Family Members Present for Testing   *Presenting Complaint(s)*

John Smith (age 38):   Father   Stress
Mary Smith (age 36):   Mother   Depression
Michael Smith (age 15):   Son   Uncooperative behavior and
                                               some alcohol abuse
Ellen Smith (age 12):   Daughter   Nonsymptomatic

Assessment Instruments and Procedures Used

I.   **Questionnaires** *(See Appendix 1A)*
     1. Locke-Wallace Marital Adjustment Scale (Locke & Wallace, 1959)
     2. Dyadic Adjustment Scale (Spanier, 1976)
     3. Kansas Marital Adjustment Scale (Schumm et al., 1983)
     4. Spousal Inventory of Desired Changes and Relationship Barriers (SIDCARB) (Bagarozzi, 1983)
     5. Exchange Orientation Inventory (Murstein et al., 1977)
     6. Conflict Tactics Scales (Straus, 1979)
     7. Family Adaptability and Cohesion Scales III (FACES III) (Olson et al., (1985)
     8. Family Environment Scale (Moos & Moos, 1981)
     9. Personal Authority in the Family System Questionnaire (PAFS-Q) (Williamson et al., 1984)

II.   **Behavioral Tasks Assigned for Observational Study of Family** *(See Appendix 1B)*
     1. Marital problem identification task
     2. Family problem identification task
     3. Marital conflict resolution task
     4. Family conflict resolution task
     5. Family planning and execution task

III.   **Special Considerations: Interview Format** *(See Appendix 1C)*
     1. Circular questioning regarding identified patient's symptom
     2. Circular questioning format (Penn, 1982)

IV.   **Observational Measures** *(See Appendix 1D)*
     1. Beavers-Timberlawn Family Evaluation Scales (Lewis et al., 1976)
     2. Marital Interaction Coding System III (MICS III; Weiss & Summers, 1983)
     3. Relational Communication Coding System (Ericson & Rogers, 1973; Rogers, 1972)

V.   **Special Considerations: Individual Measures** *(See Appendix 1E)*
     1. Mrs. Smith: Depression Inventory (Beck & Beamesderfer, 1974)

ment Scale (dyadic satisfaction, dyadic cohesion, dyadic consensus, and affectional expression) (Spanier, 1976) are shown in Table 1.2.

DAS	Factor	Mr. Smith	Mrs. Smith
Table 1.2 DYADIC ADJUSTMENT SCALE SCORES FOR MR. AND MRS. SMITH			
I.	Satisfaction	29	25
II.	Cohesion	6	8
III.	Consensus	40	37
IV.	Affectional expression	5	4

The scores for both spouses, on all four factors, fall within the severely distressed range. As with the Locke-Wallace measure of marital adjustment, Mrs. Smith's scores were slightly lower than her husband's, but these differences should not be considered qualitatively or quantitatively significant because both spouses' scores fall within the same category.

From an intrapersonal standpoint, Mr. Smith's symptoms of stress and Mrs. Smith's depression can be interpreted as intrapsychic compromises they have developed to cope with certain negative and unacceptable affects (e.g., anger, rage, and resentment). However, from both a sociobehavioral exchange perspective and an interpersonal interactionist perspective, these symptoms can be seen as both spouses' attempts to create a more equitable system of exchanges in the marriage. In this sense, the symptoms are seen as coercive maneuvers designed to reduce one's own inputs and to force one's spouse to increase the inputs into the marriage. Such negative, reciprocal exchanges are typical of severely distressed relationships. Research by Weiss and Summers (1983) has shown that positive reciprocity and negative reciprocity (i.e., the exchange of rewards and punishments) are independent dimensions of marital interaction. Therefore, the therapist must attend to both dimensions in devising a viable treatment program. Typically, the therapist helps the couple devise more equitable exchanges and increases in positive reciprocity while helping the couple decrease negative exchanges, punishments, and the like.

Spousal Inventory of Desired Changes and Relationship Barriers:

A detailed analysis of the social exchange process can be seen in the Spousal Inventory of Desired Changes and Relationship Barriers (SIDCARB) scores for the Smiths (Table 1.3; Bagarozzi & Pollane, 1983). Factor I (satisfaction with the fairness of the social exchange process in the marriage and the degree of behavioral change desired in one's spouse in the 10 areas of marital exchange) shows that Mr. and Mrs. Smith desire a considerable amount of change in their exchange system. Mr. Smith's standard score of 75 is 2½ standard deviations above the mean. Both spouses perceive the conjugal exchange system to be grossly inequitable and both desire a considerable amount of change if the marriage is to be improved. The first aspect of factor I also measures commitment. Both Mr. and Mrs. Smith scored in the moderate range on this variable. However, the degree to which each spouse is committed to making the necessary changes required to move the relationship in a more positive direction can only be measured by each spouse's willingness to negotiate differences, to compromise, and to complete homework assignments. (Appendix 1B provides examples of three basic types of behavior task assignments.)

Mr. and Mrs. Smith differ significantly in their perception of the barriers to divorce and separation in their marriage. Mrs. Smith reports a fairly strong internal-psychological barrier (factor II), whereas Mr. Smith's perception of these barriers to relationship termination approximately reflect the mean. Scores for factor II were 72 for Mrs. Smith and 57 for Mr. Smith. External-circumstantial barriers to separation and divorce (factor III) were slightly lower for both spouses, but Mrs. Smith still perceives higher barriers to relationship termination than does her husband. These scores were 77 and 65, respectively.

Table 1.3		
SPOUSAL INVENTORY OF DESIRED CHANGES AND RELATIONSHIP BARRIERS (SIDCARB) SCORES FOR MR. AND MRS. SMITH		
SIDCARB Factor	*Mr. Smith*	*Mrs. Smith*
I.	75	82
II.	57	72
III.	65	77

These scores reveal much about the power dynamics in this marriage. Mr. Smith has much more power than Mrs. Smith by virtue of the "principle of least interest." The person who perceives fewer barriers to relationship termination has more power to influence the person who perceives more barriers; the person who perceives more barriers is more dependent on the relationship than the person who perceives fewer barriers. It is not surprising that Mrs. Smith presents with depression. She is caught in what has been termed a "nonvoluntary" marriage (Bagarozzi & Wodarski, 1977) and uses a meta-strategy to influence her husband — she has become symptomatic. This interpretation reflects family systems theory as well as the sociobehavioral interpersonal interpretation offered earlier. Mrs. Smith's depression would lift if she could learn to communicate her needs and desires more directly to her husband and if she could learn how to negotiate more satisfactory and equitable exchanges.

Exchange Orientation Inventory:

A sociobehavioral exchange and contingency contracting approach should be attempted with this couple at the outset of treatment because both Mr. and Mrs. Smith scored very high on the Exchange Orientation Inventory (Murstein, Cerreto, & MacDonald, 1977), indicating that they both perceive their marriage in terms of an exchange paradigm. However, because both spouses perceive such great discrepancies in their marital exchange system, should the therapist explore with each spouse his or her viewpoint concerning distributive justice, sharing, and exchange in marriage. More than likely, Mr. and Mrs. Smith are applying different rules for exchange, and this may be at the root of their conflict.

Conflict Tactics Scale:

The therapist may wish to consider additional issues in treating this family. For example, further individual testing of Mr. Smith using measures of personal and occupational stress might be helpful in pinpointing the sources of his stress. Relaxation training may also be used in conjunction with marital and family work to help Mr. Smith reduce external life stresses. This is important because all family members, including Mr. Smith, reported on the Conflict Tactics Scales (CTS) (Strauss, 1979) that Mr. Smith has a history of being physically violent with his wife and children. Although Mr. Smith has had fewer temper outbursts in the last few years and has not been violent with his spouse for over 3 years, the threat of physical violence hangs over this family. This is another reason for Mrs. Smith's depression and the increase in Mr. Smith's stress. In the family interview, Mr. Smith recognized that he had learned to alleviate personal stress by "blowing off steam" and by being physically assaultive. However, these cathartic releases gave him only temporary relief of his chronic stress. Mr. Smith acknowledged that he must learn more functional and more prosocial ways to reduce stress and resolve interpersonal conflicts. Scores on the CTS indicate that Mr. Smith used verbal aggression more frequently than verbal reasoning when communicating with Mrs. Smith and their children. Mrs. Smith used passive-aggressive tactics to express her anger (e.g., sulking, refusing to talk, and performing acts to spite Mr. Smith). Again, these responses are typically seen in spouses who perceive themselves to be powerless and confined to a nonvoluntary marriage.

Training in more functional and direct communication, problem solving, and conflict negotiation may help to reduce stress and depression in Mr. and Mrs. Smith. Additional social skills training in assertive responding may be taught to all family members at a later time in treatment, once Mr. Smith has learned to relax and to no longer use physical violence to resolve interpersonal conflict.

Family Adaptability and Cohesion Scales III:

Perceived and ideal versions of Family Adaptability and Cohesion Scales III (FACES III) (Olson, Portner, & Lavee, 1985) were administered to all family members. These findings are reported in Table 1.4.

Table 1.4 FAMILY ADAPTABILITY AND COHESION SCALES III (FACES III) SCORES FOR THE SMITH FAMILY		
Family Member	*Perceived*	*Ideal*
Mr. Smith	Chaotically disengaged EXTREME	Rigidly enmeshed EXTREME
Mrs. Smith	Chaotically connected MID-RANGE	Structurally enmeshed MID-RANGE
Michael (IP)	Chaotically disengaged EXTREME	Structurally separated BALANCED
Ellen	Chaotically disengaged EXTREME	Rigidly disengaged EXTREME

The interpretation of FACES III will begin with a discussion of Ellen's scores because they represent the type of responses typically given by the nonsymptomatic child in a two-child family system. She perceives herself as totally isolated from all members of her family system. For example, circular questioning (Penn, 1982) (see Appendix 1C) revealed that Ellen is the least concerned with her brother's substance abuse problems.

In Ellen's view, the system itself is chaotic—leaderless and lacking direction. Her isolation, however, is self-imposed and serves defensive and self-preserving functions. By withdrawing and being inconspicuous, she has avoided being used as a scapegoat by other family members, and she has been able to avoid (to a large degree) being triangulated into her parents' struggles.

Ellen's report that she had been used as a scapegoat by her parents whenever she tried to help her brother (the identified patient [IP]) or come to his aid is a pattern frequently seen in families in which scapegoating is the central mechanism used by parents. Typically, nonsymptomatic children have learned to protect themselves from becoming the target by fulfilling the role of "good" or "model" children. Often, these model children develop a strong sense of guilt for abandoning the IP. (This sense of guilt may be seen in a variety of ways later in life.) Withdrawal from family interaction as a self-preservation strategy in families with only two children also prevents the formation of sibling coalitions, which often allow siblings to band together for mutual support, comfort, and solace. Not surprisingly, Ellen and Michael show little evidence of a sibling coalition.

Also not surprising, Ellen does not wish to become closer to other family members because the effects of closeness are not predictable; she would rather be left alone. However, her need for order and structure cause her to go to the opposite extreme in her formulations of her ideal family. This flip-flop from one extreme to the other is an attempt to compensate for the perceived lack of structure and leadership by imposing a rigidly inflexible structure. Finally, inquiries into why Ellen does not desire more closeness with other family members in her "ideal" reveal that she would like to be "a little closer" to her mother but fears becoming too involved with her father.

Because of the incestuous threat such closeness often poses to young adolescent girls who are aware of deep rifts between the parents, Ellen's desire to remain fairly isolated is understandable.

Mrs. Smith's responses concerning her perception of the family's customary way of functioning places her in the mid-range category of functioning according to the Circumplex Model of Marital and Family Systems (CMMFS) (Russell & Olson, 1982), on which the FACES III measure is based. Her ideal for how the family should function also places her in the mid-range category. Interviews with Mrs. Smith reveal that she would like more closeness with both children, especially her son, and a more predictable (structured) relationship with her husband; however, she does not desire increased intimacy with him.

Mr. Smith perceives the family to be chaotically disengaged. He would like to have closer and more intimate relationships with all family members. Unlike his daughter, who also perceives the family and herself as chaotically disengaged, Mr. Smith's isolation does not appear to be self-imposed and defensive. He sees himself as responding to rebuffs from Mrs. Smith. He refers to her as "cold" and "distant." Ellen's uneasiness with the prospect of a closer relationship with her father becomes more understandable in the light of Mr. Smith's responses.

Finally, Michael (the IP) also sees the family as chaotically disengaged. His ideal family structure, however, is one in which family members are structurally separated. Michael's ideal family design is the only one that falls within the healthy balanced range of family functioning according to the CMMFS. This balanced ideal allows for a definite family structure having designated leaders, stable roles, firmly enforced rules, and parents who are mainly responsible for making family decisions. The degree of closeness or interpersonal intimacy in structurally separated family systems is one in which personal distance is preferred; clear ego boundaries, emotional separateness, and differentiation exist among family members;

and personal time alone and separate physical space are preferred to family cohesion. In structurally separated family
systems, the individual's orientation is focused outside the
family, and individual friendships are prized more than family group friendships. Family members pursue personal interests, and recreational activities tend to be engaged in individually or with persons outside the family system itself.

The perceived views of all family members fall within the
extreme, dysfunctional range of family structure and family
process. These views coincide with the perceptions of alcoholic families and chemically dependent family systems found
in a number of clinical research studies (Bonk, 1984; Killorin &
Olson, 1984; Olson & Killorin, 1985). The Smith family, therefore, can be seen as a typical family where substance abuse is
the presenting problem.

All members of the family, except Ellen, desire more closeness and intimacy. They agree that structure is a definite need.
A straightforward behavioral-structural approach designed
to create about a much-needed family structure is indicated.
Efforts should be made to have Mr. and Mrs. Smith turn to each
other for their intimacy needs rather than to their children.
Similarly, intervention should be geared for helping Michael
gain more closeness with his father. However, Mrs. Smith has
a tendency to want to bond with her children. Therefore, the
therapist might attempt to help Mrs. Smith develop appropriate levels of intimacy with her children and not to use them to
compensate for the emotional isolation she experiences in her
relationship with Mr. Smith. Essentially, building an appropriate parental coalition with definite boundaries between the
parental and sibling subsystems should be a primary structural goal of treatment.

Another concern is how to bring Ellen into the family
system in a way that does not place her in a scapegoat position
and does not pose a threat to her by pushing her too close to
Mr. Smith. Because Ellen does verbalize a desire to be closer to
Mrs. Smith, building appropriate mother-daughter cohesion
may be the best way to begin this process.

Family Environment Scale:

Figure 1.1 shows the Family Environment Scale (FES) (Moos & Moos, 1981) profile for the Smith family. The FES was developed to measure a family member's perception of the social-environmental characteristics of the family system. The social climate perspective assumes that family environments can be accurately measured and that these environments exert a directional influence on family members' behavior. There are ten 9-item subscales that assess three underlying dimensions of family life: the relationship dimension, the personal growth dimension, and the systems maintenance dimension.

The Relationship Dimension

The relationship dimension is comprised of three subscales: cohesion, expressiveness, and conflict. Research has shown that the cohesion dimension of the FES does not correlate very highly with cohesion as measured by FACES III. Because FACES III has much more empirical support for the validity of its cohesion dimension, FACES III should be considered the measure that most accurately assesses this construct. It has been suggested that the FES cohesion dimension actually represents a measure of "family support" (Russell, 1980; Russell & Olson, 1982). My interpretation of the Smith's profile uses the FES cohesion label as an indication of the supportive atmosphere of the Smith family and not as another measure of cohesion itself.

The Personal Growth Dimension

Depending on the nature of the presenting problem, the importance of the personal growth dimension for developing treatment goals and foci varies from family to family. This dimension consists of five variables: independence, achievement orientation, intellectual-cultural orientation, active-recreational orientation, and moral-religious orientation. In using this measure, it has been my experience that parents and children usually agree on the importance of these variables in family life. Parent-child conflicts develop, however, when the parents are dissatisfied with the degree to which their children's behavior is perceived to be consistent with the family's orientation about this dimension.

The Systems Maintenance Dimension

Moos and Moos (1981) have shown that the severity of alcoholic patients' psychiatric disturbance, as measured by the Minnesota Multiphasic Personality Inventory (MMPI), correlated significantly with all three subscales of the relationship dimension (cohesion, expressiveness, and conflict) and with only one item, independence, on the personal growth dimension. Similarly, only one of the two subscales of the third dimension, systems maintenance, correlated significantly with severity of psychiatric-illness scores of alcoholic patients as measured by the MMPI. This subscale was family organization. Family control, the second subscale of this third dimension, was not significantly related to psychopathology in alcoholic patients. Keeping these findings in mind, I have limited my discussion and suggestions for intervention to information gathered from the following FES items: cohesion, expressiveness, conflict, independence, and family organization.

Analysis of the Smith's Family Environment Scale:

In looking at the FES profile for the Smith family, it becomes apparent that all generally agree about the family's social-environmental climate. Essentially, all family members perceive interpersonal relationships as low in cohesion (i.e., interpersonal support). The men, however, tend to perceive the family as more expressive than the women. We may understand this discrepancy by noting that Mr. Smith is hot tempered and that Michael, the IP, has a history of acting out.

Given the past history of physical abuse by Mr. Smith, it is possible that Mrs. Smith and Ellen are much more reluctant to express their true feelings openly. Withdrawal by the women, as manifested by Mrs. Smith's depression and Ellen's self-

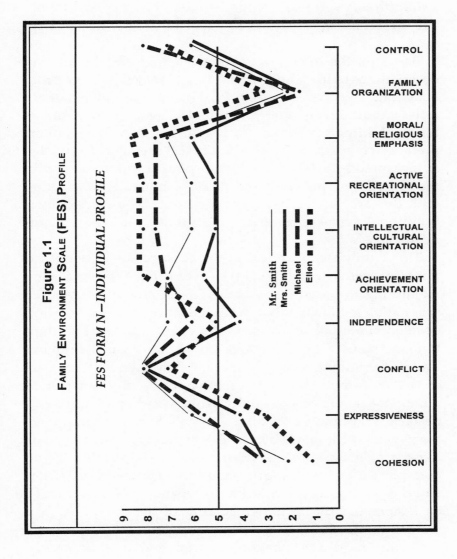

Figure 1.1
FAMILY ENVIRONMENT SCALE (FES) PROFILE

FES FORM N—INDIVIDUAL PROFILE

imposed isolation, may be a safer alternative to open disagreement with Mr. Smith. Evidence to support this interpretation was gathered during observations of the Smith family's attempts to solve problems, negotiate conflict, and plan a family project. (These observations are developed later in the chapter.)

Based on the interviews conducted with this family and observations of the family attempting to set goals, solve problems, and negotiate conflict, FES scores for independence reflect traditional gender role orientations and expectations for the children's behavior. Additional evidence for this interpretation comes from Mr. and Mrs. Smith's requests for change as measured by SIDCARB. Neither spouse desired changes in the areas of marital roles and tasks. Usually, dissatisfaction with this area of marital exchange indicates a conflict over traditional versus egalitarian role sharing and task assignments.

This family's subcultural, ethnic, and regional identifications — as well as religious values — should be considered when attempting to determine whether a traditional gender role orientation is functional or dysfunctional for the growth and development of all family members. The Smiths share a strong fundamentalist Christian value orientation, which supports traditional family gender behaviors. Any interventions perceived by family members as attempts by the therapist to modify the family's basic value orientation will probably be an obstacle to forming a trusting therapeutic relationship with the parents. Although Mrs. Smith's depression may be symptomatic of her dependent position vis-à-vis Mr. Smith, the therapist's attempts to create a more even power distribution and power-sharing relationship between the spouses should be tempered with an understanding of the Smith family's sociocultural, ethnic, regional, and religious values.

Finally, family members agree that the family is poorly organized and that interpersonal attempts to dominate, control, and manipulate others are characteristic of the family's mode of functioning. Both Michael and Ellen perceive higher levels of control than do Mr. and Mrs. Smith. This is not an unusual perception for teenagers. Adolescents frequently perceive their parents as trying to control them. However, it has been my experience that the combination of high conflict, low family organization, and high control is characteristic of chaotic and disorganized family systems. Again, this clinical observation is supported by all family members' perceptions of chaos and disorganization as reflected in their scores on FACES III. Obviously, a primary treatment goal is to help the family develop a viable organizational structure.

Personal Authority in the Family Systems Questionnaire:

The final self-report questionnaire selected for inclusion in the battery of tests given to the Smith family is the Personal Authority in the Family Systems Questionnaire (PAFS-Q) (Williamson, Bray, & Malone, 1984), which measures an adult's ability to function autonomously within the family of procreation while maintaining an age-appropriate and intimate adult relationship with the family of origin. Personal authority exists on a continuum. At the positive pole, personal authority is characterized by peerhood and relational equality with one's parents. The negative extreme is characterized by intergenerational intimidation. The PAFS-Q consists of eight fairly independent subscales: spousal intimacy, spousal fusion-individuation, nuclear family triangulation, intergenerational intimacy, intergenerational fusion-intimidation, intergenerational triangulation, intergenerational intimidation, and personal authority.

Spousal intimacy and spousal fusion-individuation can be used as validity checks for cohesion (FACES III) and support-cohesion (FES). For Mr. and Mrs. Smith, these scores were consistent with FACES III and FES findings. Both spouses perceived their relationship to be low on intimacy and low on fusion. They received similar scores for nuclear family triangulation and intergenerational triangulation. Neither spouse perceived himself or herself to be the focal point of such triangulations.

However, Mrs. Smith received very high scores for intergenerational intimacy, intergenerational fusion, and intergenerational intimidation, whereas Mr. Smith's scores on these three factors were only mid-range (i.e., average). Mr. Smith evidenced a much higher level of personal authority than did Mrs. Smith. Essentially, Mr. Smith appears to have achieved much more autonomy, independence, and personal authority than has Mrs. Smith. Mrs. Smith, on the other hand, showed many of the characteristics of one who has not separated successfully from the family of origin. She was docile, dependent, and underassertive. Under such conditions, the spouse who has separated unsuccessfully from the family of origin frequently transfers dependency to the mate and attempts to recreate the enmeshed (and sometimes symbiotic) union with the spouse after marriage. When this attempt fails, the spouse begins to feel abandoned, isolated, alone, alienated, and depressed. This spouse often turns to one of the children for closeness and intimacy. Such parent-child closeness is often found in families where incest, drug abuse, or alcoholism is present. Mrs. Smith turned to Michael. One way of understanding Michael's acting out and alcohol abuse is to view it as his attempt to separate and distance himself from Mrs. Smith. Taking this into consideration, two therapeutic goals should be considered: (a) to help Michael achieve separation-individuation in a more appropriate, socially acceptable manner, and (b) to help Mrs. Smith establish a more satisfying and appropriately intimate relationship with her husband. This will also help reduce Ellen's anxiety concerning her fears about closeness to her father.

SUMMARY OF FAMILY OBSERVATIONS

As a couple, Mr. and Mrs. Smith had no difficulty identifying problems in their marriage. In fact, they were able to do this without the aid of SIDCARB. Similarly, the Smith family had no difficulty identifying family problems that needed attention. However, the Smiths were unable to resolve the marital difficulty selected for the purpose of this assessment. Analysis of the Smiths' videotaped conflict resolution attempts showed they used punishments, coercion, and negative reinforcements much more frequently than positive reinforcements as defined by the Marital Interaction Coding System III (MICS III) (Weiss & Summers, 1983; Appendix 1D). According to the Relational Communication Coding System (RCCS) (Ericson & Rogers, 1973; Rogers, 1972; Appendix 1D), the Smiths had an interactive pattern of rigid complementarity, with Mr. Smith in the dominant position. The couple was deadlocked in a "zero sum" power struggle, with Mr. Smith in control. Mrs. Smith used passive-aggressive and manipulative strategies to gain leverage in the marriage.

Training in functional communication and "nonzero sum" conflict negotiation strategies would help Mr. and Mrs. Smith disrupt their rigid, homeostatic pattern. This straightforward structural-behavioral approach should be attempted initially. It could be used to help build the much-needed parental coalition. If this can be done, Mr. and Mrs. Smith can begin to work together as a team to bring their son's behavior under control.

The Beavers-Timberlawn Family Evaluation Scales:

Observations of the entire family's attempt to identify a problem and devise a solution on which all family members can agree proved to be a futile exercise for the Smith family. The Beavers-Timberlawn Family Evaluation Scales (BTFES) (Lewis, Beavers, Gossett, & Phillips, 1976; Appendix 1D) were used to rate the family's performance. Thirteen of the 14 BTFE scales were used in the analysis, which is reported below.

Overt Power
The Smith family was characterized as having moderate-marked dominance. Mr. Smith had the most overt power. Interventions designed to move the family toward a more fair (but not necessarily a more egalitarian) power-sharing structure in which Mr. Smith is not always in the dominant position are recommended.

Parental Coalition

The Smith family had a weak parental coalition. The parental subsystem must be strengthened.

Closeness

Again, this is was not a cohesive and supportive family system, but was characterized by isolation and distancing. Interventions should be developed that help bring about appropriate levels of closeness and separateness. Helping family members negotiate and develop mutually satisfying levels of interpersonal closeness and distance may prove a challenge for the therapist. (I do not believe that this will occur easily or swiftly.)

Goal-Directed Negotiation

This family was "poorly efficient" in this area. Training in family "nonzero sum" conflict negotiation and functional communication should also be attempted with the entire family.

Clarity of Expression

This family's ability to express itself clearly and honestly was in the vaguely clear and hidden range. Communication training may be helpful.

Responsibility for One's Own Actions

Much scapegoating occurred in the Smith family. The family was characterized by a considerable amount of speaking for others, mind reading, and projection. Michael was the only person who took responsibility for his own actions; he was highly identified with his "bad child" or "black sheep" role in the family. One way to break this pattern may be to use intervention techniques that "spread the symptoms."

Invasiveness

There was much mind reading and speaking for others in this family. Thus, the Smith family scored highly on interpersonal invasions. Structured communication training should reduce this considerably.

Permeability of Family Members

This dimension is an assessment of each family member's openness to other family members' statements, thoughts, and ideas. The Smith family was evaluated as unreceptive. Communication skills training may be helpful here as well.

Range of Feelings

The range of feelings in the Smith family was highly restricted; that is, the family members masked and hid their true emotions. The degree to which trust can be developed among family members and the degree to which family members can learn not to fear Mr. Smith will depend on how successful intervention is in teaching Mr. Smith more socially acceptable and less violent ways to express his negative emotions. To the extent that he can do this, family members may feel more secure in expressing their true feelings.

Mood and Tone

The overall affect in this family was depressed. The Smiths showed a lack of warmth, humor, and optimism.

Unresolvable Conflicts

The Smiths had numerous severe and unresolvable conflicts, which had existed for some time. A considerable amount of impairment of family functioning resulted. If the family is able to achieve success in resolving even minor conflicts, enough positive reinforcement to provide an incentive may be generated to tackle larger problems.

Empathy

All family members genuinely tried to be empathic. However, they failed to maintain empathy for any sustained period of time. In Mrs. Smith's case, what first seemed to be empathy for her son actually was identification with him. Mrs. Smith also tended to project her feelings and ideas onto both children. Again, if the child is silent, as Ellen was, Mrs. Smith's projections may go undetected, and she may appear to be truly empathic. Teaching both children to use functional communication skills may enable them to verbalize their differing opinions and perceptions, thus reducing Mrs. Smith's tendency to accept her projections as valid indicators of what her children think and feel.

Global Health-Pathology

The Smith family rated 8 on this 10-point Likert-type scale used to rate overall family pathology. (A score of 8 suggests a relatively high level of pathology.)

ANALYSIS

The Smith family is severely distressed and borderline dysfunctional. Intensive family therapy appears to be the treatment of choice. However, if the parents are unable to work cooperatively as a team and are unsuccessful in bringing their son's uncooperative behavior and alcohol use under control, professional placement for him should be considered. Although numerous underlying problems in the marital relationship require attention, once the presenting problem is resolved, Mr. Smith appears to lack sufficient motivation to improve his marriage. Mrs. Smith, on the other hand, appears to be more ready to tackle these marital difficulties.

A straightforward, social skills training, structural-behavioral approach appears to be the most appropriate intervention strategy to adopt initially. If the structural behavioral route proves to be ineffective, a strategic approach may be used later in therapy.

Based on Mrs. Smith's responses on the Beck Depression Inventory (Appendix 1E), her depression is considered moderate. Successful marital/family therapy should cause Mrs. Smith's depression to abate. But if her depression worsens, referral for antidepressant medication should be considered. If Mr. Smith is unwilling to work on the marital relationship once the presenting problem is resolved, individual treatment for Mrs. Smith may be appropriate.

In true systemic fashion, Michael's presenting problems are symptomatic of a dysfunctional parental relationship. However, his symptoms also might have assumed an existence of their own — an existence independent of their original meaning. These symptoms may now be maintained by forces outside the family system, and Michael may have become substance dependent. The therapist should investigate to what extent this has occurred and whether other treatments should be used to complement family work.

CONCLUSION

As can be seen from this sample family profile report, specific recommendations for treatment are made to the referring clinician. These recommendations are based on information gathered throughout the testing process. Traditionally, clinical psychologists have used their expertise in diagnostic testing to make recommendations to referring therapists in their psychotherapeutic work with individual clients. Similarly, intelligence and abilities tests by school psychologists have been valuable sources of information for teachers and guidance counselors in their work with children. In keeping with this tradition, family psychologists can make a much-needed contribution to the fields of family life education and marital and family therapy by providing marital and family diagnostic testing for other practitioners who work with couples and families but who have not been trained in marital and family diagnosis, assessment, and evaluation.

REFERENCES

Bagarozzi, D. A. (1983). Methodological developments in measuring social exchange perceptions in marital dyads (SIDCARB): A new tool for clinical intervention. In D. A. Bagarozzi, A. P. Jurich, & R. W. Jackson (Eds.), *New perspectives in marital and family therapy: Issues in theory, research and practice.* New York: Human Sciences Press.

Bagarozzi, D. A. (1985). Dimensions of family evaluation. In L. L'Abate (Ed.), *The handbook of family psychology and therapy* (Vol. 2, pp. 989–1005). Homewood, IL: Dorsey Press.

Bagarozzi, D. A., & Pollane, L. (1983). A replication and validization of the Spousal Inventory of Desired Changes and Relationship Barriers (SIDCARB): Elaborations on diagnostic and clinical utilization. *Journal of Sex and Marital Therapy, 9,* 303–315.

Bagarozzi, D. A., & Wodarski, J. S. (1977). A social exchange typology of conjugal relationships and conflict development. *Journal of Marriage and Family Counseling, 3,* 53–61.

Beck, A. T., & Beamesderfer, A. (1974). Assessment of depression: The depression inventory. In P. Pechot (Ed.), *Psychological measurement in psychopharmacology: Modern problems in pharmacopsychiatry* (Vol. 7, pp. 469–470). Basel, Switzerland: Karger.

Bonk, J. (1984). *Perceptions of psychodynamics during a transitional period as reported by families affected by alcoholism.* Unpublished doctoral dissertation, University of Arizona, Tucson.

Ericson, P. M., & Rogers, L. E. (1973). New procedures of analyzing relational communication. *Family Process, 12,* 244–267.

Killorin, E., & Olson, D. H. (1984). The chaotic flippers in treatment. In E. Kaufman (Ed.), *Power to change: Family case studies in the treatment of alcoholism* (pp. 116-128). New York: Gardner Press.

Lewis, J. M., Beavers, W. R., Gossett, J. T., & Phillips, V. A. (1976). *No single thread: Psychological health in family systems.* New York: Brunner/Mazel.

Locke, H. J., & Wallace, K. M. (1959). Short marital adjustment and prediction tests: Their reliability and validity. *Marriage and Family Living, 21,* 251–255.

Moos, R. H., & Moos, B. S. (1981). *Family environment scale manual.* Palo Alto, CA: Consulting Psychologist Press.

Murstein, B. R., Cerreto, M., & MacDonald, M. (1977). A theory and investigation of the effect of exchange-orientation on marriage and friendship. *Journal of Marriage and the Family, 39,* 543–548.

Olson, D. H., & Killorin, E. (1985). *Chemically dependent families and the circumplex model.* Unpublished manuscript, Family Social Sciences, University of Minnesota, St. Paul.

Olson, D. H., Portner, J., & Lavee, Y. (1985). *FACES III.* St. Paul: University of Minnesota, Family Social Sciences.

Penn, P. (1982). Circular questioning. *Family Process, 21,* 267–280.

Rogers, L. E. (1972). *Dyadic systems and transactional communication in a family context.* Unpublished doctoral dissertation, Michigan State University, East Lansing.

Russell, C. S. (1980). A methodological study of family cohesion and adaptability. *Journal of Marital and Family Therapy, 6,* 459–470.

Russell, C. S., & Olson, D. H. (1982). Circumplex model: Review of empirical support and elaboration of therapeutic process. In D. A. Bagarozzi, A. Jackson, & A. P. Jurich (Eds.), *Marital and family therapy: New perspectives in theory, research, and practice* (p. 25-47). New York: Human Sciences Press.

Schumm, W. R., Milliken, G. A., Poresky, R. H., Bollman, S. R., & Jurich, A. P. (1983). Issues in measuring marital satisfaction in survey research. *International Journal of Sociology of the Family, 13,* 129–143.

Spanier, G. (1976). Measuring dyadic adjustment: New scales for assessing the quality of marriage and similar dyads. *Journal of Marriage and the Family, 38,* 15–30.

Strauss, M. A. (1979). Measuring intrafamily conflict and violence: The Conflict Tactics Scales (CTS). *Journal of Marriage and the Family, 41,* 75–88.

Weiss, R. L., & Summers, K. J. (1983). Marital interaction coding system III. In E. E. Felsinger (Ed.), *Marriage and family assessment: A sourcebook for family therapy* (pp. 85-115). Beverly Hills, CA: Sage.

Williamson, D., Bray, J., & Malone, P. (1984). Personal authority in the family system: Development of a questionnaire to measure personal authority in intergenerational family processes. *Journal of Marital and Family Therapy, 10,* 167–178.

Appendix 1A
SELF-REPORT QUESTIONNAIRES

- *Locke-Wallace Marital Adjustment Test (LWMAT)*
  The LWMAT is a 15-item questionnaire that assesses levels of marital satisfaction, adjustment, and accommodation of spouses in their marital relationships. Scoring of items is weighted and ranges from 2–158. The mean (x) score for well-adjusted and satisfied spouses is 135.9. The mean (x) score for dissatisfied and maladjusted spouses is 71.7.

- *Dyadic Adjustment Scale (DAS)*
  The DAS is a 32-item questionnaire that assesses the quality of dyadic relationships. The mean score for adjusted couples is 114.8. The mean score for maladjusted couples is 70.7. The range is 0–151.

- *Kansas Marital Adjustment Scale (KMAS)*
  KMAS is a 3-item questionnaire that measures marital satisfaction. The KMAS controls for social desirability of responses.

- *Spousal Inventory of Desired Changes and Relationship Barriers (SIDCARB)*
  SIDCARB is a 24-item Likert-style questionnaire. The behavior and attitudes of spouses are assessed along three factor dimensions: (a) desired level of behavior change in one's spouse and satisfaction with one's marriage, (b) willingness to separate and divorce one's spouse, and (c) barriers to separation and divorce. Each factor has a standard score of 50 and a standard deviation of 10.

- *Exchange Orientation Inventory (EOI)*
  The EOI contains 44 items scored on a 5-point Likert scale. It assesses the degree to which spouses conceptualize their relationship according to the norms of equitable distribution of resources and reciprocity. The higher one's score, the higher one's exchange orientation is thought to be.

Appendix 1A
SELF-REPORT QUESTIONNAIRES
(CONTINUED)

• *Conflict Tactics Scale (CTS)*
This scale measures an individual's responses to situations within the family that often produce conflict. There are 17 Likert-like items, and subjects are asked to indicate the number of times that they have resorted to using each particular conflict resolution strategy within the last 12 months. The CTS can be administered as a questionnaire or as part of a clinical interview. There are three factor-derived subscales: reasoning, verbal aggression, and physical violence. Although scores are weighted for each of the three subscales, the scoring is less important than determining to what extent physical violence is used within a particular family system.

• *Family Adaptability and Cohesion Scales III (FACES III)*
FACES III is a self-report instrument that measures two dimensions of family process: adaptability and cohesion. Twenty items, 10 for adaptability and 10 for cohesion, yield scores that range from 10–50 for each subscale. These scores are plotted on a circumplex model yielding 16 relationship types.

• *Family Environment Scale (FES)*
The FES is a 90-item self-report scale that measures the social environments of families. This atheoretical measure is comprised of 10 subscales. Scores for each subscale range from 0–9.

• *Personal Authority in the Family System Questionnaire (PAFS-Q)*
The PAFS-Q is a lengthy 132-item questionnaire yielding eight scores: one score for each of the eight subscales (spousal intimacy, spousal fusion/individuation, nuclear family triangulation, intergenerational intimacy, intergenerational fusion/individuation, intergenerational triangulation, intergenerational intimidation, and personal authority). Ranges of scores and means for each score differ according to the particular subscale.

Appendix 1B
BEHAVIORAL TASK ASSIGNMENTS

A multitude of stimulus tasks can be assigned to couples and families so that the therapist can observe marital and family interaction for purposes of diagnostic assessment and evaluation. Depending on the information the therapist wishes to gather, stimulus tasks can be broken down into three basic types:

- *Problem identification assignment*

  This task can be a simple assignment given to the couple or family that asks the members to identify a problem all participants agree needs resolution. The interaction among family members allows the therapist to assess the system's ability to identify a problem in a way that makes resolution possible and gives valuable information about the couple or family processes that are getting in the way of problem identification. The cause of the problem can come from outside the family system (e.g., the recent unemployment of a spouse) or within the system itself (e.g., husband and wife continually argue about finances).

- *Conflict resolution assignment*

  This task assignment can be accomplished in two ways. First, if, during the problem identification assignment, the couple/family pinpoints an interpersonal conflict that comes from within the family system itself, the members of the system can be instructed to resolve the interpersonal conflict in a way that is satisfactory for all involved parties. Second, if standardized instruments have been given to the family members, the therapist can ask the couple or family to resolve a particular problem or interpersonal conflict identified as a concern by the couple, parents, identified patient, or children. The ability of the family system to solve the problem or resolve the conflict is assessed. Any structural or process dynamics that hamper successful problem solving or conflict negotiation are identified.

Appendix 1B
BEHAVIORAL TASK ASSIGNMENTS
(CONTINUED)

• *Family planning and task execution*
Many couples and families seeking therapy are unable to plan an activity and carry it out with any measure of success. Identifying an agreed-on goal and developing the leadership-followship patterns necessary to achieve the goal require some type of hierarchical arrangement. The task can be a simple directive to the family such as: "Plan an activity that everyone will enjoy and that you will be able to complete or accomplish before our next session." How well the family does with this task gives the therapist some indication of the degree to which hierarchical arrangements are successful, flexible, and functional. It also gives the therapist some indication about how responsive the couple or family will be to performing homework assignments given in therapy.

Appendix 1C
CIRCULAR QUESTIONING

Circular questioning (Penn, 1982) is a technique developed by the Milan group under the leadership of Selvini-Palazzoli. This technique is designed to give the therapist valuable information about how the family functions as a system and how the unique interactions of family members maintain the family's problem, symptom, and so on. The focus of the interview is the family's here-and-now (current problem). This is an extremely difficult technique to master because it requires translating all statements made by family members into relationship dynamics; therefore, the therapist must have a thorough understanding of family-systems theory.

A basic assumption about this approach is that the presenting problem is paradoxically maintained by the family members' attempts to resolve it! The therapist asks questions formulated to assess faulty hierarchical power arrangements, coalitions, triangular patterns, and dysfunctional behavioral sequences in which the problem or symptom is thought to be encased. The therapist uses the information gathered from the family to formulate hypotheses about the family's dysfunctional style and to devise ritual prescriptions or paradoxical methods to free the family from its dysfunctional cycle.

Appendix 1D
OBSERVATIONAL MEASURES

* *Beavers-Timberlawn Family Evaluation Scales (BTFES)*
These scales consist of seven subscales (14 items) that are loosely derived from systems theory. A considerable amount of supervised training is required to use this observational rating scale. Each subscale is a Likert-type scale that has nine separate anchoring points (e.g., 1, 1.5, 2, 2.5, 3, 3.5, 4, 4.5, 5). Variables assessed include family structure, family mythology, goal-directed negotiation, autonomy, family affect, and global family health-pathology.

* *Marital Interaction Coding System (MICS)*
The MICS is a behavioral observation coding system that requires a considerable amount of training and supervision before one can competently use it. The latest version has 32 separate codes that cover verbal and nonverbal realms of marital interaction. Speaker and listener are both coded in 30-second units. This observational coding system is suited for research settings but is impractical for everyday clinical practice.

* *Relational Communication Coding System (RCCS)*
The RCCS is based on systems theory and the work of Gregory Bateson and colleagues (Ericson & Rogers, 1973). It was designed to measure the control dimension of ongoing messages in dyadic relationships. This is a highly sophisticated coding system that requires extensive training to use and interpret. Although there is a considerable body of empirical support for this procedure's reliability and validity, it is so time-consuming that its use as a clinical tool is questionable. However, once a person is trained in this coding procedure, he or she should be able to make a fairly good estimate of the control pattern that characterizes a particular dyad. Translating these observations into clinical strategies, however, requires a considerable degree of clinical competence and experience.

Appendix 1E
BECK DEPRESSION INVENTORY

This 21-item questionnaire was developed by Aaron Beck to assess the severity of the respondent's depression. There are no arbitrary cutoff scores because any cutoff points are determined by the characteristics of the sample under consideration. Nevertheless, Beck offers the following scores as guidelines.

Range 0–63

Normal range	=	0–9
Mild depression	=	10–15
Mild/Moderate	=	16–19
Moderate/Severe	=	20–29
Severe depression	=	30–63

Source: Beck, A. T., & Beamesderfer, A. (1974). Assessment of depression: The depression inventory. In P. Pechot (Ed.), *Psychological measurement in psychopharmacology: Modern problems in pharmacopsychiatry* (Vol. 7, pp. 469-470). Basel, Switzerland: Karger.

2

Counseling Children of Divorce

Paul J. Ciborowski, PhD

Dr. Ciborowski is Associate Professor of Counseling, Long Island University, C. W. Post Campus, Brookville, NY, and Chair of the Brookhaven [NY] Youth Board.

KEY POINTS

- More than 12 million children in the United States have been affected by the experience of divorce. Children have various negative reactions to divorce, including absenteeism from school, unwanted pregnancies, substance abuse, academic and social underachievement, depression, and suicide.

- The first 3 years after divorce are the most critical for children; during this period, behavioral problems may develop. A "delayed reaction" to divorce is also possible, especially in boys.

- The predominant feeling that most children of divorce experience is the desire to reunite their parents.

- In 90% of divorces, the mother is granted custody. It is important to involve older children in custody decisions. Therapists should be aware of changes in child custody laws.

- Kübler-Ross's four-stage model for coping with difficult emotional events may be applied to children's experiences of divorce: denial, anger and guilt, depression, and acceptance. This four-stage cycle can take 2–3 years to complete—or even longer if the parents remarry.

- Each psychological stage of reaction and its appropriate therapeutic intervention are examined. Counseling strategies are summarized.

INTRODUCTION

Young people experience many crises. In the United States, a crisis that confronts many children is divorce; more than 12 million children have experienced divorce in their families (Statistical Abstracts, 1993) and show its strains. Being the children of a divorcing couple may have many side effects, including increased absenteeism from school, running away from home, drug abuse, unwanted pregnancies, childhood depression, underachievement in school, and suicidal thoughts (Ciborowski, 1984; Doherty & Needle, 1991; Neighbors, Forehand, & Armistead, 1992; Wallerstein & Johnson, 1990).

The past decade has produced an abundance of literature concerning the effects of divorce on children. This chapter summarizes several of the latest findings. For more detailed information, the reader may consult the references and suggested reading list at the end of the chapter.

In my experience as a practicing therapist, divorce produces no winners. However, if there are any losers, they are the children. The parents may be overly concerned about their own interpersonal difficulties and divorce negotiations, thereby forgetting that their children are active participants in the divorce. However, the concern for children and their welfare becomes important when behavioral problems develop. Although young people are full participants in a divorce, they are rarely consulted or given adequate warning of what to expect.

The goals of this chapter are to provide mental health professionals with relevant psychological information concerning children of divorce, describe typical feelings experienced by these children, and discuss counseling techniques that may be effective in helping youngsters process their feelings.

CRITICAL YEARS FOR CHILDREN

The first 3 years after a divorce are the most critical for children

(Francke, 1983). During this time, behavioral problems may become evident. For example, some young people may experience a significant drop in school grades. In one such instance, a student achieved solid marks through the 8th grade and underachieved through 9th and 10th grades while his parents were getting a divorce and battling over custody. Only in the 11th grade did he start to put his academic and emotional life together (Ciborowski, 1988).

Many other problems experienced by children today (e.g., drug use, suicide attempts, and dropping out of school) start with parental separation and divorce. Suicide attempts among young people (ages 15–24), for example, have increased dramatically in the past two decades (Brody, 1992). During this same period, the number of children in divorced households more than tripled (Baird & Sporakowski, 1992). The loss of a parent—so typical in divorce—was a strong determinant in many suicide attempts by adolescents (Ciborowski, 1984).

Some groups of children do not show immediate changes after a divorce. However, for these youngsters, a "sleeper effect" is often at work; 2 or 3 years later, well within the "3-year rule," a delayed reaction may appear. In working with groups of boys, for example, I have frequently noted this effect (Ciborowski, 1984). After initial denial to the therapist that "nothing's changed," adjustment difficulties are acknowledged. They may be caused by financial pressures on the single-parent family or the personal and social problems created by a move to a different neighborhood, a new school, or the effort to find new friends. Boys seem to have a higher incidence of the "sleeper effect" than girls (Wallerstein & Kelly, 1980).

WHO IS THE CUSTODIAL PARENT?

Although fathers have become more active in seeking custody of their children, statistics show that 90% of the time, the mother becomes the custodial parent (Ciborowski, 1988). Mental health professionals are more likely to be working with a single-parent family headed by a mother. There may or may not be active paternal involvement.

The decision concerning which parent should be granted custody of the children after a divorce always has been a reflection of cultural and historical attitudes. So far in the 1990s, the mother is usually awarded child custody in the majority of cases. Yet this has not always been so. Until the early 1900s, the father was the custodian of choice for most children. Men, in general, were assumed to be the more stable parent. This belief reflected the strong "pro-male" bias of 19th-century jurisprudence (Chesler, 1985). However, this has changed with an enhanced judicial appreciation of the role of the mother in child development.

Judges generally examine each parent to determine which one is more capable of supporting and raising a child. More often, in recent decisions, judges are favoring joint custody arrangements. Research findings support this trend. Maccoby, Buchanan, Mnookin, and Dornbusch (1993) indicated that even after controlling for education, income, and conflict, both boys and girls function better in dual residences. (For an explanation of custody terms, see the glossary in Table 2.1.) Therapists must keep abreast of the fast-moving decisions being made in the legal arena (Lowery & Settle, 1985).

Custody cases should involve older children. Judges may grant children standing in court so that their rights are represented in custody hearings. The "Gregory K" case in Florida set a new precedent. Gregory, although underage, was permitted to petition the court to be allowed to live with his foster parents. In granting the petition, the court overruled the request of his natural mother (Rohter, 1992). Therapists should be extremely sensitive to this issue: the rights of the child must be heard. As pro-child advocates, therapists have no other choice (Pearson & Thoenness, 1990).

CHILDREN'S FEELINGS AFTER A DIVORCE

Mike, age 15, was frequently absent from school. His grades

during the first half of the year dropped 10–15 points in every major subject. Each teacher had similar comments on his report card: "inattentive," "does not do homework," and "is not prepared." Also, Mike had been involved in a number of fights with classmates and had been insubordinate to teachers and administrators.

Although Mike was in need of counseling, the therapist may not necessarily relate Mike's problems to divorce. Mike may appear no different from other teenagers with adjustment problems in school; however, the divorce is a wrenching trauma that sets him apart. The impact of his parents' divorce and the time needed for readjustment are both painful and disruptive. Mike's academic record and disruptive school behavior only hint at the powerful undercurrents at work.

PSYCHOLOGICAL STAGES

As witnesses to their parents' divorce, children may experience many conflicting feelings. In addition to the initial shock and surprise are denial, grief, fear, guilt, and anger. To better understand these feelings, it is useful to examine a model originally designed for use with terminally ill cancer patients. Developed by Dr. Elisabeth Kübler-Ross (1974), the stages model places feelings about death within an understandable pattern.

Adapting this model for the child of divorce, the first "feeling" stage is one of *denial*. The child does not want to, or simply cannot, accept the reality that a break-up is occurring.

The second stage involves feelings of *anger, resentment,* or *guilt*. Acting-out behavior is fairly common during this stage.

The third stage is *depression*, which usually occurs when the young person realizes that he or she cannot change the situation or immediately reunite his or her parents.

The final stage is *acceptance*. This stage comes about only gradually and occurs when a child realizes certain things cannot be changed and he or she perceives some positive

---

Table 2.1
GLOSSARY OF CUSTODY TERMS

Alimony/Maintenance: Money paid by one ex-spouse to the other for support after a divorce. The payment of alimony lasts for a specific time or until the ex-spouse remarries. It is not automatic.

Child support: Payments made by an absent parent to the custodial parent to pay for a child's expenses, such as education, trips, and medical bills. Child support continues until the child marries, finds full-time employment, reaches a certain age, or finishes college.

Contested divorce: When one or the other parent does not want the divorce or cannot agree on a property settlement, child support, or custody. The judge rules in such cases.

Custodial parent: The parent with whom the minor children legally live, as agreed to in the divorce decree.

Custody:

Sole custody—All decisions are made by the custodial parent; the noncustodial parent can have visitation rights.

Joint physical custody—Both parents share responsibility for their children and alternate custody for periods of time. . . sometimes called alternate or divided custody.

Joint legal custody—Both parents have equal input into decisions that affect children even if the children live with one parent. This includes decisions about religion and schooling.

Split custody — Each parent receives a child (or some of the children) and makes all decisions about the child(ren) in his or her care.

Equitable (Fair) distribution of property: Marriage is viewed as a partnership, and judges can divide it without regarding who holds the legal title to property, pension funds, or medical benefits.

Legal separation: The couple no longer lives together and has formalized the terms of living apart, but the marriage is not ended legally. This is usually the first step to a divorce.

Uncontested divorce: The couple has agreed to the divorce and go to court already in agreement. A mediator may be needed for an uncontested divorce to be successful.

Visitation rights: The agreed-on visits by the children to the noncustodial parent, which are subject to change.

aspects to the divorce (e.g., no more parental fighting at home or the fact that there can still be a relationship with both parents despite the divorce (Sonnenshein-Schneider & Baird, 1980). The stages may evolve over 2 or 3 years, and if there are other subsequent life-transition events (such as a parental remarriage), the cycle may be repeated.

Children are obviously more than observers during a parental divorce. Because they are, in fact, full participants, they should be told the truth by both parents. Teens, especially, should be involved in planning their postdivorce future, including custody. However, more than 80% of children are not told in advance that a divorce is pending (Francke, 1983).

DENIAL

Denial is usually the first reaction children experience. Children use denial to protect themselves from mental anguish. No child does this deliberately; it is an unconscious process.

In fact, it is not always easy to detect denial. Children may react to a separation with a great deal of calm; parents may be surprised at the ease of acceptance. Only later may a child ask, "When is Dad (or Mom) coming back?" Telling the child that Dad or Mom will not return seems to make no impression, and the child continues to await the parent's return.

Denial occurs most often in younger children, who may fantasize that they will spend time with their father or mother in the evening and make excuses when he or she is not there. A young girl may pretend that "Mommy leaves for work before I get up in the morning and gets home after I fall asleep."

Therapeutic Intervention:

How can therapists intervene with denial? First, denial is not completely negative. It is a protective buffer between the child's self and reality and should not be suddenly stripped away. Direct confrontation is also not advisable; it may cause more anxiety and create further maladjustment.

A more useful approach is to talk with the child about a "make-believe family" in which a divorce or separation has occurred. The child can be asked to add to the story, which helps the youngster discuss his or her own fears. Talking about important feelings that other families are experiencing prevents anxiety. Bibliotherapy (the use of books in counseling) may be helpful as well.

Furthermore, therapists should communicate with parents; they should remind parents to reassure their children continually that they will not be deprived of care, food, clothing, or shelter. This reassurance, in addition to therapy, gradually will help them accept the reality of the divorce.

GRIEF

Grief is another common reaction to divorce. Although a parent is not actually lost, the child's perception may be that he or she may never see or live with that parent again. At times, grieving can be healthy (except in a family in which turmoil is so rampant that a separation is welcomed with a sigh of relief). A child who is old enough to understand what is going on should, in fact, grieve over the loss.

Therapeutic Intervention:

A therapist's compassionate reaction to the child's crying, remorse, or regret enables the child to realize that it is acceptable to react in this way. Therapists should *never* discourage the expression of such feelings, especially by comments such as "Big boys and girls don't cry" or "Be strong." Such comments are inappropriate and simply prolong the grieving process. Children need to express their feelings in a protected environment, which therapists can (and should) provide.

GUILT

A third major reaction is guilt. Young people frequently accuse themselves of having caused the divorce, with the reaction that "I am a terrible person for what I have done." Children are rarely the cause of a divorce, yet they may feel precisely that way if, for example, they heard their parents argue over money spent on them or about their disruptive behavior. These guilty feelings often have no basis in reality. One example is a boy who firmly believed he was the cause of his parents' divorce. Frank was 10 years old when he described an incident that sparked his feelings of guilt.

Frank had come home from school, gone to his room to change his clothes, and went outside to play with his friends. When

Frank's father came home from work, he found that Frank had not returned the empty garbage cans to the garage. "Why don't you do what you are told, Frank?" asked his father, who then shouted, "Now, bring those cans into the garage and go upstairs to your room for the rest of the day!" Frank did as he was told and then went upstairs. The next day, he went to school, as usual, came home, and went upstairs to do his homework.

That evening when Frank came down for supper, he noticed that his father wasn't there. "He's not coming back soon, Frank," his mother said. "Dad is going to be living on his own for awhile." With that, she discouraged any further talk on the subject. Frank soon found out that his parents were getting a divorce. As a consequence, he thought: "If only I had returned the garbage cans to the garage, Dad would not have gotten angry at me. He would not have left."

Therapeutic Intervention:

Helping a young person work through guilty feelings can be one of the most difficult tasks for therapists. Guilt can cling to the psyche and resist the usual cognitive techniques; its strength is in its irrationality.

Parental assistance can be helpful in diminishing and eliminating feelings of guilt. The parent(s) should explain why the divorce occurred. Acting as a facilitator, the therapist should try to make it clear that the divorce is not the child's fault. Within the context of family therapy, the child should start to realize the more complex reasons for the divorce decision. Time and patience are also needed. Younger children are particularly susceptible to feelings of guilt; often, guilt can be outgrown if insight and understanding grow as well. If not, guilt can fester and develop into the most unlikely phobias and compulsions.

ANGER

Children of divorce must deal with many frustrating experiences that are sources of anger: the conflict between their parents; physical changes (new friends, school, or neighborhood); and emotional tensions (less money, a working mother, and a parent not taking them for a visit when promised).

Anger can be hidden or displayed. Repressed anger can be extremely dangerous. Rather than releasing the feeling in a healthy way, children may keep it bottled up: "My anger was eating me up," said a 16-year-old girl. "It was making me claustrophobic. I wanted to feel free and all I felt was anger toward both my parents. It was all inside me." Most of the time, this "bottling up" is done unconsciously. When upset by a parent's actions, for example, children simply will excuse the behavior rather than express their anger toward the parent.

> Elaine, age 10, waited dutifully by the door of her house for her father. He promised to pick her up on Friday evening at 7:00 for a weekend visit. He never came. Elaine told her therapist: "I'm not really bothered by it. I know Dad is very busy at work. He didn't have time to call me or to take me for the weekend."

Is inhibited anger wrong? Not always. Each of us meets with frustrating situations every day. We cannot always express our anger. We have to think of the effect it will have on ourselves or others. Thus, we bring it under control.

Therapeutic Intervention:

Therapists do not want children to express anger in unhealthy ways. For example, many children become very tense — and stay that way. They are more irritable, cry easily, and even develop nervous tics (blinking, twitching, or other uncontrolled muscle movements).

When working with someone like Elaine, the therapist should assist her in eventually admitting her feelings of anger and then being able to discuss them *directly* with her father. The use of a role-playing technique would help the child verbalize her angry feelings. The therapist could play the father and Elaine could play herself, or the roles could be reversed.

However, often a youngster may be angry about things that cannot be resolved. A child may be upset, for example, by a custodial mother's work, which takes her away from the child. Therapists faced with this situation should help reduce the child's anger by discussing alternatives with both the parent and the child. Perhaps they spend more time together doing something special during the week or on the weekend to make up for the parent's absence. Or perhaps the baby-sitting arrangements could be changed, and the child could play at a friend's house some days after school while the parent is working. By exploring alternatives in a family-therapy setting, the therapist can defuse the child's anger. This counseling technique can be applied to many other situations, such as parental dating, a new home, or disappointments during a noncustodial parent's visit.

FEAR OF ABANDONMENT

Feelings of abandonment are particularly prevalent among younger children. They firmly believe that both the noncustodial and custodial parent are leaving them forever. These fears are understandable. Remember that for a child, parents represent security. When this security is shattered by divorce, insecure feelings can be strong. Very young children may regress in behavior by sucking a thumb, wanting to sleep in the parent's bed, or wetting the bed.

In one case, a parent was particularly frustrated by her 8-year-old daughter's fears. "I kept reassuring her that I would not leave like her father. This didn't seem to help. All it did was make her worry that I, too, would leave." An insecure child will cling vigorously to a parent or teacher. One teacher related a story about a 7-year-old boy who took a can of soup to bed with him each night because he was afraid that his mother would leave home and he would have nothing to eat.

Fears of abandonment usually recede with time. As children live each day with one parent and visit the other parent, the fear diminishes. The children realize that although Dad and Mom are no longer living with each other, they still love them. However, in some cases, there *is* actual abandonment and one parent leaves entirely; in this case, the abandonment is real and cannot be easily explained away.

Therapeutic Intervention:

Therapists must allow children to talk through their feelings of being left alone. Trying to explain rationally that this will not happen is *not* a fruitful counseling technique. More effective is the therapist's acknowledgment of the fear and suggestions to eliminate it. In a family-therapy session, behavioral techniques can be suggested if the child experiences anxiety when the parent goes out and leaves the child alone or with a baby-sitter. The parent could reward a youngster with a special treat for remaining in the home alone. The amount of time a child is left alone (or with a baby-sitter) could be extended gradually. This behavioral technique, reinforced by counseling, should help to effect change so that loneliness does not become a problem in adulthood (Murphy, 1991).

SADNESS AND DEPRESSION

For a time after a divorce, most children become sad. This sadness, when severe, can lead to depression (Hoyt, Cowen, Pedro-Carroll, & Alpert-Gillis, 1990). One way to detect that children are very sad is by their inability to enjoy themselves. It is not useful to ask children directly about their feelings toward a divorce; they may respond by simply saying, "It doesn't bother me" or "I'm fine and happy." However, a careful observer will notice moodiness. For example, a teacher would say, "Jeannie cries a lot in class" or "She's not enthusiastic anymore. She just stays by herself during recess."

In many instances, children shake off this feeling and adjust to the reality of life after a divorce. They slowly regain enthusiasm for life, school, and extracurricular activities. However, sadness can lead to depression if turmoil continues in the house (e.g., custody battles or financial arguments). It also can be prolonged by unhealthy postdivorce difficulties, such as one parent no longer visiting the child, parents arguing over child support, or children moving frequently to different neighborhoods.

Therapeutic Intervention:

> Soon after her parents divorced, 13-year-old Gail started therapy. She was living with her mother. Soon after her father left the house, she stopped eating, lost interest in school, was critical of herself, and became a loner. Gail's weight and physical appearance changed dramatically within a few months. Initially, Gail refused to admit she had a problem. Only later, as trust developed in the sessions, did she discuss her sadness. A custody battle was in progress at the time, and Gail was anxious about its outcome. With these pressures, she withdrew.

> Through family counseling, Gail's depression lifted. Her mother, who also suffered from bouts of depression, gradually regained her own control. This, in addition to custody resolution, was a major factor in helping Gail overcome *her own* depression.

Depression also can be linked to suicide. Therapists must be aware of the warning signs of suicide so that appropriate action can be taken. However, if a child simply talks about his or her feelings, the type of build-up that leads to suicidal thoughts may be prevented. "Being there" for the young client is the key.

THE DESIRE TO REUNITE PARENTS

Any discussion of feelings is incomplete without mentioning

one predominant feeling experienced by most children of divorce: a desire to reunite their parents. Reconciliation fantasies can be strong in children of all ages but are more pronounced in younger ones. A child may say, "Please come back. I promise to be good!" Another attempt may be, "If you don't come back, I'm not going to school anymore."

Other children try to manipulate their parents to reunite. A 10-year-old boy once said to his mother, "Why can't we invite Dad to my birthday party on Saturday? He would love to come." In school, a youngster could misbehave or earn low grades deliberately so that a parent-teacher conference would be necessary with *both* parents.

The power of this feeling should not be underestimated. One graduate student described to her professor some strong reconciliation feelings she had about her divorced mother and father; her parents had been divorced 12 years and she was 31 years old!

Therapeutic Intervention:

Although therapists should listen and provide support, they should not attempt to attack this feeling directly as being irrational. Once children develop healthy coping skills, they can perceive themselves as successful. With this success, such feelings should diminish appreciably.

SUMMARY OF COUNSELING STRATEGIES

The strategies for counseling children of divorce discussed in the literature can be summarized as follows:

- Children should be encouraged to talk through feelings of anger and guilt and to do so in an open and rational manner. With reassurance and encouragement, therapists as well as parents can discuss stressful issues with youngsters (Steinberg, 1991).

- Encourage children to have outside activities (e.g., sports, academics, community and school involvement) to channel their drives and feelings. An important concept involving an increase in the activity level is the necessity of significant adults to "think small" and accept small gains. If the activities the child chooses are fun, the response will be more immediate and effective. Involvement of the child in selecting and planning the activities will improve the likelihood of success.

- Try to help children develop relationships with strong adult role models; role models can be helpful to youngsters as they process their feelings about the divorce. Strong adult role models, who may very well be the parents themselves, also can provide the needed encouragement and positive reinforcement. Adult models must be patient—and not get too discouraged—when their efforts do not achieve immediate success (Baumrind, 1991).

- The positive qualities of both the custodial and noncustodial parent should be emphasized. Sometimes, involvement by an absent parent is not possible; however, do not encourage negative feelings about such a parent because research has demonstrated that positive adjustment is related to smooth joint decision making between parents and youth (Maccoby et al., 1993). Try to keep perceptions "upbeat." Children also might benefit from a discussion about how the parents were separate individuals, each with a life of his or her own well before they met each other and married. In other words, they were men and women before they were parents. Their love for the child will continue whether or not they stay together.

- The "divorce monologue" technique (Wallerstein & Kelly, 1980), which the therapist uses to tell the child what other children his or her age in the same situation feel, may be useful in counseling sessions. The child can relate his or her own feelings to those of other children without initially talking about the divorce. Later, as a child develops a positive relationship with the therapist, he or she may be able to discuss the feelings associated with the divorce.

- Perhaps the single most important intervention strategy involves ensuring daily successful experiences in the child's life (Hetherrington & Clingempeel, 1992). Therapists may have to work with parents and school officials in either lowering expectations or providing positive feedback to the youngster. Care must be taken not to lower expectations too much because this might either worsen or trigger depression or other negative behavior.

- Children can be taught to be aware of their feelings and behavior. Most children can learn ways to avoid the problem, if not the feelings and ideas. They can change negative thoughts and feelings to positive ones by redirecting their thoughts to pleasant experiences. Therapists should help youngsters develop their coping skills so that they can initiate change themselves. Such self-initiated behavior is more productive because the child chooses it himself or herself (Ciborowski, 1986).

- Another important coping skill for managing guilt or depression associated with parental divorce is to teach children to use their natural ability to daydream and fantasize in a positive, productive way. Therapists can encourage the use of this technique by discussing and supporting the use of the procedure. Children can be expertly guided in the use of fantasy and in planning when and how to use certain daydreams (Phillips, 1978).

- Therapists can also help youngsters gain self-control by using positive affirmations (Downing, 1986). The use of these affirmations is a powerful technique with which children can influence their own patterns of thoughts and actions. Positive self-talk can help induce relaxation and reduce fear and anxiety. For example, youngsters may be able to limit depressive thoughts and, thus, be less anxious. With the decreased anxiety, they may be able to become more assertive at home and in school.

CONCLUSION

Divorce is a reality in today's world. Marriage and family therapists are in an excellent position to intervene for children of divorce. Therapists can also educate parents and school personnel regarding the effects of divorce on children and what the appropriate adult responses should be.

All children will react to their parents' divorce—most will react negatively. Although talking about feelings is important, counseling experience indicates that learning tools for change, in addition to exploring feelings, is ultimately far more productive (Cantwell & Carlson, 1983). The most effective intervention strategies involve preventive education of children (McKnew, Cytryn, & Yahraes, 1983).

Every child, with the help of counseling, can be taught the depression-coping and control techniques discussed in this chapter. There is no limit to the creative ways therapists—and children themselves—can use behavioral, affective, and cognitive systems to feel better.

REFERENCES

Baird, G. W., & Sporakowski, M. J. (1992). *Taking sides*. Guilford, CT: Dushkin Publishing Group.

Baumrind, D. (1991). Effective parenting during the early adolescent transition. In P. A. Cowan & E. M. Hetherington (Eds.), *Family transitions* (pp. 111-116). Hillsdale, CA: Erlbaum.

Brody, J. E. (1992, June 16). Suicide myths cloud efforts to save children. *The New York Times*, p. C1.

Cantwell, D. P., & Carlson, G. A. (1983). *Affective disorders in childhood and adolescence*. New York: Spectrum Publications Medical and Scientific Books.

Chesler, P. (1985). *Mothers on trial: The battle for children and custody*. New York: McGraw-Hill.

Ciborowski, P. J. (1984). *The changing family*. Port Chester, NY: Stratmar Educational Systems.

Ciborowski, P. J. (1986). *The changing family II*. Port Chester, NY: Stratmar Educational Systems.

Ciborowski, P. J. (1988). *Survival skills for single parents!* Port Chester, NY: Stratmar Educational Systems.

Doherty, W. J., & Needle, R. H. (1991). Psychological adjustment and substance use among adolescents before and after a parental divorce. *Child Development, 23*, 25–36.

Downing, C. J. (1986). Affirmations: Steps to counter negative, self-fulfilling prophecies. *Elementary School Guidance & Counseling, 20*, 174–179.

Francke, L. B. (1983). *Growing up divorced*. New York: Simon & Schuster.

Hetherrington, E. M., & Clingempeel, W. G. (1992). Coping with marital transitions: A family systems perspective. *Monographs of the Society for Research in Child Development, 57*, (2-3, Serial No. 227).

Hoyt, L. A., Cowen, E. L., Pedro-Carroll, J. L., & Alpert-Gillis, L. J. (1990). Anxiety and depression in young children of divorce. *Journal of Clinical Child Psychology, 19*, 26–33.

Kübler-Ross, E. (1974). *Questions and answers on death and dying.* New York: Macmillan.

Lowery, C. R., & Settle, S. A. (1985). Effects of divorce on children: Differential impact of custody and visitation patterns. *Childhood Education, 62*, 130–136.

Maccoby, E. E., Buchanan, C. M., Mnookin, R. H. & Dornbusch, S. M. (1993). Postdivorce roles of mothers and fathers in the lives of their children. *Journal of Family Psychology, 7*, 24-38.

McKnew, D. H., Cytryn, L., & Yahraes, H. (1983). *Why isn't Johnny crying? Coping with depression in children.* New York: Norton.

Murphy, P. (1991). Parental divorce in childhood and loneliness in young adults. *The Journal of Death and Dying, 23*, 25–36.

Neighbors, B., Forehand, R., & Armistead, L. (1992). Is parental divorce a critical stressor for young adolescents? *Adolescence, 27*, 639–648.

Pearson, J., & Thoenness, N. (1990). Custody after divorce: Demographic and attitudinal patterns. *American Journal of Orthopsychiatry, 60*, 233–250.

Phillips, D. (1978). *How to fall out of love.* New York: Fawcett.

Rohter, L. (1992, July 10). Boy wins right to sue parents for separation. *The New York Times*, p. A13.

Sonnenshein-Schneider, M., & Baird, K. (1980). Group counseling children of divorce in the elementary school: Understanding process and technique. *Personnel and Guidance Journal, 59*, 88–91.

Statistical Abstract of the United States (1993). U.S. Department of Commerce, Economics and Statistical Administration. Washington, DC: Bureau of the Census.

Steinberg, L. (1991). Autonomy, conflict and harmony in the parent-adolescent relationship. In S. S. Feldman & G. R. Elliott (Eds.), *At the threshold.* Cambridge, MA: Harvard University Press.

Wallerstein, J., & Kelly, J. (1980). *Surviving the break-up: How parents and children cope with divorce.* New York: Basic Books.

Wallerstein, J., & Johnson, J. R. (1990). Children of divorce: Recent findings regarding long-term effects and recent studies of joint and sole custody. *Pediatrics in Review, 11,* 197-204.

FOR FURTHER READING

Bienenfeld, F. (1987). *Helping your child succeed after divorce.* Claremont, CA: Hunter House.

Dodson, F. (1987). *How to single parent.* New York: Harper & Row.

Hodges, W. F. (1986). *Interventions for children of divorce.* New York: Wiley.

Mowatt, M. H. (1987). *Divorce counseling.* Toronto: Lexington Books.

Wallerstein, J., & Blakeslee, S. (1989). *Second chances.* New York: Ticknor & Fields.

Weitzman, L. J. (1985). *The divorce revolution: The unexpected social and economic consequences for women and children in America.* New York: Free Press.

3

Working with Families Headed by Single Fathers

Geoffrey L. Greif, DSW

Dr. Greif is Professor, School of Social Work, University of Maryland at Baltimore.

KEY POINTS

- Recent data show that single fathers are raising more than 2.25 million children in the United States today.

- The increase in the number of single fathers can be attributed to the women's movement, the increased expectation that women should have careers, a profound shift in the court system's view of women, and fathers' expression of interest in raising their children.

- Challenges facing single fathers include a lack of role models, the tendency to be isolated and not included in parenting discussions to the same extent as women, and being praised for being good fathers while, paradoxically, also being regarded as less competent than women as parents.

- In general, older fathers and those involved with child care before a separation, divorce, or death, those who obtain custody after a court contest, and those with social support from friends and family tend to make the adjustment to single fatherhood more readily than others.

- Several issues are important when working with single fathers, including normalizing the experience of single fatherhood, teaching fathers how to handle children's feelings, providing support to fathers who have begun to socialize again, and referring clients to support services.

INTRODUCTION

The last 20+ years have witnessed an explosion in the number of fathers raising children alone after separation and divorce. Whereas there were 341,000 single male heads of households raising at least one child under age 18 alone in 1970, the number tripled to 1,283,000 by 1992, with fewer than 10% of these fathers being widowers (U.S. Bureau of the Census, 1993). Recent data show this trend continues: in 1993, single fathers were raising more than 2.25 million children (U.S. Bureau of the Census, 1994).

Gaining an understanding of this type of single-parent family is important for three reasons: (a) as the number of these families increases, they represent a more substantial portion of the single-parent landscape and an increasingly viable form of custody; (b) single fathers can teach us more about fathering in general; and (c) mental health professionals may be increasingly treating single fathers and their children, thereby necessitating their having a psychological framework with which to work (Greif, 1995).

The reasons for the increase in single-father-headed families are many. Chief among them has been the burgeoning women's movement, which has opened up numerous options for women. With greater access to the workplace, women no longer necessarily have to stay in a marriage for financial reasons. Generally, women are free (and encouraged) to find fulfillment through work rather than primarily through motherhood. This trend has precipitated a profound shift in the view of women in the court system. As custody cases are being decided less frequently on the basis of gender, the presumption that a child's primary caretaker should be female has been weakened.

One consequence has been the increase in joint or shared custody. The increased frequency of this arrangement, which presumes that both parents should be involved with child rearing after a marital break-up, has moved the courts closer to affirming the benefits of having fathers participate actively in the child's development. An additional significant reason for the increase in awarding sole custody to fathers is that many fathers are expressing a greater interest in raising children than before and believe they can win custody in court.

What happens, then, to single fathers when they gain custody of their children after a separation, divorce, or death? To understand them, we must first examine who they are and then some of the major tasks with which they are confronted.

CHARACTERISTICS OF SINGLE-PARENT FATHERS

Fathers who gain custody of their child(ren) come from a variety of backgrounds. Indeed, they are of every class, religion, and occupation. This represents a change from 20 years ago, when fathers who raised their children (often middle- or upper-class men) were generally regarded either as making a political statement (as a reaction to the women's movement) or as living in extraordinary circumstances in which the mother was absent. As a consequence, it was more difficult at that time for fathers to gain sole custody.

Although the research into the lives of these fathers tends to draw from those of the middle- and upper-classes (who seem to be more apt to participate in requests for surveys) (Grief, 1995), a comprehensive examination of their demographic characteristics shows that this population also includes fathers with lower incomes. In fact, one analysis states that 20% of these men receive some income maintenance assistance (Meyer & Garasky, 1993). Fathers, perhaps contrary to popular belief that they only raise older boys, do raise girls and very young children as well (Meyer & Garasky, 1993). However, the underrepresentation of persons of color in the descriptive studies may hinder an accurate demographic analysis at this time.

One significant finding of these surveys has been the identification of key differences between single fathers and single mothers, although it is impossible to determine definitively whether single-parent childrearing is harder or easier for men than women. On average, women earn significantly less than men; single custodial mothers are two and one-half times as apt to live in poverty as single fathers (U.S. Bureau of the Census, 1995). In addition, although single mothers are not generally afforded any special treatment when they gain custody, men often report they are.

One difficulty that single fathers currently encounter is a paucity of role models. Although this situation may be ameliorated as more fathers are awarded sole custody of their children, as recognition is increasingly forthcoming from the community, and as support groups for single fathers become more numerous, fathers do tend to be isolated and are not included in parenting discussions to the same extent as women.

Finally, fathers tend to receive conflicting messages about their role—they are praised on the one hand for being caring fathers while, on the other hand, they are usually regarded as less competent than women (Greif, 1990). The response to them is often, "You are wonderful for raising your children alone—but you must be getting help from your mother or sister. Men really can't do this on their own." Although these comments are often well-intentioned, fathers tend to respond to this reaction as an insult to their parenting abilities.

THE TASKS OF PARENTING

The various tasks of single fatherhood that men generally face every day in their home and work circumstances include:

- Dealing with child care and housework

- Balancing work and child care

- Coping with children's emotions

- Starting a social life

- Resolving the ongoing relationship with an ex-wife

- Navigating through the court system

Each of these areas is discussed below.

Dealing with Child Care and Housework:

Every parent, whether single or married, male or female, must, at some point, make child care arrangements for young children. Single-parent fathers are no exception. Finding child care has proven to be a major concern across several studies of single fathers (Bartz & Witcher, 1978; Chang & Deinard, 1982). Because the vast majority of fathers in these studies were working outside of the home and living without any other adults in the home, day care and sitters for young children were used extensively, with relatives used less often.

The problems posed by children vary by age. Arranging child care is the most difficult for fathers with children in the 7–11-year-old range because of the temptation to leave them on their own when they may not be prepared for such independence. Younger children clearly need child care, and older ones can be left on their own (Greif, 1985a). Day care and out-of-home sitters are more satisfactory than in-home situations in some families because there tends to be more consistency in the adults providing care (Mendes, 1976). Time management (having enough time for the children) has also been reported as a problem for the fathers (Chang & Deinard, 1982).

With occasional exceptions, fathers seem to have few problems handling housekeeping, and they rarely hire housekeepers (Bartz & Witcher, 1978; Gasser & Taylor, 1976; Risman, 1986). Men appear to adjust to housework after an initial period of confusion. Some share the housework with their children, whereas others report feeling it is important to handle the chores on their own as a way of proving their competence. One study of the division of chores within the single-father home found that children helped out more as they aged and that daughters assisted more than sons (Greif, 1985b). At the same time, a number of fathers admitted that the house did not look as neat as it did when their wives were still living in the home. This is most likely due to men traditionally not placing as much emphasis on the appearance of the home as women have.

Balancing Work and Child Care:

One of the more difficult areas for single fathers is balancing work and child care. Because men have traditionally defined themselves by their careers, a father who must divert his attention from work to child-care demands may suffer an identity crisis. Many fathers, when married, leave the care of the children to their wives (who also often work). At that time, their self-concept is often derived mainly from their career success.

When such fathers are awarded sole custody, they must adapt to becoming the children's primary caretaker. Because they are usually unable to concentrate on work to the same extent they had before the divorce or death of a spouse, their career often suffers as a direct result of their divided attention. They cannot as easily assume an overtime assignment, travel, or take a client to dinner. Over 80% of single-parent fathers reported that working while rearing a child was "difficult" or "very difficult." Although co-workers were generally per-ceived as supportive of the single father, supervisors are not always as helpful. One study found that some fathers quit their jobs when they became sole custodians, and a handful were fired. Self-employed fathers experienced the least amount of employment-related complications (Greif, 1990).

One recent analysis of the careers of single fathers identi-fied several characteristics that facilitated balancing work and child care. Older fathers, those who had been involved in child care before a break-up, those who had obtained custody after a court contest, and those with sufficient social support from friends and family, made the transition to single fatherhood more successfully (Greif, DeMaris, & Hood, 1993). Some problems identified in this study include taking time from work to deal with child-care issues, being unclear how to handle telephone calls from their children while at work, the need to attend after-school events, and the transportation of children to a doctor's appointment. However, others seemed to welcome the opportunity to limit the pressures of career ambitions and concentrate on their children's needs.

Coping with Children's Emotions:

Can fathers handle the diverse emotions their children display? What about fathers raising daughters alone? According to more than 15 years of research on these fathers, single fathers report feeling quite comfortable raising their children. Observations of these fathers and their children tend to confirm this assertion (Greif, 1990). Research on children raised by single mothers and single fathers, while varying in its results throughout the years, tends to support the parenting abilities of fathers. Few clear discrepancies have been found in the functioning of children raised by mothers and children raised by fathers. One comprehensive analysis of data indicates that no significant differences exist between boys and girls raised by the same-sex parent (Downey & Powell, 1993).

Fathers tend to give themselves satisfactory ratings as fathers and to be satisfied with how their children were developing in most areas of their lives. The research does show that a minority of fathers experience difficulties with their children and that raising children alone has improved their relationship with their children (Greif, 1985a).

However, daughters pose a unique challenge for many men. Anecdotal reports show that some fathers are unclear how to handle discussions of female development, shopping, and role modeling. They tend to ask their own mothers, sisters, teachers, and friends to deal with these areas. But although daughters pose challenges to these fathers, they also can fulfill parenting needs. In one study, fathers who were raising preadolescent daughters reported the greatest satisfaction with the parent-child relationship, when compared with fathers raising children in other age ranges. The reason was thought to be a special bond that daughters often form with fathers before the girls reach puberty (DeMaris & Greif, 1992).

These daughters sometimes occupy a unique position in the home in terms of the kind of housework and child responsibilities they assume. Although it may be believed that fathers in these nontraditional families would tend to treat their children in nontraditional ways, the opposite is the case. One study reports that daughters do more housework than sons. This may be caused by either a continuation of the role they were playing when the mother was in the home, with the daughters seeking these tasks so they feel worthwhile, or others encouraging them to assist their fathers (Greif, 1985b).

Starting a Social Life:

After the break-up of a marriage or the death of a spouse, many fathers wait a number of months before they start dating again; the typical father waits about 6 months. When they do begin relationships with other women, it is with some frequency, but not with a great deal of satisfaction. In one study, almost half the fathers reported dating once a week or more with another quarter dating once or twice a month. Yet the majority reported dissatisfaction with their social lives (Greif, 1990).

In divorces that result in custody being awarded to the father, it is more often the wife who has initiated the dissolution of the marriage (Greif, 1985a). As a result, the father is typically "gun shy" of new involvements. When he does resume dating, it is usually after being out of the social scene for many years. Because the expectations for men's and women's dating behaviors have undergone continuous change over the last few decades, he may be unclear how assertive to be, whether to pay for the date, and how to react to being asked out by a woman. With perhaps a more limited income than when he was single, he may be unable to entertain in the manner to which he was accustomed. If he wants to entertain in his home when the children are present, he may find it impossible to serve a romantic dinner while, for instance, the children are watching television in the next room.

The father has to manage more than his own discomfort when he resumes socializing. One reason children may initially refuse to accept their father's socializing is that it dashes any hope that their parents will reunite. This may manifest itself as specific complaints about the father's choice in dates. As children perceive an unpopular relationship becoming more serious, they may threaten to move in with their mother if such an arrangement is possible.

The new woman involved with the father may also be in a delicate position. She may be unclear whether she is being sought after as a friend, potential mother to the children, a future wife to the father, or as a transition object to help the father cope with the loss of his marriage. The father will often be unclear himself about what he is seeking, but he will tend to place the needs of the children above those of the woman, thereby placing her in a more precarious position.

Many fathers do remarry. Those who do not remarry and have difficulty in accepting their potential long-term single status may be most in need of psychological services.

Resolving the Relationship with the Ex-wife:

Single fathers must work on resolving their relationship with their ex-wives and finalizing the legal proceedings that often involve custody and child-support disputes. Even though the marital relationship has ended, single parents have to work out the continuing co-parental relationship for the benefit of the children. When the father and mother have divorced on good terms and are continuing to have an amicable relationship, the children and the father appear to benefit. This is especially true if the father views the mother as a competent parent, a view that is unfortunately rare (Greif, 1985a). Conversely, if the father and mother are battling and using the children as pawns, everyone suffers.

The most damaging element in this scenario seems to occur if the mother's involvement is sporadic rather than consistent. Fathers report that they have the easiest time establishing a satisfying relationship with their children when the children's mother visits either frequently or not at all. If visitation is occasional and unpredictable, the relationships tend to be unsettled and the father has difficulty preparing himself and the children (Greif & DeMaris, 1990).

Navigating the Court System:

When court experiences of single-parent fathers are compared with those of single-parent mothers, the fathers' complaints tend to be stronger, their stories of financial problems more significant, and their worry about losing custody more fervent. Although the majority usually have gained custody without a court battle, those who do go to court may frequently have to spend thousands of dollars to gain and retain custody. Even though they have "won" in court, they often see the process as being biased against men. Many worry that, because of this bias, their ex-wives will be able to find a sympathetic judge and reverse the custody arrangement. However, data reveal that this occurs infrequently (Greif, 1987).

Child support is rarely awarded to fathers and, when it is, the chances of collecting the full amount owed are worse than the chances of a single mother collecting from an absentee father (Meyer & Garasky, 1993). In addition, the amounts awarded to fathers tend to be lower, largely because of the lower income of the noncustodial mother. Some fathers do not even seek child support, feeling that the noncustodial mother is unable to pay (U.S. Bureau of the Census, 1995).

THERAPEUTIC CONSIDERATIONS

When counseling the single father with custody, it is important to keep several principles in mind:

- Because the time pressures on single fathers (like single mothers) may be stringent, a short-term approach may be the most efficacious.

- It is important to accept and understand single-parent fathers' nontraditional position in society. These men often feel as if they have no role models. They need to hear that the practitioner appreciates the potentially uncomfortable situation in which fathers find themselves.

- To facilitate their growth, the fathers may need to have their experiences normalized. This can be undertaken by a therapist who is knowledgeable about some of the tasks with which the father may be struggling. Using a teaching role about these tasks, as well as about the expected developmental stages for children, can be reassuring.

- Fathers who are struggling with housework may need permission from the family therapist to delegate chores appropriately to the children. Some fathers exonerate children from having to do anything around the house as a way of dealing with their own guilt about the departure of the mother. A more appropriate approach is to include the children in daily chores and to guard against overburdening daughters.

- If child care is required, the father may need help in ascertaining the extent to which children can or cannot be left on their own, how outside child-care workers can be interviewed, and under what circumstances he can be called at work. Clear guidelines in this area can allow the father to focus on his own work when away from his children.

- For the father who is suffering a blow to his self-esteem because of work and home conflicts, directly addressing the conflict and perhaps exploring family of origin issues can be helpful. The messages the father received about work when he was growing up may factor into the current situation.

- Fathers tend to struggle with how to handle their children's feelings. They tend to believe that discussions about the divorce or death need to be brought up only once or twice before they are settled. The therapist can teach the father that feelings change as the children grow and that the children will benefit from ongoing discussions as each new developmental stage raises anew the need to talk.

- It is important to support the father, when he is ready, to socialize with friends or dates. Needlessly staying home sends a message to the children that they, in turn, should not be with friends—a message that is potentially damaging. If the father has not already told his children he will be dating at some point in the future and that such action is a normal part of moving on with one's life, he should be encouraged to do so. This normalizes the event so the children are not taken by surprise by their father's dating.

- Consideration must be given to the pros and cons of including the ex-wife in the therapy sessions with or without the children. One danger of inclusion is that it resurrects the children's fantasies of their parents' reconciliation. In addition, including the mother with the other family members may heighten the volatility of the situation. On the other hand, not including her may preclude important systemic information from being gathered. The best course is to make an assessment of the father and his family first and, if warranted, interview the mother by telephone before making a decision about her inclusion.

- Other services such as supportive legal counsel and support groups for the fathers may be helpful. Legal counsel will help the father to feel that his rights are being protected; support groups may provide a forum for learning how other single parents are coping with their situations.

CONCLUSION

The single-father-headed family has, in many situations, proven to be a viable alternative to the more common single-mother family. As the numbers of such families increase, mental health practitioners will increasingly be asked to treat these fathers and their children. Understanding the issues faced by single-parent fathers as they move into nontraditional roles is instrumental in helping them and their children cope with the challenges and rewards of family life.

REFERENCES

Bartz, K. W., & Witcher, W. C. (1978). When father gets custody. *Children Today, 7*(5), 2–6, 35.

Chang, P., & Deinard, A. S. (1982). Single-father caretakers: Demographic characteristics and adjustment processes. *American Journal of Orthopsychiatry, 52,* 236–242.

DeMaris, A., & Greif, G. L. (1992). The relationship between family structure and parent-child relationship problems in single-father households. *Journal of Divorce and Remarriage, 18,* 55–77.

Downey, D. B., & Powell, B. (1993). Do children in single-parent households fare better living with same-sex parents? *Journal of Marriage and the Family, 55,* 55–71.

Gasser, R. D., & Taylor, C. M. (1976). Role adjustment of single-parent fathers with dependent children. *The Family Coordinator, 25,* 397–401.

Greif, G. L. (1985a). *Single fathers.* New York: Macmillan/Lexington Books.

Greif, G. L. (1985b). Children and housework in the single father family. *Family Relations,* 353–357.

Greif, G. L. (1987). A longitudinal examination of single custodial fathers. *American Journal of Family Therapy, 15,* 253–260.

Greif, G. L. (1990). *The daddy track and the single father.* New York: Macmillan/Lexington Books.

Greif, G. L. (1995). Single fathers with custody following separation and divorce. *Marriage and Family Review, 20,* 213-232.

Greif, G. L., DeMaris, A., & Hood, J. (1993). Balancing work and single fatherhood. In J. Hood (Ed.), *Men, work and family* (pp. 176-194). New York: Sage.

Greif, G. L., & DeMaris, A. (1990). Single fathers with custody. *Families in Society, 71,* 259–266.

Mendes, H. (1976). Single fathers. *The Family Coordinator, 25,* 439–444.

Meyer, D. R., & Garasky, S. (1993). Custodial fathers: Myths, realities, and child-support policy. *Journal of Marriage and the Family, 55,* 73–90.

Risman, B. J. (1986). Can men "mother?" Life as a single father. *Family Relations, 35,* 95–102.

U.S. Bureau of the Census. (1993). *Household and family characteristics: March 1992.* (Series P-20, No. 407). Washington, DC: U.S. Government Printing Office.

U.S. Bureau of the Census. (1994). *Marital status and living arrangements: March 1993*. (Series 20-478). Washington, DC: U.S. Government Printing Office.

U.S. Bureau of the Census (1995). *Child support for custodial mothers and fathers: 1991*. (Series 60, No. 187). Washington, DC: U.S. Government Printing Office.

4

Understanding and Treating the Remarriage Family

Florence W. Kaslow, PhD

Dr. Kaslow is Director, Florida Couples and Family Institute, West Palm Beach, FL; Visiting Professor of Medical Psychology in Psychiatry, Duke University Medical Center, Durham, NC; and Visiting Professor of Psychology, Florida Institute of Technology, Melbourne, FL. She was the first president of the International Family Therapy Association.

KEY POINTS

- The number of remarriage families has increased rapidly in the past several decades.

- Remarriage families vary widely in structure, goals, and the issues and symptoms they present; therefore, clinicians need to have a range of treatment strategies at their command.

- Therapists should be able to differentiate clinical issues and syndromes from remarriage issues.

- "Ghosts" from previous marriages can haunt new families through contact with ex-spouses, visiting children, ex-in-laws, old friends, and the like. In addition to healing, a significant psychological and emotional divorce

should occur before a new marriage is considered.

- In remarriage families, adults must tend to the needs of children from previous marriages and preserve ties with them even though the temptation is to be extremely involved with the new marriage. For the remarriage couple, it is important to establish a foundation (environmental *and* emotional) for the marriage before having children.

- In-laws, holidays, and finances are important areas for consideration by remarriage families. Changes in financial management should parallel changes in family-systems transaction patterns.

INTRODUCTION

The number of remarriage families has increased rapidly in the past several decades — and continues to do so today (Visher & Visher, 1991). These complex families are entering therapy in increasing numbers, and it behooves clinicians to understand their different formations, dynamics, and functioning. In addition, because remarriage families (Sager et al., 1983) are so varied in structure, goals, and the issues and symptoms they present, the therapist needs a broad theoretical lens to encompass the kaleidoscopic fragments as these families attempt to combine into a cohesive unit. Therefore, clinicians should have a wide range of treatment strategies at their command for the different situations that may arise.

This chapter addresses the many terms used to designate remarriage families, the various important components of these families, and frequent themes in the problems and issues they present. A typical case example is presented, and intervention strategies are discussed.

Although there are many documented difficulties that remarriage families may confront, approximately 83% of divorced men and 75% of divorced women remarry; approximately half of these marriages end in divorce (Kaslow & Schwartz, 1987). The odds may seem overwhelmingly stacked against the happiness and longevity of remarriage families because those whom we see clinically and on whom much of the available data are based (Goldner, 1982; Kaslow, 1988; Sager et al., 1983) are distressed and involved in negative cycles of interaction. Knowing how to intervene effectively can reverse the negativity, hostility, and pessimistic outlook of some families and decrease the odds that they will need to divorce.

TERMINOLOGY

No term in the English language accurately depicts the remarriage family. Many people, such as Visher and Visher (1979), prefer the designation "stepfamily." Yet, for others, this term conjures up visions of the "wicked stepmother," about whom children learn from fairy tales. They dread this person as a result of an early distorted exposure to the term and its negative symbolism. In addition, "step" seems to connote "one step removed," which may imply a barrier to the establishment of a close relationship. Unfortunately, the myth of the wicked stepmother persists and seems to create a scenario for a "self-fulfilling prophecy" in that children may anticipate their father's new bride will be nasty, cruel, demanding, and rude (Kaslow, 1988); as a consequence, the children may relate to her based on this expectation rather than on her actual personality and behavior.

"Reconstituted" or "recoupled" are words favored by others. However, the dictionary definition of "reconstitute" is "to restore to a former condition" (*Mirriam-Webster's Collegiate Dictionary,* 1993, p. 977). "Recouple" denotes a similar meaning. These terms are thus inaccurate because the marriage of two people, at least one of whom has been previously wed to someone else, constitutes a new relationship rather than a return to an earlier condition.

Likewise, numerous problems arise from the designation "blended family." Blending entails mixing together so that the constituent parts become unrecognizable. It is important in remarriage families for the prior parent-child(ren)-grandparent constellation to maintain its special ties and earlier history so that this identity is not lost or camouflaged. The new family may attempt to act as if the other biologic or adoptive parent never existed so that the new family can become more cohesive. Living in such an artificial world is virtually always detrimental to children because it is predicated on deception and obscures one's roots (Boszormenyi-Nagy & Spark, 1973/1984). The idea of blending, although often well-intentioned, can cause some children to have a diminished sense of self, a lack of clarity about their heritage, and a loss of contact with the nonresidential biologic parent (Ahrons & Rodgers, 1987; Saposnek, 1983). Therefore, blending should be avoided except under very extreme, compelling circumstances.

The word "remarriage" literally implies a situation in which divorced spouses reunite. However, to me, it is the best option because it conveys both that a marriage has occurred and that it is not an original union. Nonetheless, when most applicable and to avoid repetition, the other terms elucidated above are used interchangeably as synonyms in this chapter, as is done in much of the current literature. A more accurate term for this varied and complex family form will hopefully be coined in the future.

FAMILY COMPOSITION

Although each remarriage family is unique, all remarriage families share some characteristics (Kaslow, 1988). Indeed, these families are intriguing in their complexity and diversity.

If first marriages are hard to define and depict, remarriages are even more complicated. Many possible pairings exist:

- Both partners previously married and divorced; neither has children

- Both previously married and divorced; each has children

- Both previously married; one has children from the prior marriage

- Both previously married (one divorced, one widowed); each has children from the previous marriage

- One previously married and has children; one never married

- One previously married and has children; one unmarried with an out-of-wedlock child

- One unmarried with no children; one divorced with children

- Both widowed; each has children

PRECURSORS TO THE REMARRIAGE

Entrance into the new marriage may be accompanied by uninvited "ghosts from the past." This includes ex-spouses who call or send messages, children who were not expected to "live in" or visit often, ex-in-laws, old friends, and even bill collectors. The fantasy that they will vanish or fade away is rarely realized: they are alive and influential—and must be dealt with.

Unresolved items from the earlier marriage, such as a lingering sense of pained rejection and rage, almost always exist. Often financial entanglements with the former mate remain until all child and spousal support payments end. The economic divorce from the former mate (Bohannan, 1970; Kaslow, 1990) is not coterminus with the legal divorce; rather, it continues until the last amount of money that is to be sent by the payor to the recipient ex-spouse is made. Frequently, connection with the past extends beyond this period as both parents remain involved in supporting their children. This may stir up or keep alive earlier dissension and hostility, which can spill over into the second family in numerous ways. (See case study and discussion of themes.)

Many people who remarry have been badly wounded and see themselves as having failed. Although they may not like being without a partner, they do not want to risk another painful parting that culminates in divorce. If the person believes or knows with certainty that the former mate betrayed him or her by having an affair or lying about money or other important matters, he or she is apt to have difficulty trusting a spouse again. Generally, if someone has effective therapy during or after the divorce, and allows ample time for the healing to occur (Kaslow & Schwartz, 1987; Kessler, 1975; Wallerstein & Kelly, 1980), then the psychic divorce will be accomplished and the person will be more ready and able to invest emotionally in a new, committed relationship (Kaslow, 1995). Putting one's life in order and feeling confident and optimistic again — even when one is quite emotionally healthy — usually takes 2–5 years after the physical separation has occurred. Thus, it is rarely a good idea for a person to remarry soon after a marriage is terminated, before he or she deals with the sense of failure and the need to prove his or her attractiveness and desirability.

In light of the often-devastating impact of divorce on couples and their children, many people are reluctant to make a total commitment to a new marriage. In addition, it is typical for those contemplating second or third marriages to have amassed some assets, and they wish to protect them from becoming "marital property" on the day of the wedding. This prospect looms menacingly to those who feel that they lost too much in their previous divorce and who fear another divorce or the advent of death and the channeling of assets to their new spouse's family instead of their own. Such valid concerns have led to increasing usage of prenuptial agreements (Dreyfus, 1990) and, more recently, postnuptial agreements, which elucidate the financial arrangements that the two parties are willing to make with one another (Du Canto, 1991).

Because such documents often are formulated by the wealthier member of the potential couple with an attorney, they may be used to intimidate and control. At times, an overt or covert threat appears that one spouse will cancel the wedding if the other does not sign. When this occurs several weeks before a scheduled wedding, the party receiving this document and the accompanying declaration may be astonished and disconcerted at the seeming lack of recourse. Trust (or lack thereof) may surface as an issue and threaten the upcoming marriage; yet, surprisingly, few people alter their plans at this point.

Pre- or antenuptial agreements become a blueprint for the marriage and can be valuable if prepared through a process of mutual dialogue. I suggest to clients that they first evolve a "psychosocial prenuptial accord" (Kaslow, 1991). This is done by discussing, over a period of several weeks to several months, what each partner wants and needs in the relationship, what each is prepared to offer (Sager, 1976), and which wants or needs the other has that he or she cannot or does not wish to fulfill. Such honesty and integrity in making one's attitudes known to the other fosters the building of a mutually open and respectful relationship. It enables each to honor comfortably the commitments previously made to an ex-spouse or children both verbally and in the divorce agreement. Once the couple understands why they are marrying again, and why they have chosen each other, they can negotiate the financial issues so that the prenuptial agreement facilitates the creation of the type of marriage they desire. From such discussion they can create a fair plan (with or without the aid of a skilled therapist), and then have a lawyer draft the plan—preferably in easily understandable language with minimal "legalese." Once crafted, the other takes the plan to separate legal counsel for fine-tuning.

Such a process is noncontentious, empowering, and growth oriented (Kaslow, 1991). Once this agreement is signed, the couple can proceed into the new marriage with a more informed picture of the pleasures and possible pitfalls that lie ahead. Romance can flourish more fully in an atmosphere pervaded by truth.

The following case analysis and discussion of the treatment process highlight some of the typical dilemmas that remarriage families confront. It illustrates a remarriage family that is a composite of many we have treated at the Florida Couples and Family Institute in Palm Beach County from 1981–1993. Certainly, not every concern confronted by remarriage families was expressed by the family in the following example, nor do all blended families exhibit all of this family's problems.

CASE STUDY

Bill called to ask that I see him and Gail, his spouse of 10 months. He was distressed because he discerned that his choice of a second wife was an error and wanted help in deciding whether to try to improve his turbulent marriage or to end it quickly and "cut" his and his children's pain and discouragement.

In the initial interview, Bill, a 40-year-old administrator in a medium-sized hospital chain, presented as a fastidious, attractive, and highly controlled person. His voice was calm; he seemed rational, articulate, and pleasant. Gail was a 33-year-old nurse's aide in the same organization. She was somewhat untidy, highly reactive, tense, and anxious. They appeared mismatched or the embodiment of "opposites attract." Bill had an MPH degree from a well-regarded university; Gail had a high school diploma equivalent. He seemed to be "classy" and upwardly mobile; she appeared to be from a lower socioeconomic background and to have a dependent and angry personality. All of her energy went into "just keeping her head above water."

The summary of their relationship history during the first few sessions indicated that they had met at work and been almost immediately attracted to each other. Gail was previously divorced and had custody of her 10-year-old daughter, Kyle. They had reluctantly moved back to Gail's parents' home — from which she had run away 16 years earlier because she could not tolerate her parents' abuse. Both parents still were alcoholics and lived a squalid existence.

When Gail ran away, she took menial jobs to support herself and then "married the first man who proposed." He turned out to be physically abusive, and Gail sought relief in drugs and alcohol. She had an affair with a drug dealer to obtain drugs and money. Two years before she came to my office for marital therapy, Gail mustered enough courage to leave her husband and file for divorce — despite his strong protests. Her family called her a deserter but let her move back home. Three months after their divorce, her ex-husband committed suicide. His suicide note blamed her for deceiving and abandoning him and for stealing Kyle. Both families (hers and her ex-husband's) blamed her. Gail felt bewildered, horrified, and terribly guilty. Her ex-husband's death was a subject she could not discuss with Kyle; it was therefore shrouded in mystery. Despite the fact that, after her divorce, Gail had become a licensed practical nurse, her earnings were too meager to provide for Kyle and herself. She detested living with her parents because she found their drinking and quarreling obnoxious. When she met Bill at work, they "fell for each other." Hearing her desperate need to move from her parents' home, Bill's sympathies were aroused, as was his ardor. He invited her and Kyle to move in with him temporarily. Gail considered herself lucky and appreciatively accepted his offer.

When they first met, Bill had been divorced for approximately 1½ years. He had primary custody of his 11-year-old daughter, Suzy, and his 15-year-old son, Greg. He was an involved, devoted father; the three of them were a close and interdependent trio. Greg and Suzy resented the intrusive entry of Gail and Kyle into their lives. Because they adored their father, they placed all their blame on "that seductive witch." By the time Bill and Gail arrived at my office, they had been married almost a year, and resentments had intensified.

Gail's substance abuse escalated after she moved in. The children often saw her "under the influence." She became sloppy and did few of the homemaking tasks. Bill's ex-wife, Tina, sought a change of primary residence because she did not want her children living with "that drunken whore." Bill, an empathic rescuer, captivated by Gail's helplessness and wanton charm, was unable to ask her to leave. Tina gained custody of the children and he projected all blame for this loss onto Gail. He insisted that Gail enter a residential treatment program, which she did for 1 month. While she was there, Bill cared for Kyle and saw his own children frequently. The two girls became friendly and began to regard each other as sisters. Bill was relieved that some benefit was being derived from the relationship.

When Gail was discharged, her prognosis was deemed "cautiously optimistic." Her reentry into the pseudofamily put everyone on guard because the three children and Bill feared her volatility and a possible relapse. Because she desperately wanted to marry her lover and protector, and because Bill was still fascinated by her beauty and sexiness, he agreed to wed if she promised to stay clean, be receptive to his children, and go to work steadily. Bill, governed by his compassion, married her after 1 month of sobriety. His children were furious and felt as if he had spurned them in favor of Gail.

Because Bill was lenient with Greg and Suzy, partially to appease his guilt, they rarely adhered to the set visitation times. Both of his children had rooms at his marital home — Greg had his own room, and Suzy shared one with Kyle — they visited and left whenever they desired. Whereas Gail needed the structure of a visitation schedule to feel safe and in charge, Bill wanted flexibility so he could see the children whenever they were available. His indulgence of their whims unnerved Gail and played havoc with her tenuous recovery program.

The children's dissatisfaction with Gail contributed to the escalation of the marital conflict. Bill finally called to enter therapy. Gail wanted the marriage to continue, but wasn't confident. She was a month short of a year of sobriety and was proud of her progress. Her success afforded me an area in which to affirm her determination and her growth. But her lifelong emptiness was so acute that she needed to possess Bill totally and felt competitive with his children — and even Kyle — for his attention. When thwarted, she became uncontrollably angry and further alienated everyone; Bill was embarrassed by her outbursts. The more he gave, the more she seemed to require. Like many spouses of a "borderline personality" (American Psychiatric Association, 1994), he realized that "he never could give enough" to satisfy and appease her. He could no longer tolerate her jealous attacks when he wanted to spend time alone, such as hiking or playing golf with his son on the weekend. Meanwhile, she felt that he undermined her recovery by insisting she prepare special dinners on the nights his children came to visit — even if this interfered with her attendance at a Narcotics Anonymous (NA) or Alcoholics Anonymous (AA) meeting. He refused to go to Al-Anon because he saw the addiction as her problem — not his — and did not want to be further "sucked into" the substance abuse/recovery world.

The couple also quarreled over money. Gail resented his generosity to Greg and Suzy; he felt she overindulged Kyle and did not contribute her salary to the household budget. Bill regretted having married "beneath his level" and thought his wife might inadvertently block his chances for rapid career advancement. Even though she still "turned him on," he was ashamed of her. He was ambivalent about staying married and was often cool to Gail, which provoked her wrath.

THEMES IN TREATING THE REMARRIAGE FAMILY

Children Predate the Marriage:

In this case, as in many remarriage families, children existed before the "remarriage" and were an integral part of their parents' lives (Ahrons, 1981). Bill's and Gail's special bonds with their respective children after their divorces had become stronger. This often occurs because the parent and the child support each other during the mourning period and try to fill the void in each other's lives. Sometimes they cling together simply to survive the upheaval. When a live-in relationship occurs, the warm, close-knit parent-child unit is often overshadowed by the passionate intensity of the new love relationship. The delightful intimacy of a one-on-one adult psychosexual adventure causes the parent-child ties to recede from prominence — fostering resentment in bewildered children who once again feel abandoned. Because their stability had again been disrupted, it is not surprising that Greg and Suzy, who lost their beloved father as a primary residential parent to "her," resented Gail. Her arrival into their home led to their return to their mother's house and a significant loss of Dad's daily caretaking. To them, Gail personified "the wicked step-mother." Meanwhile, Kyle acquired an intelligent and nurturing father, a nicer, more solid home, and a much-wanted sister. Bill and Gail had never had a chance to live alone together and become acclimated to one another; they had not established a foundation for the marriage before acquiring a family, and the relationship was strained because they lacked a shared history.

Ghosts from the Past and Persistent Rivalries:

Unfinished issues from prior marriages often haunt the stepfamily. In this case, Bill's first wife petitioned successfully to become the primary residential parent of Greg and Suzy. She periodically called Bill to reemphasize the children's criticisms of Gail and to disparage her as a "wanton whore." Not wanting to further antagonize her and risk additional alienation of his children, Bill swallowed her criticisms and permitted total flexibility regarding visitation. His attitude and behavior enraged Gail and interfered with her efforts to bring calm and structure into her chaotic life.

Meanwhile, Gail was haunted by guilt over insisting on her divorce, thereby deserting her ex-husband, and perhaps having ignited his suicide. Her own family hurled these accusations at her. Whenever she spoke to them, they degraded her. Her unwillingness to discuss honestly Kyle's father's death with Kyle prevented the establishment of a trusting relationship.

The unwanted presence of both former partners in Bill's and Gail's thoughts exacerbated the ongoing tensions and heightened competition between Bill's first and second wife. The first wife had not remarried, and, despite her periodic antagonistic behavior, she wanted to reunite with Bill. Ex-husbands often remarry before their ex-wives do, and a similar pattern ensues; the two wives establish an uneasy truce because they share a husband (albeit sequentially), children, and money. Sometimes open warfare ensues, making the establishment of a happy marriage virtually impossible.

Money—The Unfinished Financial Aspect of Divorce:

The economic divorce only ends simultaneously with the legal divorce (Bohannan, 1970; Kaslow & Schwartz, 1987) when the marriage has been short-lived, there are no children, and the financial settlement is completed at the time the divorce decree is issued. Ordinarily, child support continues (as it usually should) as part of postdivorce parenting, at least until the youngest child is 18 years old, and often until completion of postsecondary school and beyond. Many divorced persons desire to provide for their children and give them a good start into young adulthood. However, often a second spouse resents the outflow of funds or feels deprived of what he or she wants. The second spouse may have been led to believe he or she would receive the funds for himself or herself and the new family, especially when there is insufficient money for everyone involved or if this person has a very empty/needy/jealous personality. Because sending money is a frequent, repetitive, court-mandated occurrence, the disgruntlement is periodic—if not continuous. Every time the exspouse or children overtly ask or subtly convey the desire for more, pressure is exerted on the relationship of the remarriage couple.

All of these factors were present in this case. By the time they began therapy, Greg was attending a local community college and his father had volunteered to pay for his tuition and books. Gail admonished Bill for "wasting our money on your lazy, stupid, ungrateful son." Having had to fend for herself, she believed that if Greg wanted to go to college, he should earn the money and pay his own way. Because Kyle expressed no interest in attending college, Gail was not worried about setting a precedent that would adversely effect her daughter.

When long-term alimony payments have been imposed by a judge, even if fully warranted, the seemingly permanent economic encumbrance often enrages a second wife (or husband, if the wife is the payor). She may be unable to comprehend: (a) why he should keep supporting "her" when he gets nothing in return except aggravation (usually, she doesn't want him to get anything positive in return); (b) why the ex-wife can refrain from working due to the amount of child *and* spousal support her husband sends, while she has to work so they have enough income; (c) how he can say "no" to her when she or her child wants or needs something (including more time and attention) but he must either succumb to the ex-wife's demands or be summoned back to court (Kaslow, 1988). Such conflicts of interest do not create a context for harmonious living in many blended families; it certainly did not in the case of Bill and Gail. Gail grudgingly worked because of financial necessity; she harbored no desire to express herself through a career. Her disdain for the idle and seemingly pampered former wife of her husband was always simmering, just as it is in other remarriage families.

Focus on Annoying Behaviors and Traits:

All the unresolved emotional "baggage" a person carries is brought into the new marriage. Some couples are mature and wise enough not to allow small things to disturb them because they do not wish to hurt each other or the relationship. Pettiness was often a major source of tension in their earlier marriages, so they try to be accepting and tolerant. But the minute annoyances accumulate over time, particularly when time alone together is scarce, and many disagreements surface regarding handling and being with (or away from) the children.

Gail disliked Greg's "vegging out" silently and alone behind closed doors in his room. She detested his liberty to come and go without a schedule. She disliked Suzy's challenging manner and her "sassy" retorts. Gail expected obedience and compliance from Bill's arrogant teenagers; they wanted her to "quit nagging." His submission to his ex-wife's and children's demands, combined with his critical tirades about her earlier addictive behavior and her increasing rigidity about his children's actions, were chronic irritants to her. Bill disdained her need to take part in an AA program and treated her as inferior and sick. The threads that held their recent marriage together were precariously strung; this is frequently true of the remarriage families who present for treatment, because they find it hard to tolerate each other or their partner's offspring.

Sexuality and Sexual Attractions — Incest in the Stepfamily:

The taboos against mother-son, brother-sister, or father-daughter sexual relationships are not as definitive in remarriage families as they are in nuclear families (Phipps, 1986). An adolescent stepsister and stepbrother may appeal to each other enormously, particularly in the atmosphere of heightened sexuality that may initially infuse a blended-family home when Mom and Dad are overtly very much in love. Inadvertently, the new parent couple may facilitate this by evincing great pleasure and relief at how much the two teenagers like each other and by encouraging them to do things together. If the teenagers are left home alone together and impulsively or deliberately become "lovers," they are then faced with living with their tantalizing and disturbing secret or revealing their sexual involvement and causing their parents enormous consternation. If the daughter becomes pregnant, it wreaks havoc in the family. When one loses interest in the other, they must still live together and face the actuality and memory of what has transpired. So, although this may be only "pseudo-incest," the consequences can be devastating (Fuller, 1993), and the situation needs to be avoided.

Similarly, the mother may be pleased that her new husband likes her daughter and is willing to coach her in playing sports, driving a car, or learning geometry. She may be grateful for the affection they develop for each other, never suspecting that her daughter has become her competitor for her husband's sexual, not parental, attentions. Although this theme was not present in the case study, it appears often enough to merit mention as a major issue.

The Lack of Anything That is "Ours":

When couples remarry, often one or both already have their own residence. A dispute may arise over whose home to keep and whose to sell or lease. Regardless of which home is kept, the newcomer who moves in is apt to feel like an interloper; he or she must take over closet and drawer space previously used by others. Frequently, the new arrival will want to bring along some personal possessions or redecorate, so that the house will partly reflect his or her personality and spirit. When this does not occur, the newcomer generally feels like an unwelcome outsider. Yet when he or she does imprint the existing home with personal touches, prior residents may feel they are being disregarded and intruded on. Clearly, this was part of the resentment Bill, Suzy, and Greg felt when Gail and Kyle moved in, mainly because space that had accommodated three people now had to accommodate five.

Whenever possible, couples in a new union should create a *new* shared environment that belongs to *this* marriage and that affords it a sheltering context in which to flourish. This may mean placing emotional considerations above financial ones and selling both separate properties to purchase a new one jointly. If this is not financially feasible, then the couple should, by agreement, make ample changes so that both feel that the home is theirs. Possessions each has acquired should be pooled and some of each person's should be used. If any item is closely associated (in the minds of the children or one of the adults) with a former spouse, it should be replaced so as not to keep memories alive. For example, children are alarmed when Mom's new husband comes to sleep in "Dad's bed." Therefore, at a minimum, the bedroom should be refurnished.

However, children who reside in the house should be allowed to keep their rooms as they were, if they so desire, and to keep pictures of their other biologic parent on display, because this person is important to them. The new stepparent may be uncomfortable with this but should honor the child's identity, parentage, and preferences. If not, a no-win battle may ensue.

Other Prevalent Themes:

Other prominent issues include dealing with in-laws, deciding where children are to spend holidays, and handling finances. Generally, it seems to me that a "yours, mine, and ours" system of accounts works best to preserve the sense of individuality and independence, while also substantiating the commitment to the marriage. Sound and sensitive financial planning that accounts for separate and shared interests is recommended (Moreau, 1993). Therapists can suggest this because changes in financial management can and should parallel changes in family systems transaction patterns.

THE COURSE OF TREATMENT

Phase I:

The first phase of treatment with the case-study family consisted of two history-taking sessions, in which each partner constructed a genogram in my office to promote spontaneous discussion about the significant people who populated their complicated family tree and their feelings toward them (Kaslow, 1986; McGoldrick & Gerson, 1985). This graphic family portrait depicted who "belonged to" and responded to whom. Many mixed emotions and bittersweet memories arose in this process, fostering some ventilation and catharsis.

I inquired whether they had discussed their expectations of each other and of the relationship before deciding to marry. They had not done so then, nor since that time. Therefore, three sessions were used for exploration of: (a) what they wished for and craved, (b) what they were willing to give to the other, and (c) what expectations they did not think they were capable of fulfilling. This contracting process (Sager et al., 1983) helped them articulate why they had chosen one another, what needs were and were not being met, and their current — as opposed to their earlier — emotional state. By shifting their focus to the present, they were unfrozen from their stagnant positions — Bill from continuing to criticize her about her substance abuse and rudeness to his children, she from nagging him about his preference for his children over her and his indifference to her wishes, particularly for time alone together. By the third session, Gail decided to go to at least one AA meeting a week. Bill finally agreed to go to Al-Anon a minimum of once each month. Both acknowledged that she had done well in staying sober and that this was to remain a major objective. Bill's long-overdue recognition of her "clean time" was valuable to her, and I was able to convey to him the urgency of his accepting that she had moved beyond her "drunken whore" stage and was living a sober and respectable existence. It was suggested that he talk to Greg and Suzy about acknowledging Gail's changed behavior and that he urge them to stop treating her like an unsavory "slut." In grateful response, Gail volunteered that she would stop nagging Greg about his room and try to be more flexible about visitation. They designated at least one night per weekend to go out as an adult couple — with friends or alone — and Gail tried fervently to keep her impulsivity and temper under control by such actions as using self-imposed time outs and jogging when she felt like yelling.

Phase II:

Once a better homeostasis was established between Bill and Gail, a double session was held with both of them and the three children. To the family's astonishment, Gail was able to listen attentively and not react defensively. Kyle looked young for her age and was giggly and shy. She seemed to have copied her mother's pattern of not dealing with emotionally charged issues. However, Suzy responded to issues such as: what it felt like when Gail and Kyle moved in, when she and her brother had to return to live with their mother, when Gail went to the hospital for treatment, and when her father decided to marry Gail. Her disillusionment with her father and her rage at and dislike of Gail were revealed rapidly. Despite her sadness, sense of loss and rejection, and bewilderment at her father's actions, a bright, responsible, and candid adolescent emerged. I commented on her admirable truthfulness.

Then, Greg, who had maintained an aloof presence, entered the dialogue. He initially stated that his father's actions had not mattered to him and that his dad had a right to do whatever he wanted. He then added that he was becoming fond of Gail because she had stopped "drinking and drugging" and expressed a willingness to be more cooperative. He was pleased that their expectations had been clarified and asked that they address his concerns about college, a career, and what support he could count on from them. Bill stated that he would support him, just as he would have if the original marriage had not been dissolved. Gail became visibly but quietly distraught at Bill's additional financial pledge to his son, especially if he were to attend college, which would have resulted in room-and-board expenses. This issue needed continued processing in phase III of treatment with this couple, just as recurring disagreements about expenditures do for many remarried families. These problems are more complex in remarried families than in first-time couples because of divided loyalties.

Greg and Suzy both emphasized that they wanted to spend time *alone* with their father on weekend visits, that he was aware of this, and that Gail was jealous when he did. They were angry at Gail's resistance and protests. We discussed the validity of their respective desires and the importance of each set of *biologic ties* within the remarriage family unit. Trembling, Gail told of her fear that Bill and his children would form too tight an alliance from which she and Kyle would be excluded. She revealed her worries about the children poisoning Bill's attitude toward her again and persuading him to desert her.

After everyone had a say on this perplexing issue, it was agreed that Bill could spend part of each Saturday that the children visited alone with them. In addition, they all decided that Friday evening was to be "family night," and Bill and Gail would go out as a couple on Saturday night. Although Gail was uneasy with this plan, she agreed to try it for a month in return for the children promising not to complain about her to Bill, but to try to talk with her directly and politely when they had something to straighten out. Nevertheless, Gail's starvation for nurturing still caused her to feel uneasy at the thought of sharing Bill in this way.

As in most remarriage families, the commitment to one's own children must be balanced with the commitment to one's new spouse (Kaslow, 1988); this often necessitates structuring time so that there is "something for everybody."

Phase III:

In succeeding sessions, attention was focused on other ways Gail could fill her inner emptiness, such as participating in AA, acquiring a sponsor, enjoying time with Kyle while Bill was busy with his children (something she had never done), making friends whose company she might enjoy, and asking Bill to devote some time and positive energy to her exclusively throughout each week when she would be an interesting and fun companion/wife/lover.

Sometimes I hold family of origin sessions with each of the spouses in the remarriage couple and their respective parents and siblings to help them recapture and rework unresolved issues from the past that are having a negative impact on their current lives (Framo, 1981). However, this seemed counterindicated in this case. Both Bill and Gail believed that Gail's efforts to repair her relationship with her parents and become a respected adult in her original family had only resulted in their ridiculing her for becoming "Miss Prim and Proper," and thinking she had become too fancy for their family. Being in their company, she said, led her to regress.

During this stage, some of the therapeutic dialogue focused on Bill's passive controlling machinations, his extreme permissiveness with his children, and his ambivalence about wanting to be in the relationship, which blocked his ability to achieve closeness and intimacy with Gail. Whereas some people enter a remarriage believing that they should do all they can to make the marriage work, Bill fell more within the other group of persons who think, "If I don't like it, I can leave," and, "The second divorce has to be easier than the first."

The therapist's role combined "multidirectional partiality" (Boszormenyi-Nagy & Spark, 1973/1984) in the attentive listening and in the circular questioning, clarification and interpretation, confrontation, provocative and paradoxical comments, behavioral suggestions, restructuring, ego support, and questions regarding where the couple wanted to be in their relationship 1–3 years into the future. Although the primary modality was couples therapy from a family systems perspective to strengthen the parent/spouse unit, individual sessions were held with each spouse as needed. In phase III, the treatment format included one family session per month so that the entire remarriage family had an opportunity to engage in productive interchange and resolution of troubling issues. As they conversed in the format of the therapeutic conversation and dealt with the anger through ventilation, apologies, and forgiveness, they were able to bond more closely into a compatible unit. This approach emanates from the "diaclectic" or integrative model of Kaslow (1981).

The therapist made an effort to dispel the myth of the "wicked stepmother," a role into which Gail had been cast and had initially fit well. Two other destructive myths also were explored, dissected, and seemingly eradicated: (a) that there should be instant love, affection, and respect between members of the recently created remarriage family (Einstein, 1982) and (b) that "ghosts from the past" would vanish, never to be seen or heard from again.

Remarriage families should be helped to understand that loving bonds only evolve over time and when a sense of humor prevails. They must also accept the fact that former spouses and in-laws, as well as one's own parents, are alive and will reappear, asking for something, making unwanted statements, and perhaps deliberately causing turbulence. Children who are not in residence will also call and visit. The real issue is not how to make them vanish, but how to cope with them most effectively and exercise some choice on the nature of the present relationship (Visher & Visher, 1991). These myths are apt to surface in the treatment of most remarriage families and must be eradicated to make substantial progress.

Unresolved mourning regarding the ending of the prior marriage must be completed before enough psychic energy and trust are available to invest deeply in a new commitment. Power and control issues often burst forth, as they did with the case study. After having the couple address the power imbalance and their respective needs for control, therapy may use a psychoeducational model to teach them how to develop effective problem-solving techniques to use when future battles for control erupt. Only then do conflict-ridden remarriage families have a good prognosis for their "third chance" families to co-evolve well and to live reasonably satisfying lives together. Family conferences for planning and problem resolution should ultimately replace therapy sessions (Kaslow, 1988).

SUMMARY

When treating remarriage families, it is important to recognize that people enter second or third marriages with high hopes and much caution. They harbor their unfulfilled dreams from the past and bring much "excess baggage." The therapist, in formulating a systemic hypothesis, must be able to differentiate the clinical issues and syndromes (such as Gail's substance abuse disorder and extreme dependency) from step issues (such as children's resistance to and sabotage of a parent's new partner and love interest). Therapists who are not conversant with the existential realities and core dynamics of the establishment of blended families may find themselves searching for the right clinical diagnosis for one or several family members that label the difficulty. In reality, the ways in which reconstituted families deal with the special dilemmas created by their step structure is predicated on both intrapsychic distress *and* difficulties that create a new, close system of family relationships following the pain and chaos of divorce or the death of a parent/spouse. All of these become intertwined issues, meriting attention in therapy.

Personal issues and dysfunction can heighten the marital dissension and make the process of building a new life together more difficult. For example, when an adult who was imbedded in a family triangle as a child becomes a stepparent through marriage to a rebellious biologic parent, he or she is likely to recapitulate the insider-outsider experiences. In treating remarriage couples, therapists must help them understand how the stepfamily structure initially contributes to a high level of stress for all and that this situation is normal.

If the adults' new relationship with each other began before either or both were divorced, resentment by the children is apt to be extremely strong and will be harder to overcome because this is a transgression many children of all ages find almost impossible to forgive. In such cases, therapy is even more complex. (See Kaslow [in press] for the treatment protocol that I use.)

With efforts at cooperation made by everyone, including patience, tolerance, and the ability to perceive and laugh at the absurdity inherent in this extended family form, the remarriage family can flourish and succeed, particularly when the individual members also accept responsibility for their own growth and development.

This chapter has attempted to distill the essence of the remarriage family—looking at and differentiating the personal/clinical from the stepfamily issues they present. Cautious optimism has been expressed about the viability of the majority of remarriage families, providing they are highly motivated to make their amalgamated unions happy and satisfying for *all* members.

REFERENCES

Ahrons, C. R. (1981). The continuing coparental relationship between spouses. *American Journal of Orthopsychiatry, 51*(3), 415–428.

Ahrons, C. R., & Rodgers, R. H. (1987). *Divorced families: A multidisciplinary developmental view.* New York: W. W. Norton.

American Psychiatric Association (1994). *Diagnostic and statistical manual of mental disorders* (4th ed.). Washington, DC: Author.

Bohannan, P. (1970). The six stations of divorce. In P. Bohannan (Ed.), *Divorce and after: An analysis of the emotional and social problems of divorce* (pp. 29–55). New York: Doubleday.

Boszormenyi-Nagy, I., & Spark, G. (1984). *Invisible loyalties.* New York: Brunner/Mazel. (Original work published 1973)

Dreyfus, E. A. (1990, October). Antenuptial agreements revisited: Intimate negotiations. *Independent Practitioner,* pp. 27–30.

Du Canto, J. N. (1991, March). Passing your wealth on to others: How to avoid financial pitfalls. *USA Today,* pp. 82–83.

Einstein, E. (1982). *The stepfamily: Living, loving and learning.* New York: MacMillan.

Framo, J. (1981). The integration of marital therapy with sessions with the family of origin. In A. S. Gurman & D. P. Kniskern (Eds.), *Handbook of family therapy* (pp. 133-158). New York: Brunner/Mazel.

Fuller, B. (1993, September). I'm in love with my stepbrother. *YM,* p. 36.

Goldner, V. (1982). Therapeutic techniques for remarriage families. In J. Hansen & L. Messinger (Eds.), *Therapy with remarriage families* (pp. 195–206). Rockville, MD: Aspen.

Kaslow, F. W. (1981). A diaclectic approach to family therapy and practice: Selectivity and synthesis. *Journal of Marital and Family Therapy, 7*(3), 345–351.

Kaslow, F. W. (1986). An intensive training experience: A six-day postgraduate institute model. *Journal of Psychotherapy and the Family, 1*(4), 73–82.

Kaslow, F. W. (1988). Remarried couples: The architects of stepfamilies. In F. W. Kaslow (Ed.), *Couples therapy in a family context: Perspectives and retrospective* (pp. 33–48). Rockville, MD: Aspen.

Kaslow, F. W. (1990). Divorce therapy and mediation for better custody. *Japanese Journal of Family Psychology, 4*, 19–37.

Kaslow, F. W. (1991). Enter the prenuptial: A prelude to marriage and remarriage. *Behavioral Sciences and the Law, 9*, 375–386.

Kaslow, F. W. (1995). Dynamics of divorce therapy. In R. H. Mikesell, D. D. Lusterman, & S. H. McDaniel (Eds.), *Family psychology and systems therapy.* (pp. 271-284). Washington, DC: American Psychological Association.

Kaslow, F. W. (in press). A therapeutic remarriage ritual. In T. Nelson & T. Trepper (Eds.) *Favorite family therapy interventions* (vol. III). New York: Haworth.

Kaslow, F. W., & Schwartz, L. L. (1987). *Dynamics of divorce: A lifecycle perspective.* New York: Brunner/Mazel.

Kessler, S. (1975). *The American way of divorce: Prescription for change.* Chicago: Nelson Hall.

McGoldrick, M., & Gerson, R. (1985). *Genograms in family assessment.* New York: Norton.

Mirriam-Webster's collegiate dictionary (10th ed.). (1993). Springfield, MA: Merriam-Webster.

Moreau, D. (1993, August). Yours, mine, and ours. *Kiplinger Personal Financial Magazine,* pp. 70–75.

Phipps, E. (1986). Sexual tensions in a remarried family. *Contemporary Family Therapy, 8*(3), 208–216.

Sager, C. J., Brown, H. S., Crohn, M., Engel, T., Rodstein, E., & Walker, L. (1983). *Treating the remarried family.* New York: Brunner/Mazel.

Sager, C. J. (1976). *Marriage contracts and couples therapy: Hidden forces in intimate relations.* New York: Brunner/Mazel.

Saposnek, D. T. (1983). *Mediating child custody disputes.* San Francisco: Jossey-Bass.

Visher, E. B., & Visher, J. S. (1979). *Stepfamilies: A guide to working with stepparents and stepchildren.* New York: Brunner/Mazel.

Visher, E. B., & Visher, J. S. (1991). *How to win as a stepfamily* (2nd ed.). New York: Brunner/Mazel.

Wallerstein, J. S., & Kelly, J. B. (1980). *Surviving the breakup: How children and parents cope with divorce.* New York: Basic Books.

5

The Role of Family-Treatment Approaches in Adolescent Substance Abuse

William H. Quinn, PhD

Dr. Quinn is Associate Professor, Marriage and Family Program, Department of Child and Family Development, University of Georgia, Athens, GA.

KEY POINTS

- Family life is a significant treatment variable with substance-abusing adolescents. The individualistic focus on adolescent behavior, unfortunately, often excludes the family.

- Substance use provides the adolescent with a sense of belonging to a peer group, promotes thrill-seeking behavior to tempt fate, and induces emotional numbness and feelings of immortality or hopelessness.

- Drug use is an unhealthy means of separating from the family. If autonomy is attempted in this way and no reconciliation with the family occurs, the adolescent will most likely search for identity in a group of peers experiencing the same (or similar) type of family dysfunction.

- The family of the drug abuser should not be a group to which treatment providers simply report the status of the adolescent's progress; rather, the family has an important role in intervention and prevention of the abuse.

- Family therapy can be more effective in curbing adolescent drug abuse than adolescent group therapy or family education; accordingly, parents and adult family members should participate in intervention.

INTRODUCTION

> Our young people seem now to love luxury. They have bad
> manners and contempt for authority. They show disrespect for
> adults and spend their time hanging around places gossiping
> about one another. They are ready to contradict their parents,
> monopolize the conversation in company, eat gluttonously,
> and tyrannize their teachers.
>
> —Socrates

The adult perception of adolescent behavior as a break in social norms is hardly a 20th-century phenomenon. However, more recent concerns regarding adolescent functioning and well-being are unique in many ways and should be seriously considered by therapists who deal with this age group.

ADOLESCENTS IN A CONTEMPORARY CONTEXT

In the 1940s, the major school problems reported to the National Committee on Schools were gum chewing, rude behavior, and walking in the halls during classes. In the 1980s and early 1990s, the major school problems reported were violence and drug abuse. In 1992, a conference organized by the Carnegie Council on Adolescent Development entitled "Crossroads: Critical Choices for the Development of Healthy Adolescents" (Califano, 1992) concluded that there are progressively more adolescents younger than age 15 who experiment with illegal drugs and consume alcoholic beverages regularly (often five or more drinks in a session).

Furthermore, Antonia Novello, then U.S. Surgeon General, reported that of the nation's 20.7 million students in 7th through 12th grades, 8 million drank alcohol monthly and 454,000 had five or more consecutive drinks at least once a week (Califano, 1992). According to this account, many of these adolescents are progressing toward alcoholism. Of these individuals, 41% are female. Furthermore, according to the

Monitoring the Future Study (Youth Indicators, 1993) among high school seniors in 1992, 33% reported having tried marijuana, 6% reported using cocaine, and 9% reported using LSD. More than 40% reported using some illicit drug. Almost 88% of these youth reported having used alcohol. In the prior 30 days, 51% of youth reported using alcohol and more than 14% reported using an illicit drug. The report takes issue with the influence of the media, but it unfortunately virtually ignores the role of the family. Yet there is significant evidence, as well as common agreement, that the family is a salient treatment variable (Huberty & Huberty, 1986; Kaufmann, 1979).

Adolescents and the Family Unit:

Although peers are significant to the development of adolescents, the family remains crucial to a young person's well-being (Eccles et al., 1993; Quinn, Newfield, & Protinsky, 1985). Family life with adolescents is a misunderstood phase in the evolutionary cycle of events that underlie stability and change in social groups; it is a time of what anthropologist Victor Turner (1969) calls "social drama." He defines a social drama as a unit of aharmonic or disharmonic social process arising in conflict situations.

The social drama contains four elements — all of which are affected directly by adolescent drug behavior:

- A breach of predictability governing social relations between persons within a social system (in this case, the family).

- A phase of mounting crisis moving toward a visible cleavage in these relations. This periodic bickering, or sparring, is normal and inevitable across cultures and primate groups.

- A regressive action operationalized in response to a

concern to limit the spread of crisis. This is conducted by prominent members of a disturbed social group (in this case, the parents).

- A "reintegration" of the disorganized social group and a "legitimation" of the irreparable schism between the contesting parties. (A number of events and altered views might occur that contribute to a reconciliation in time, such as leaving home successfully, undergoing psychotherapy, gaining or losing a family member, forcing a shift in roles, or recognizing new information about another family member. Several family process characteristics symbolize these four dimensions of the social drama and form the basis of a treatment model that builds on the therapeutic implications of the drama.)

The breach of a crucial norm in adolescent-family social relations is the break in an agreement between parents and the adolescent that a dominant-submissive dichotomy be accepted. This break is a temporal shift, stimulated by the developmental changes of adolescents. Such a breach must essentially be either blatant disobedience or an obvious nonfulfillment of some crucial norm. Generally, adolescents actively violate these norms.

DRUG BEHAVIOR AND FAMILY SYSTEMS

The individualistic focus on child behavior (including the drug abuse) often has excluded an important phenomenon — the family (Minuchin, 1985). Although the family provides a context for the developing child, it simultaneously incurs transformations through the participation of the child. Considering the family life cycle, the marital life of the parents, and the current life circumstances (financial resources, housing, educational circumstances, and health status) of the adolescent and family, some adolescents are at higher risk for developing problems than others. Yet the reconciliation of problematic life circumstances is the process by which such life stressors are managed adequately.

Some family systems lack a process or context in which to allow for reconciliation. This may be a function of interpersonal conflict and often may be driven by the premise that alcohol and other drug abuse by an adolescent is embedded in family conflict and that interpersonal dynamics must be considered in association with physiological concerns (Todd & Selekman, 1991). Unfortunately, taking drugs is a seemingly useful mechanism of action because it injects a powerful message into the informational channels of families. Therefore, drug behavior represents a symbolic trigger for confrontation.

It is unfortunate and destructive that this breach cannot be addressed in less harmful ways. Some families are unable to acknowledge breaches in patterns of communication and thought that promote adolescent autonomy; however, at the same time, an adolescent naturally desires a sense of belonging to a group. Without a family resource, adolescents are forced to seek a sense of belonging on the streets with peers who may be embedded in similar family dysfunction.

The Role of Adolescents:

In our culture, rites of passage in adolescence are scarce (Quinn et al., 1985). The social relevance of adolescence is vague and confusing — if not meaningless — in a cultural context. Adolescence is a by-product of industrialization in which the economic value of youths essentially has evaporated; instead, their economic value has been reduced to their value to producers, who prey on their consumer-laden tendencies. Teenagers generally are eager to be perceived as physically mature. Yet they desire to maintain a carefree existence, without significant responsibility, as if to say, "I want to be in the world, but don't expect me to know how to be part of it."

For many in contemporary society, the adolescent experience partly consists of abrasive interactions with authority (such as parents and teachers) and partly of an overcompensating peer group, which attempts to counter strife and add meaning to turmoil. These relationships are normal because physiologic, emotional, and social changes confuse identity and roles.

One way adolescents counter these unresolved interactional conflicts with adults is to take drugs. In so doing, they achieve a sense of belonging with peers and an emotional numbness to compensate for the emotional alienation or conflict in the family. Drug taking may also be a manifestation of thrill-seeking behavior to tempt fate for immediate pleasure, reflecting the adolescent's sense of immortality or feelings of hopelessness stemming from a deprived environment.

This social drama does not necessarily lead to a physical separation (although runaways, street gangs, and homeless youth represent that possibility). However, the drama does involve a negotiation or reconstruction of roles, thereby representing the changing goals of the social group. For the adolescent, a changing goal is a push for autonomy — independence in thought and emotion as well as physical separation. However, some families are unable to move beyond the mounting crisis; they cannot suggest an appropriate alternative to keep the group together. A successful countermove by parents, incidentally, should not be an adamant push to return to prior family patterns.

The following examples describe family dysfunction with drug-involved adolescents:

- An 18-year-old male adolescent heavily used drugs in the hope that he would be such a worrisome problem that his parents, who had been divorced for 5 years, would reunite, although his father had remarried. We recommended that the parents participate in treatment with their son and his 23-year-old sibling.

- A 15-year-old girl abused drugs because she was smothered by a set of overbearing parents. The mother reminded her to clean her room each day so her allergies would not flare up although her daughter contended that her allergies only flared up when her mother failed to make regular appointments with the allergist. The mother constantly reminded her to eat vegetables and checked the cleanliness of her daughter's bathroom daily. When a therapist requested that the mother take a brief "vacation" from parenting and the father take over, the daughter came home one night inebriated; her mother found her asleep with wet clothes from the rain and guided her in removing them. None of these actions on their own might be considered inappropriate but, taken collectively, they reflect the family's denial of this social drama. In addition, the father passively supported the mother's desperate need to control their daughter's behavior; he punished the girl when she made attempts to gain self-control. This family is mired in outmoded and rigid interactions that stifle growth and development.

- A daughter and single-parent mother took drugs together to help the mother soothe her grief about her marital break-up and loneliness.

An intergenerational pattern of alcohol and drug use in the family is well-documented. Recent data suggest that more young children are using drugs, possibly indicating the effects of drug use on siblings and these children's pleas at a young age for help (Califano, 1992).

Traits of Families with Adolescent Drug Abusers:

Families with evidence of adolescent drug abuse are over-represented with characteristics of developmentally outmoded, often rigid patterns of operation. The family ecology contains interactional patterns that do not allow the members to satisfy individual needs or establish acceptable distance-regulating mechanisms to rectify these breaches. Furthermore, they do not demonstrate effective shared group experiences to tie members together in a meaningful way.

Studies and clinical observations of families of adolescent drug abusers have yielded the following conclusions (Quinn, 1993):

- Adolescent substance abusers are overrepresented in families with extreme family conflict (i.e., hostility or apathy in marital relations, bitterness and ineffective divorce adjustment between divorced parents, or disturbing interaction between the adolescent and one or both parents).

- Substance abuse is associated with family disruption and transitions (i.e., divorce, death, or remarriage, and the subsequent adjustment to a stepparent). Adolescents are vulnerable to these disruptions because their abilities to express feelings honestly — and to receive effective responses from other family members — often are limited. Furthermore, some parents fail to acknowledge or modify the consequences of adding further instability to an adolescent's already unstable universe.

- Because family rituals or rites of passage are nonexistent or limited in our culture (Quinn, et al., 1985), few visible markers exist to confirm or validate adolescent competencies and associated responsibilities and privileges. For instance, some adolescents consider driving a car an achievement for surviving adolescence rather than a privilege to accompany their sense of responsibility. Some drug-abusing adolescents perceive themselves as useless because they have few experiences of success at home, at school, or in the community. Therefore, they behave below their creative levels and full potential. It is much rarer for adults in society to expect too much from teenagers as opposed to too little. There are many false claims in society regarding the incompetence of youth; such claims culminate in paternalism (Quadry, Fischhoff, & Davis, 1992) and a view of teens as unable to govern their own actions or make significant contributions to their social context. (In the case of a 14-year-old adolescent who abused drugs and whose single-parent mother had been diagnosed with degenerative joint disease, the teenager was directed to apply his woodworking interest and skills by building a ramp for his mother to enter the house more easily.)

- Parental relations are in conflict and, therefore, the parents are ineffective in managing or remedying the child's substance abuse.

- Substance abuse is associated with emotional problems and becomes a metaphor for these problems. Typical nonverbalized statements representative of incongruent family roles and counterproductive family environments include: "I don't feel wanted/ significant here in this family"; "I am worried about your grief"; "I am tense or anxious with your new husband/wife in the house with me"; "I am confused about how to grow up"; "How can you make me stop my drug abuse when you abuse yourself?"; and "You hypocrite!"

- Substance abusers have limited social involvements (i.e., extracurricular activities or peer involvements with adolescents who do not abuse drugs). Parents tolerate or even condone an adolescent's inactivity or passive involvements, such as excessive use of television or video games. Parental life stressors intrude on the desire of parents to initiate interaction or physical activity with adolescents. The adage "no news is good news" is too often a mind set of anxious and personally troubled parents.

- Adolescent substance abusers have a disproportionate number of parents who also are substance abusers. This results from acquiescence or modeling and the parents' demonstration of similar maladjustments in their own development. Such parents provide little guidance related to coping with hardship or disappointment. Therefore, these adolescents view adversity as intolerable rather than integrative to life experience.

- Families of adolescent substance abusers are not unlike families with other adolescent problems with regard to intensity of conflict, occurrences of family transitions or disruptions, outmoded or inflexible interactional patterns, or a dearth of family rituals or rites of passage. Clinical data indicate that families being treated for different adolescent problems demonstrate similar dysfunctional characteristics (Reilly, 1984).

The Role of Parents:

Criminologists report that the "war on drugs" attacks the problem from the wrong angle (Gottfredson & Hirschi, 1989). To them, parents—not the police—are the key to the drug crisis. Their research indicates that drug abusers are not any different in profile from those who perform other criminal acts and that children who are taught to respect the property of others, to delay gratifications of the moment if they conflict with long-term goals, and to understand the negative consequences of drug and alcohol abuse are less likely to abuse drugs or commit criminal acts regardless of the strength of the criminal justice system.

Siblings of drug-abusing adolescents are also more prone to substance abuse; they belong to the same families who have susceptible characteristics. One study of family therapy with adolescent substance abusers who had been arrested showed that they were significantly less likely to be arrested again for any crime, including drug-related events, than adolescents who did not receive family treatment (Linne, 1984).

A severe limitation in intervention is the view that parents and families are not important to health care. Families often have been neglected by treatment centers, researchers, and policy makers. Modern health care, including mental health in the 20th century, has centered on a tradition of individualism, with the primary obligation placed on the status of the individual. If a secondary obligation exists, it relates not to the family but to the public health of the community (including disease transmission and the well-being of political agenda). If the majority of substance-abuse disorders are not intergenerationally transmitted (two thirds of alcoholic individuals do not have a family history, and children of alcoholics are likely to be younger when first intoxicated than children of nonalcoholic parents [Bennet, Wolin, Reiss, & Teitelbaum, 1987]), prevention and intervention efforts logically should include the family.

A more recent problem is the modest attention directed to families of adolescents in treatment. The family is used as a "parole board" by which members are "informed" about the adolescent's problems and health progress, rather than as a contributing part of the problem and the solution. Given the description of family influences in adolescent substance abuse, families clearly should have a more vital role. Family members should be active ingredients in any intervention, and, more important, in any prevention.

A FAMILY TREATMENT MODEL

The model presented in Table 5.1 is a blueprint for family

treatment in cases of substance abuse; it contains elements of structural therapy (Minuchin & Fishman, 1981) and strategic therapy (Haley, 1987). Three stages are delineated with an approximate number of sessions indicated for each stage. This number varies depending on the level of family motivation, the complexity of problems, and the level of family resources. The model is structured so that the initial phase is focused directly on the drug behavior because of possible risks to physical well-being, threatened status in school, and potential negative legal outcomes. Family goals are established, woven into the initial phase of treatment, and brought to the fore in stages II and III (Quinn, Kuehl, Thomas, Joanning, & Newfield, 1989).

Treatment or intervention programs for adolescent substance abuse should *require* family participation (during or after detoxification, if necessary). Family therapy can be a more effective treatment in curbing adolescent drug abuse than adolescent group therapy or family education (Joanning, Quinn, Thomas, & Mullen, 1992). Family members should be active participants in solving the problem. Intervention requires an understanding of the larger system. Sometimes, this involves even more than the family, such as schools or the court system.

Parents and other adults (i.e., grown siblings or grandparents) in the family should be required to participate routinely in intervention. Programs for adolescent substance abuse should not ignore the family because the adolescent ultimately will return to the family environment. Without family participation, treatment success frequently disappears after the adolescent is discharged from therapy. Family treatment should include an assessment of parental substance abuse and the origin of family conflicts.

Families must be engaged in treatment to supervise adolescent substance-abuse patterns. We have had success with a "home detoxification" program in which parents are obligated to supervise the adolescent when he or she is not in school and to ensure that schools monitor non–substance -abuse behavior (Quinn, Kuehl, Thomas, & Joanning, 1988). This is particularly

Table 5.1 FAMILY SYSTEMS THERAPY		
Family Goals	*Contextual Goals*	*Therapist Activity*
Stage I (1–5 sessions)		
Adolescent drug-free behavior	Therapist-family relationship	Joining — accommodation Nonblaming — positive connotation Convening strategies
Adolescent involvement	Parental coalition	Coaxing negotiation of rules Significant relatives or cotherapist in single-parent families
Stage II (5–9 sessions)		
Eliminating parental drug abuse	Open split — familial discord	Unbalancing — raising intensity Enactment — changing reality Complimentarity Identifying strengths
and/or		
Marital harmony	Balancing marital power Contracting with parental identified patient above	Opening conversational space
and/or		
Conflict resolution skills		
Stage III (9–12 sessions)		
Developmental shifts (separation)	Constructing rites of passage	Prescribing rituals Pairing adolescent achievement with status and privilege
		Family role negotiation
Networking	Sparking competencies	
Sibling strengths	Engaging extra-familial systems	Prescribing community attachment

crucial because inpatient treatment must be of a limited duration, given the financial constraints of families and health insurance limitations. If constant supervision is perceived to be necessary for curbing drug-using behavior, and family members are unable or unwilling to do so, an off-duty security guard or college student may be a more cost-effective alternative than inpatient facilities. We have found these options, as well as the use of the court system, to be effective.

The traditional once-a-week psychotherapy sessions should not be the staple of treatment. When necessary, inpatient treatment should include family therapy several times per week. Outpatient family therapy, which some insurance companies are now encouraging, should be more frequent and include a multiple-family format when possible. Other research studies (Bernal & Flores-Ortiz, 1991; Todd & Selekman, 1991) indicate that outpatient treatment and partial hospitalization can be as effective as inpatient hospitalization at significantly lower cost.

Just as parents and siblings are crucial to treatment, schools are essential to continued success. Schools require drug-free behavior although they are not always successful. The dilemma is that social control can be antithetical to adolescent treatment because to suspend or dispel students is to strip away their normal environment. We must be cautious about using institutions primarily for social control for long periods. Furthermore, a family's financial well-being (Anmis, 1986) and future plans (i.e., college tuition and medical care) must be protected. Flexible solutions must be discovered with school assistance to protect the adolescent's necessary resources for future success.

Marital relationships, family rituals, rites of passage, sibling development, and inappropriate family roles (e.g., the effects of a recent gain or loss of a family member) must be the foci of treatment. It is important to identify the available resources to alter the family transactional patterns in a way that is beneficial to the adolescent and that improves the life situations of other family members as well.

Family approaches to adolescent therapy are valid treatment models because they contain a prevention focus. Siblings who may be vulnerable to substance abuse and mental health disorders—as well as to the family as a group—may benefit from the effects of treatment on family processes, which may deter potential crises in the future. Family treatment is also preventive because it can limit the possibility of relapse.

CONCLUSION

When asked about the most important improvement needed in adolescent substance-abuse treatment, many treatment providers and colleagues answer without hesitation, "More family involvement." However, some treatment providers do not consider family involvement essential and, in fact, passively accept the family's apathy or fear of active participation. Can an adolescent be treated without the family being present in treatment? Intervention personnel must demand such inclusion in policy making and program development. Otherwise, the ability of therapists to bring about drug-free behavior will be limited.

Based on various research findings, individual treatment as the primary intervention for the adolescent substance abuser cannot be responsibly justified. I believe that it is not possible to reduce significantly the number of adolescent substance abusers without the family's participation. Promoting a "reintegration" of separately connected adolescents in a family system may help to make substance abuse unnecessary.

REFERENCES

Anmis, H. M. (1986). Is inpatient rehabilitation of the alcoholic cost effective? Con position. *Advances in Alcohol and Substance Abuse, 5,* 175–190.

Bennet, L., Wolin, S., Reiss, D., & Teitelbaum, M. (1987). Couples at risk for transmission of alcoholism: Protective influences. *Family Process, 26,* 111–129.

Bernal, G., & Flores-Ortiz, Y. (1991). Contextual family therapy with adolescent drug abusers. In T. C. Todd & M. D. Selekman (Eds.), *Family therapy approaches with adolescent substance abusers* (pp. 70-92). Boston: Allyn and Bacon.

Califano, J. A. (1992). *Adolescent health: A generation at risk.* New York: Carnegie Corporation.

Eccles, J. S., Midgley, C., Wigfield, A., Buchanan, C. M., Reuman, D., Flanagan, C., & MacIver, D. (1993). Development during adolescence: The impact of stage-environment fit on young adolescent's experiences in schools and families. *American Psychologist, 48,* 90–101.

Gottfredson, M., & Hirschi, T. (1989, September 24). War on drugs attacks problems from wrong angle. *Atlanta Journal-Constitution,* p. D3.

Haley, J. (1987). *Problem-solving therapy.* San Francisco: Jossey-Bass.

Huberty, D. S., & Huberty, C. E. (1986). Sabotaging siblings: An overlooked aspect of family therapy with drug dependent adolescents. *Journal of Psychoactive Drugs, 18*(1), 31–41.

Joanning, H., Quinn, W. H., Thomas, F., & Mullen, R. (1992). Treating adolescent drug abuse: A comparison of family systems therapy, group therapy, and family life education. *Journal of Marital and Family Therapy, 18,* 345–356.

Kaufmann, P. (1979). Family therapy with adolescent substance abusers. In E. Kaufmann & P. Kaufmann (Eds.), *Family therapy of drug and alcohol abuse,* (pp. 71-93). New York: Gardner Press.

Linne, G. T. (1984). *The impact of structural family therapy on the recidivism rate of adolescents arrested for substance abuse.* Unpublished doctoral dissertation, U.S. International University, San Diego, CA.

Minuchin, S. (1985). Families and individual development: Provocations from the field of family therapy. *Child Development, 56,* 289–302.

Minuchin, S., & Fishman, H. C. (1981). *Family therapy techniques.* Cambridge, MA: Harvard University Press.

Quadry, M. J., Fischhoff, B., & Davis, W. (1992). Adolescent (in)vulnerability. *American Psychologist, 48,* 102–116.

Quinn, W. H. (1993). The role of family treatment approaches in adolescent substance abuse. *Directions in Marriage and Family Therapy, 1*(5).

Quinn, W. H., Kuehl, B. P., Thomas, F. N., & Joanning, H. (1988). Systemic interventions in families with adolescent drug abusers: Attainment of drug-free behavior. *American Journal of Alcohol and Drug Abuse, 14,* 65–87.

Quinn, W. H., Kuehl, B. P., Thomas, F. N., Joanning, H., & Newfield, N. A. (1989). Family treatment of adolescent drug-abuse transitions and maintenance of drug-free behavior. *American Journal of Family Therapy, 17,* 229–243.

Quinn, W. H., Newfield, N. A., & Protinsky, H. O. (1985). Rites of passage in families with adolescents. *Family Process, 24,* 101–111.

Reilly, D. M. (1984). Family therapy with adolescent drug abusers and their families: Defying gravity and achieving escape velocity. *Journal of Drug Issues, 14,* 381–391.

Todd, T. C., & Selekman, M. (1991). A structural-strategic model for treating the adolescent who is abusing alcohol and drugs. In W. Jones & T. Ooms (Eds.), *Empowering families, helping adolescents: Family-centered treatment of adolescents with alcohol, drug abuse, and mental health problems.* Rockville, MD: U.S. Department of Health and Human Services, Office for Treatment Improvement.

Todd, T. C., & Selekman, M. D. (Eds.) (1991). *Family therapy approaches with adolescent substance abusers.* Boston: Allyn and Bacon.

Turner, V. (1969). *The ritual process: Structure and antistructure*. Chicago: Aldine.

Youth Indicators (1993, October). *Trends in the well-being of American youth*. Washington, DC: U.S. Department of Education, National Center for Educational Statistics.

6

Family-Therapy Interventions with Inner-City Families Affected by AIDS

Gillian Walker, MSW

Ms. Walker is a senior faculty member of the Ackerman Institute for Family Therapy, New York, NY.

KEY POINTS

- Families living with AIDS require counseling to work through issues such as medical management, infection-related fears, disclosure guidelines, parenting infected children, coping with the reaction of siblings, creating support systems with extended kin, and planning for a patient's imminent illness or death.

- Other areas in which the clinician can provide assistance include finding medical and social service resources, helping patients decide how and when to disclose HIV status to others, helping patients adopt safer sex and drug-taking behaviors, helping family members adapt to the strains of caretaking and fears of loss, and opening communication pathways within the family.

- Psychological intervention with children whose parents have HIV/AIDS is essential to ameliorate or prevent psychosocial disruption. As the virus progresses, children often feel increasingly bereft of caretaking and frightened by the events taking place.

- Fear, shame, guilt, and social stigma have a demoralizing effect on the psychosocial functioning of persons with AIDS and their families. Engaging patients in a family context can be an important part of creating natural support systems and ameliorating the psychological effects of the disease.

- Several family treatment approaches are discussed, including psychoeducation, conventional family therapy, and network link intervention.

INTRODUCTION

The emergence of acquired immunodeficiency syndrome (AIDS) has challenged the ways in which the mental health community regards illness, social deviance, and the organization of health care services. In disrupting the lives of thousands of inner-city families, the AIDS epidemic has flooded most health care and social service agencies with especially taxing case loads. The pressures currently bearing on social service agencies are overwhelming; effective service delivery to infected persons requires the creation of productive partnerships between health care and social service professionals as well as families and community groups.

Fear, shame, guilt, and social stigma have a demoralizing effect on the psychosocial functioning of persons with AIDS and their families. If these issues are not resolved, they can create additional stress for patients (which may jeopardize treatment efficacy) and possibly have repercussions for several generations. Engaging the families of persons infected with the human immunodeficiency virus (HIV) is therefore essential to creating natural support systems for these patients and minimizing the destructive psychological effects of the disease.

The family therapy setting provides a unique opportunity to empower family members, extended kin systems, and friendship networks to solve problems, provide adequate and loving care, and even provide support and advice for other families. In the context of AIDS, however, it differs from traditional family therapy in that it usually includes helping families negotiate with care providers so they receive accurate information about treatment options, nutrition, and social services.

PROVIDING RESOURCES TO SOCIOECONOMICALLY DISADVANTAGED PERSONS

The demands of urban poverty create adversarial relationships between poor families and the larger institutions with which they must interact. For example, those working for service organizations may regard such families as requiring an inordinate amount of services; health care providers are sometimes dismayed by what they perceive to be a lack of change on the part of the family despite intensive efforts to help them. As a result, care providers—like the families themselves—feel overwhelmed by the myriad problems presented by the families and may regard their clients as burdensome and unrewarding. Providers' frustrations are further exacerbated when they try, often futilely, to negotiate for the families' welfare, disability, and housing benefits through complex mazes of bureaucracy.

Adopting a Systems Perspective:

Moynihan's (1965) paper, "The Negro Family: The Case for National Action," which viewed social ills as a result of "the steady disintegration of the Negro family structure," became the dominant perspective for human service providers who worked with economically disadvantaged people of color. Adapted from Moynihan's paper, the label "multiproblem family" involved examining family pathology rather than intervening to change the social context to which these families had to adapt.

This perspective is starting to shift in favor of more systemic thinking about the nature of families and communities. Rather than emphasizing what is wrong with the family, the systems thinker searches for cultural assets that may be used as key elements of the therapeutic process. Studies of the cultures of some ethnic minority groups have demonstrated their extraordinary resourcefulness and family strength. For example, the African-American family has been cited in the literature for strengths such as strong kinship bonds, work and achievement orientation, adaptability of family roles, and strong religious beliefs (Boyd, 1989).

Mental health professionals may not realize that concealed in the seemingly disorganized structure of the poverty-stricken family are tools for coping that can make the health care provider's task immeasurably easier. A systems perspective advocates studying the various strategies historically used by families that enabled them to survive economic or psychological oppression. This perspective enables counselors to help families use resources such as the power of loyal kin ties, rituals of faith and belonging, and traditions of hard work and mutual aid. The community of poverty can thus be viewed not as a deficient, pathology-ridden culture, but as a rich and varied group of individuals who have strong capacities for effectively meeting their needs.

One reason family members may not initially disclose their true abilities is that they may believe the etiquette of the relationship with the health care provider requires a show of deference or even helplessness. If the professional is able to change the family members' perceptions of the role they can play in their own care, the clinician may be surprised at the family's resourcefulness in the face of immense adversity.

The large family networks characteristic of many ethnic groups can be used in various ways to facilitate care. In fact, a study by Reiss, Gonzalez, and Kramer (1986) indicates that patients in seemingly disorganized poor families may survive longer than those in middle-class families. They hypothesize that these families seem to have the flexibility to manage trauma, whereas middle-class families may be more rigid about their goals and have less capacity for flexible organization.

CHARACTERISTICS OF DRUG-USING FAMILIES

Drug use is the most common precipitant of HIV infection in inner-city families (Drucher, 1986; Turner, Mille, & Moses, 1989). Therefore, the mental health professional treating AIDS patients must be aware of the dynamics that operate in this environment.

Substance abuse is a multigenerational phenomenon affecting all family members, even if they themselves do not use drugs. Family system theorists, such as Stanton and Todd

(1982), have demonstrated that intravenous drug use often is reinforced by the patient's familial context. Moreover, clinical findings demonstrate that when the identified drug user who seeks treatment is an older sibling, younger siblings in the family also are at risk of developing a chemical dependency (Coleman, 1980). Furthermore, a daughter or son who has an important caretaking role in the family or is attached to the drug-using parent may attempt to emulate that caretaking relationship by becoming the partner of a drug user (Stanton, 1985).

Although the drug user frequently denies having regular contact with his or her family, research suggests that users have a far higher than average degree of contact with families of origin (Stanton & Todd, 1979, 1982; Vaillant, 1966); thus, the family setting provides a logical context for intervention. I have found it noteworthy that some drug users have a close relationship with their mother despite their mothers' anger and disappointment over their children's drug-using behavior. Indeed, drug use often is correlated with difficulty relinquishing a child-like role in favor of adult autonomy (Stanton, 1985).

Another key finding in the family drug abuse literature, which has a special resonance for the culture of poverty and the multiple losses occasioned by AIDS (Coleman, Kaplan, & Downing, 1986; Coleman & Stanton, 1978; Stanton, 1985; Stanton & Todd, 1982), is that the onset of drug-related behavior frequently coincides with loss or threatened loss in the family of origin. The conditions of poverty and the violence of inner-city life clearly provide a context of constant loss that often precipitate drug use. Normal separation becomes more painful, and traumatic losses may increase the parents' need to dedicate themselves to repairing the earlier loss symbolically through incessant attempts to rescue the drug user. However, these attempts may inadvertently function as enabling behaviors.

Incest and sexual abuse within the context of poverty leave a child vulnerable to developing a chemical dependency and to tolerating sexual abuse in adulthood. Furthermore, the lowered self-esteem engendered by the incest or physical abuse makes a woman more likely to view prostitution as an acceptable means of obtaining drugs. In my clinical experience, I have observed many male family members who later become drug users reporting sexual abuse by same-sex family members.

Research also indicates that the children of immigrants show an unusually high level of addiction (Alexander & Dibb, 1975; Stanton & Todd, 1982; Vaillant, 1966), which suggests that the disparity between parents and children in level of acculturation may lead to a diminution of parental control and the rejection of traditional values — and thus to drug use. Equally important is the fact that the immigration experience involves loss of kin systems and other natural networks on which one generally relies for support; this loss creates a context that is potentially conducive to substance use and subsequent chemical dependency.

Indeed, the success of a treatment program for some addicts may depend on the degree to which therapy can mitigate the loss of old familial networks. Mental health professionals can be instrumental in helping clients develop new networks or strengthen existing ones; such efforts might include starting a community group in which members who are experiencing the same issues can learn from and support one another. Support networks also can emerge from work with persons in fragmented family networks who have not been actively or consistently involved with their families.

The drug users served by the Ackerman Institute for Family Therapy in New York City generally come from families that have suffered traumatic loss(es) or that have endured a history of abuse of alcohol or other drugs. In most environments, drug users represent a stigmatized and feared group. Even drug treatment programs warn clinicians not to trust drug users because they often manipulative and unreliable.

The stigma of addiction, unfortunately, often eradicates the counselor's sense of the person. However, programs that incorporate the user's family into treatment have evidenced statistical success in helping the user reduce or terminate drug use (Stanton, 1985). Seeing the client in the context of the family also helps counselors place the drug use in a more useful therapeutic perspective; it can illuminate the various complex issues intertwined with the substance abuse.

Stanton and Todd (1979) have explored the ways in which the family may actually enable or facilitate continued drug use. Family assessment of a drug user can accomplish four main goals:

1. Identify the ways in which family members are involved with the drug user and may inadvertently support ongoing drug use

2. Identify family caregiving resources if the drug user becomes ill and requires family care

3. Identify sexual partners who are at risk for infection and start a process of safer sex intervention and pregnancy counseling

4. Identify caretakers who may provide continuity of care in the event of the drug user's death or subsequent illness and death of his or her spouse

HIV INFECTION AND SUBSTANCE ABUSE

Effective family treatment approaches for intravenous drug users have become even more important in the context of AIDS because drug use has the potential to kill not only the user but also his or her partner and children through transmission of HIV.

Active Users:

Needle sharing among intravenous drug users has been a major factor in the rapid spread of HIV. Moreover, the majority of drug users are heterosexual, and many of them have families that include young children (Drucher, 1986). Before the advent of AIDS, partners of substance abusers certainly experienced significant stress in managing the chemical dependency in the context of the relationship. This stress is now compounded by the fact that engaging in a sexual relationship with a substance abuser constitutes a major risk for contracting AIDS and transmitting HIV to one's children.

Active users often regard a diagnosis of AIDS as a death sentence. Such persons not only may continue to use drugs but may even intensify their use because they feel that living with AIDS is an insurmountable burden for them and their families. They actually may think they are saving themselves and their families from the horrors of a protracted illness. In fact, of course, it is exceedingly difficult for family members of substance abusers to watch them deliberately self-destruct.

The clinician can help the drug user identify such maladaptive thinking and behavior patterns and concentrate on important issues, even if the user is unable to refrain from active drug use. For example, the clinician may focus on issues such as future planning for the abuser's family. If the clinician respects that drug use does not eradicate the person and that the drug user often values his role as a son, husband, or father, the clinician can help him maintain a sense of dignity by engaging him in decision making on family matters. Although this therapeutic endeavor may motivate him to seek treatment, many times it will not. If the family members and counselor fail to motivate the drug user to seek help, the family will need assistance in coping with ongoing drug use and the emotions it generates.

Recovering Users:

Former addicts embarking on the recovery process must begin to confront the responsibilities they had avoided (career, children, relationships with family and friends, etc.). Partners who are in recovery together may find it difficult to balance the repair of their relationship and the renegotiation of relationships with their families of origin. Unresolved issues with their own families can create difficulty for the couple in maintaining a boundary around their fledgling drug-free life. In addition, safer sex is a more difficult task for recovering addicts than for those without a history of drug use, because drug users are especially accustomed to instant gratification.

When partners recovering from intravenous drug use discover that one or both of them have AIDS, the difficulties of the transition from active drug use to recovery are further complicated. AIDS creates a sense of urgency in assuming responsibilities for which the person in recovery may not yet be ready. Such persons often find themselves caught between wanting to parent their children and wanting to be parented themselves.

FAMILY THERAPY IN THE MANAGEMENT OF AIDS

The family therapist's main challenge in working with families affected by AIDS involves the development of a realistic (and, if possible, optimistic) view of life with HIV/AIDS. The family must understand that AIDS is a preventable chronic illness that requires alert management and changes in lifestyle to maximize immune resistance to viral replication.

To become effective partners in care, families require counseling in working through a broad range of issues:

- Managing medical issues

- Coping with infection-related fears

- Assessing disclosure guidelines

- Maintaining a "normal" life in the context of AIDS

- Parenting infected children

- Coping with the reaction of noninfected siblings

- Creating support systems with extended kin

- Planning for a parent's imminent illness or death

The complex illness pattern associated with AIDS and the proliferation of available medical protocols require that families comprehend medical information that is seldom presented in plain language. They may not be aware of all the available medical options, and they may have a fatalistic attitude toward the illness. They may be afraid to ask questions, especially because they do not know what types of questions to ask.

If family members are to be partners in care, the clinician must help them develop an optimistic outlook about the course of the illness with the primary physician and other medical staff members. Optimism may involve exhibiting the appropriate hope and resourcefulness that can augment the quality of life for the patient. This most likely will foster a cooperative, rather than adversarial, relationship with health care providers.

For those in the immediate family of the patient, the episodic course of the disease requires continual adaptation and role change. Strain on the family is caused by both the frequency of shifts between crisis and noncrisis modes of operation and the pervasive imminence of the next medical crisis. Although the family or the person's network of significant others must remain "on call," they also must learn to balance illness-generated needs with day-to-day family needs and functions.

Areas in which the clinician can provide a vital function include:

- Finding resources for medical information and other social service benefits

- Helping patients decide when and how to disclose HIV status to others

- Helping patients understand and adopt safer sex and drug-taking behaviors

- Helping family members adapt to the strains of caretaking and fears of loss

- Opening communication pathways within the family so that family members can deal most effectively with the patient's condition

- Mobilizing the family's extended kinship networks to resolve problems in the present and plan for the future

THE COURSE OF AIDS

Those who provide services to families affected by AIDS must understand the developmental tasks for families in the crisis, chronic, and terminal phases of AIDS (Rolland, 1984, 1987a, 1987b, 1987c).

Crisis Phase:

The crisis phase is marked by the onset of the first opportunistic infection, which signals the transition from HIV infection to full-blown AIDS. Although a positive result at testing may precipitate a psychological crisis, the asymptomatic phase of HIV infection has an indefinite time frame, which allows space for denial of mortality. Diagnosis of an opportunistic infection forces the patient to face the probability of a vastly shortened life and to anticipate an illness frequently marked by a downhill course of serial illnesses between shorter respites. The crisis created by an opportunistic infection raises questions of disclosure to intimate partners who comprise the illness management network. For parents, it raises the question of future planning for their children's care. For many persons, it means increasing difficulty with work and negotiating entitlement systems. For all, it means learning to negotiate complex medical systems. Psychosocial tasks during this phase include learning to:

- Grieve for the loss of a pre-illness family identity and an individual identity

- Reorganize family tasks and roles to deal with crisis

- Manage AIDS-related symptoms

- Deal with the hospital environment

- Create a cooperative team consisting of health care providers and family members

- Create an outlook about AIDS that preserves dignity and facilitates competence

- Incorporate permanent change while maintaining a sense of continuity between the past and the future

- Develop the flexibility to deal with future uncertainties

Chronic Phase:

In the chronic phase, when the course of the disease is marked by alternating patterns of deterioration and improvement, the family's primary tasks involve:

- Maintaining a semblance of a normal life under the disruptive presence of AIDS and heightened uncertainty

- Maximizing autonomy for all family members in the face of contradictory pulls toward mutual dependency and caretaking

- Dealing with issues such as home care and the gradual incapacitation of the family member

- Helping children with the transitions of care when a parent is hospitalized

AIDS may cause periods of mental impairment that alternate with periods of lucidity in which, without much warning, the patient wishes to resume normal ways of functioning. Family members must be able to shift from a "severe illness mode" of functioning to a framework in which the person with AIDS resumes normal life tasks and the usual role in the family system.

Such rapid changes present major challenges for most family members. The therapist must help family members deal with complex feelings ranging from anger, despair, and actual wishes for the patient's death, to compassion and hope. These feelings should be normalized and accepted by family members as appropriate responses to a difficult, chronic disease.

Terminal Phase:

In the terminal phase, the family and patient must make peace with each other (if their relationship is adversarial) and arrive at an acceptance of the inevitability of death. The practitioner must ensure that all family members receive adequate care during the terminal phase, when caregivers may be extraordinarily overtaxed by the crisis. This may involve helping the family find resources outside its immediate system to alleviate some of the caregiving burden, particularly if the family also has young children who need care when the rest of the family is focused on the dying patient's needs.

The clinician should be aware that family members often are out of synchronicity with the patient in terms of their acceptance of death. The patient, for example, may have already accepted the inevitability of death and wish to share this with the family. However, family members may refuse to discuss death with the patient and, instead, relentlessly pursue exhaustive or questionable treatments to prolong the patient's life.

To avoid this potential disruption of the terminal stage, patients may need to discuss with family members their wishes in advance by preparing a living will. As the patient approaches death, the health care provider often must help family members make decisions about discontinuing life-prolonging measures. Such decisions may be extremely challenging, especially because "[m]uch of the way physicians deal with terminal illness is the result of habit; they have been taught to diagnose and treat" (Misbin, 1994). Thus, it is imperative for both the patient and family members to be knowledgeable consumers of medical services. Misbin suggests that if the patient is dying, it may be rational to request that life-prolonging treatments—especially those that serve "no real purpose other than to preserve physiologic function"—not be initiated (or should be discontinued if they are already in effect).

If the dying patient was a drug user, as is common in inner-city families, family members may experience tremendous difficulty letting go because so much of their lives has been organized around rescuing the user from life-threatening situations. When the user becomes terminally ill with AIDS, the family experiences intense failure, impotence, and a reawakening of unresolved mourning issues connected with earlier losses. Surviving spouses of drug abusers may themselves be HIV positive and have one or more children with AIDS. As they mourn the death of their spouse, they are likely to feel anger and helplessness at the certainty that they themselves and others in the family will die as well.

Bereavement:

In communities of poverty, AIDS often kills parents who have families with young children; therefore, death may cause the dislocation of an entire family. Secrecy about AIDS complicates the normal mourning process. When parents die of AIDS, their children often are bewildered about how to mourn the parent's death because sometimes family members' attitudes toward the disease prevent it from being named publicly. Furthermore, secrecy isolates nuclear families from other kin and community members who may be able to help.

How the family counselor manages the bereavement process can have enormous impact on the future of the family. Families of drug users often have suffered multiple losses (Stanton, 1985). In these families, silence and stoicism may replace the open expression of feelings.

A family session is an opportunity to encourage the family to share memories and experiences and resolve conflicts that have emerged during the illness. If the person who died was a drug user, the family may have been torn apart by the conflicts that naturally emerge when dealing with a family member's drug use. Children need to experience the family as healing itself just as they need a safe place to share their grief.

AIDS AND INNER-CITY CHILDREN

Children Whose Parents Have AIDS:

Psychological intervention with children whose parents have AIDS is essential to ameliorate or prevent psychosocial disruption as the disease progresses and children feel increasingly bereft of caretaking or frightened by the events taking place. During the time when the parent is experiencing the physical and mental deterioration of the terminal stages of the disease, the children may not have adequate parental supervision. Support and care from family members or others who are prepared to supervise or assume responsibility for raising the children after the parent's death must be ensured during this period.

When a parent dies, the children may be removed from familiar surroundings, extended family, and even one another. During the terminal phase, siblings often grow exceptionally close to one another, especially if older children assume primary care responsibilities for their younger siblings. After the death of a parent, the sibling system may be divided, thereby disrupting the support they have built for one another. This presents additional losses that need to be healed. The intervention of a family counselor (or any mental health or health care professional) can be crucial in avoiding the breakup of the family. If this proves to be impossible, the counselor can help ensure that the new family system affords the survivors maximum contact with one another.

Children who have been raised by substance abusers and have experienced the trauma of a parent's death may present with psychological disturbances (e.g., delinquency, school failure, disruptive behavior) that make their behavior difficult for their new caretakers to understand and manage. (These children frequently have already experienced a number of deaths to AIDS.) As one teenager said after five aunts and uncles and two young cousins had died of AIDS, "Everyone's dying . . . Who's next?" Shortly afterward, he began to speak openly about suicidal fantasies — after all, suicide would permit him to join all those beloved people whom he had lost and would stop the terrible pain he was feeling (Walker, 1995).

Family intervention before a parent dies helps the family prepare to manage the trauma of parental loss and provides the children with a more secure future. In one case, for example, the children had been in an abusive relationship with a drug-using father. When both parents became ill with AIDS, the Ackerman team helped the family identify competent and willing caretakers. Along with the caretakers, we then worked through problems that the children had developed (e.g., stealing, violence) in response to their abusive environment and loss of parents. With counseling, the children began to function better than they had previously. By working together with the counselor, the family was able to provide the children with an opportunity for achievement and functioning that had been unavailable in their previous environment.

Children Who Have AIDS:

As the prevalence of AIDS among women continues to increase, the number of children with AIDS will continue to rise commensurately — especially among minorities (Shelton et al., 1993). The majority of HIV-infected infants are born to women who are intravenous drug users or are sexual partners of drug users and are mostly African-Americans or Latinas. Infected women who choose to have a child require understanding and compassion, as well as good prenatal care (taking azidothymidine [AZT] reduces the chance that the baby will be born with HIV) (Altman, 1994).

Issues affecting families with infected children include:

- The effects of secrecy on family functioning

- Strategies for appropriate disclosure

- Concomitant parental diagnosis and its effect on the children, whether it is disclosed or kept secret

- The psychological effects on noninfected children

- The need for parents to find means of alleviating their own feelings of shame and guilt

- The need for dying children to discuss fears and emotions

- Difficulties in handling social isolation, stigmatization, and discrimination in the community when the child's HIV status is disclosed

- The need to develop appropriate support networks of other parents and people dealing with AIDS

Noninfected children who have a sibling with AIDS may present with the following concerns:

- Terror about an uncertain future

- Jealousy when a parent's attention is consumed by the ongoing medical demands of the infected sibling

- Confusion about the meaning of AIDS and the secrecy surrounding it

- Acting-out or violent behavior

The family practitioner can demonstrate ways in which parents or other family caregivers can discuss with their children fears that the sibling is dying. In addition, clinicians can help children express their resentments about their parents' needing to devote the majority of their time and energy to the ill child.

FAMILY THERAPY APPROACHES

Family-centered models use a number of approaches, including psychoeducation, conventional family therapy, and network link therapy.

Psychoeducation:

The illness process disrupts normal family structure by creating emotional coalitions and exclusions within the family that may lead to destructive and divisive family interactions (Gonzalez et al., 1987). Psychoeducational models have been used successfully with people who have chronic medical conditions and their families to normalize their experiences and help them understand that negative feelings are common to all families coping with any disease (Gonzalez et al., 1987). The goals of the psychoeducational approach are to:

- Facilitate a shift from blaming and adversarial attitudes within the family to an attitude of mutual support and problem solving

- Impart information about the etiology, symptoms, expected course, and environmental determinants of exacerbation of the disease and the conditions conducive to optimal quality of life

- Help the family find a balance between illness-generated needs and the need to attend to normal family developmental demands and priorities not related to the illness

Conventional Family Therapy:

Developing a Systemic Hypothesis about Family Functioning and Interaction

A systemic hypothesis provides an explanatory framework for understanding the meaning and function of all behaviors and interactions of family members related to the cohesiveness and evolutionary development of the family system through time. The behaviors themselves arise out of the family's deeply structured belief systems and determine the family's approach to illness.

Families also develop a history of shifting coalitions and alliances; shifts often are triggered by critical stress events such as illness, death, dislocation, or even pregnancy. A careful tracking of critical dates and the changes in family structure that coincide with them can direct the therapist to problem issues. Beliefs about illness as well as past family interactions around illness may predict the way the family and patient will handle illness in the present. These coalitions often shift when a family confronts stress.

Example

Steve, in his late 30s and the father of three children, dies of AIDS. His wife, Mary, is HIV positive but asymptomatic. She keeps the cause of Steve's death secret from her children and her family of origin, which adds to the stress of her medical condition and her status as a single parent. Her 13-year-old son has developed behavior problems at school.

Family History

1964   Mary's younger brother, Peter, begins using drugs. Family life becomes centered on Peter's problems.

1970   Peter dies of an overdose. Mary's parents drift apart. The cause of Peter's death is not revealed to those outside the family. Mary meets Steve, a recovering drug user, in a program where she works.

1972   Mary marries Steve. She does not reveal Steve's drug use to her family of origin.

1974   Mary gives birth to Michael, their first child. Steve returns to using drugs.

1982   Mary and Steve have their third child.

1984   The third child dies of leukemia. Steve reveals to Mary that he is HIV positive. Mary does not tell anyone about Steve's diagnosis.

1984   Michael begins to act out in school. The fight-

ing between Steve and Mary intensifies. As
Steve becomes more ill, Mary asks him to leave.
Their children do not know of Steve's drug use
or his diagnosis. The family enters therapy.

1987   Steve dies of AIDS. Mary tests positive for HIV.

Developing a family time line helps the therapist and family
identify which problems originated prior to the diagnosis and
facilitates the tracking of issues that emerge during therapy.
Therefore, conflicts that may surface in the future can be
anticipated as the family understands previous patterns of
family interaction and devises strategies for managing them.
It can also help family members gain insight into their patterns
of behavior.

Shame and unresolved mourning dating back to Peter's
death shaped Mary's relationship with Steve, her difficulty in
reconnecting with her family of origin, her fears about Michael's
future, and the secrecy she maintained. The secrecy about
information that could not be shared or even inwardly acknowledged was frightening to her surviving children and
alienated them just when they most needed her support.
Treatment included conversations about the meaning of this
crisis for the entire family, which helped facilitate the creation
of a family support system for Mary and her surviving children as she became more ill.

A family assessment provides the mental health professional with information about these interlocking beliefs, fears,
and behaviors as well as the power to intervene in changing
destructive patterns.

Example:

A substance-abusing patient with AIDS was exhibiting symptoms of depression. His mother continued to give him money
for drugs despite his illness.

Although it may not be unreasonable to attribute an AIDS

patient's depression to the physiologic effects of his disease, it is wise to examine other factors that may contribute to the depression. In fact, the therapist in this case discovered that a large part of the patient's depression resulted from his inability to respond to the conflicting messages expressed by his mother. Although she constantly implored him to stop using drugs, her giving him money essentially constituted implicit approval of his drug use.

The patient interpreted his mother's nonverbal message as, "I need you to die to spare the family the stigma of the revelation of your illness." Depression (which correlates negatively with immune system functioning [Borysenko, 1989]) became the drug user's adaptive response to the family's "problem." By neglecting his health, the patient exacerbated his condition and perhaps accelerated his own death, thus sparing the family the stress of a prolonged illness. Research by Reiss and colleagues (1986) has shown that death often follows a "set point," at which both patient and family "give up" when the stress of illness on all those concerned outweighs the desire for survival.

Example:

> Louann and John, newlyweds, entered couples therapy complaining of fighting. Their 8-month-old infant had AIDS, and Louann was HIV positive; John was HIV negative. Louann has a 7-year-old child, Samantha, from a previous, very brief relationship. Samantha's father is uninvolved.

A clinician using a linear hypothesis (i.e., "A leads to B") to diagnose the couple's problem might advise John and Louann that stress often results in conflict. This is logical advice, and it is probably true that stress has something to do with the escalation of conflict. However, in this case, attempts to stop the fighting by direct intervention, relationship tasks, and extra care for the child all proved futile.

The Ackerman therapists then undertook a more systemic

investigation of the premises governing the fighting and the significance it held in the lives of John and Louann. The couple first was asked what would happen if the fighting were to continue; the couple answered that they would probably break up.

Louann felt too guilty about the possibility of infecting her husband to risk staying in the marriage, particularly because he desired her sexually. By losing him, she would also be able to punish herself for what she perceived to be her past sins. John felt that leaving his new wife was not a viable option for him because he himself had grown up without a father. He felt that being a good father was extremely important; leaving his wife and child would mean violating his strongly held paternal principles.

The systemic hypothesis brought the couple's hidden motivations into the open: their fighting was a futile attempt to resolve an unsolvable problem. Louann's fighting and provocative acts were attempts to protect her husband by making the relationship virtually unbearable at times. For John, the fighting represented an attempt to resist Louann's intention to push him out of the relationship. Whatever ambivalence John felt about staying in their tempestuous relationship could not surface because it conflicted with his conviction that he must remain active in parenting his ill child.

Once John and Louann realized the issues behind their fighting, it became unnecessary, which freed them to find productive solutions to their problems. The treatment plan developed by the therapist provided Louann with a ritual that connected the fighting to her guilt and her wish to punish herself and protect her husband. She began to reconnect with her family of origin so that she could have a support system; this afforded her more options about separating from John and would ensure caregiving as her condition worsened.

John had to distinguish between his wish to stay in the relationship with Louann and his desire to remain a father to his child. Once John was able to face his ambivalence, he realized that his determination to be a good father was more operative in maintaining the relationship than his desire to be a husband to Louann.

They were able to separate amicably. Louann moved back in with her family of origin, who provided support during the illness and subsequent death of her child. John remained in constant contact with his child and was able to perform valuable paternal duties without the stress of his marriage (Kaplan, 1987).

Developing a Family Resource Genogram

Therapists frequently use *genograms,* or family trees, to diagram important family information. Genograms typically include names of the client's family members, their birth and death dates, critical events such as mental or physical illnesses, substance use, accidents, and divorces or moves away from home. Genograms can be used to diagram affiliation, coalitions, areas of conflict, emotional cutoffs, and over- and under-involvements.

A *resource genogram* focuses on areas of potential support to the client such as the family of origin; extended kin networks; friendship networks; cultural institutions, such as churches; and social service agencies, including professionals with whom the family has contact. The resource genogram also illustrates the relationship between these people and/or institutions. It can be used as a map to determine who should attend meetings convened by therapists in which persons engaged in helping the client come together and collaborate on meeting the client's needs.

Mental health care providers often have limited knowledge about the resources available to families caring for AIDS victims. Preparing a family resource genogram can help practitioners assess the following information:

- Who has been informed about the disease

- Who in the family can be called on for help during a specific crisis

- Who in the family can be called on to provide continuity of care to young children in the case of the death of one or both parents

In the example of Louann and John, Louann felt isolated from her family of origin. When Louann was 12, her older brother, the family "star," was killed in military action. Her mother was consumed by grief and emotionally abandoned her adolescent daughter. Louann became a troublemaker and dropped out of school at age 16.

Louann's resource genogram revealed the strengths and weaknesses of her family resource system. Both her mother and John's mother and one of Louann's sisters were potential avenues of support for Louann and Samantha, although conflict between Louann and her mother and sister had to be resolved. Her church could provide support to Louann's mother and was a potential source of support to Louann and for Samantha should Louann die. The school was a support to Samantha, but Louann's relationship to the medical system treating her baby had to be addressed. Louann had a sporadic relationship with a Gay Men's Health Crisis (GMHC) intervention team and attended a GMHC support group. She needed encouragement to consolidate these relationships, which proved useful in alleviating her fears of being alone.

Network Link Intervention:

Developed by Judith Landau-Stanton in her work with families in cultural transition (Landau-Stanton, 1982), network link intervention has been used with people with AIDS (Landau-Stanton et al., 1993). This type of therapy identifies certain family members with leadership capacities and asks them to become liaisons between professional systems and the family and to act as family problem solvers.

Network link therapy uses family members to reach the maximum number of people, build family and community networks, disseminate information, enhance family members' capacities for problem solving, and empower families to heal themselves. In this model, families are asked to organize a network session consisting of as many family members and significant others as are needed or with which the family is comfortable. The network session is used to pool information, identify problems and resources for dealing with those problems, and discuss difficult issues openly. The aim of the network session is to consolidate family bonds and transform them into resources. At this meeting, the family designates one or more family members who will continue to work with the therapist and family system to solve the identified problems. The family must vest authority in the liaison, who, in turn, works to bridge the gap between professional care providers and the family and community.

Example

> A patient has AIDS dementia. His wife, also HIV positive, is overwhelmed by the demands of caring for young children in the context of her husband's illness and her own medical condition. The wife's mother has always been a powerful figure in the family, and it is she who meets with the therapist to gather information and strategies for managing the care of her son-in-law and the emotional and psychological problems created by the situation. She is encouraged by the therapist to organize a family care network, convene meetings, and provide advice and counsel. Her willingness to become the "link" between family and medical system reduces the need for family meetings with the professional and empowers the family to manage its problems with minimal outside intervention.

PREVENTION

Because few programs exist that effectively reach the sexual partners of intravenous drug users, a family assessment can be an important first step toward prevention in an at-risk population.

Engaging both partners in sexual counseling can help overcome the complex emotional, interactional, and cultural barriers that prevent them from practicing safer sex. For example, in some cultures of poverty, fertility is a major source of self-respect and pride for men and women. At the same time, "macho" mores may make some women afraid to demand safer sex practices from their sexual partners for fear of inciting anger, alienation, rejection, or outright violence. However, because such communities also deeply value their children, helping a couple face the possible effects of HIV infection on the entire family may motivate them to practice safer sex.

Family intervention also can enhance the efficacy of safe sex counseling, which is currently the most effective known means of preventing the spread of HIV. Providing a forum to discuss these issues — a forum in which a woman's voice, needs, and goals are given equal weight with those of her partner — can be enormously helpful in identifying barriers to safer sex and helping the man place future-oriented family goals ahead of his wish to control the sexual arena. Dealing with sexuality issues is difficult and often time consuming; however, it tends to be more effective than educating a single partner because it allows for the resolution of conflictual issues. Families often include more than one person at risk for contracting HIV; network link therapy encourages family members to counsel one another about safer sex. The transmission of such advice from a respected family leader rather than a health professional increases the probability that such advice will be heeded.

SUMMARY

Because AIDS is a disease that always affects families (whether it be the family of origin or family of choice), it makes sense to identify the "family" as the unit of care. Strengthening family care networks, attending to family needs both during the course of illness and in the aftermath of death, has obvious salutary effects in terms of quality of life for the ill person and in terms of family life, including the prevention of psychosocial damage resulting from the traumatizing losses of AIDS. Family interventions are cost effective in that the appointment of a single family case manager or therapist reduces the need for the multiple care providers who gravitate to the ill person and the family. A family case manager has an organizing and consulting role, mobilizing the family to assume the bulk of caretaking and future planning responsibilities in the most life-preserving and enhancing manner possible. The overall effect of productive family work is the empowerment of families to find spiritual and emotional resources in the face of this most devastating and tragic epidemic.

REFERENCES

Alexander, B. K., & Dibb, G. S. (1975). Opiate addicts and their parents. *Family Process, 14,* 499–514.

Altman, L. (1994, August 17). High HIV levels raise risk to newborns, two studies show. *New York Times,* p. C8.

Borysenko, J. (1989). Psychoneuroimmunology. In C. Ransey (Ed.), *Family systems in medicine.* New York: Guilford Press.

Boyd, F. N. (1989). *Black families in therapy: A multisystems approach.* New York: Guilford Press.

Coleman, S. B. (1980). Incomplete mourning and addict family transactions: A theory for understanding heroin abuse. In D. Lettieri (Ed.), *Theories of drug abuse.* Washington, DC: U.S. Government Printing Office.

Coleman, S. B., Kaplan, J. D., & Downing, R. W. (1986). Life cycle and loss: The spiritual vacuum of heroin addiction. *Family Process, 5,* 5-23.

Coleman, S. B., & Stanton, M. D. (1978). The role of death in the addict family. *Journal of Marriage and Family Counseling, 4,* 79–91.

Drucher, E. (1986). AIDS and addiction in New York City. *American Journal of Drug Abuse, 12*, 165–181.

Gonzalez, S., Steinglass, P., & Reiss, D. (1987). *Family centered interventions for people with chronic disabilities*. Washington, DC: George Washington University Press.

Kaplan, L. (1987). AIDS and guilt. *Family Therapy Networker, 12*, 44–45.

Kaufman, E., & Kaufman, P. (1979). From a psychodynamic orientation to a structural family therapy approach in the treatment of drug dependency. In E. Kaufman & P. Kaufman (Eds.), *Family therapy of drug and alcohol abuse*. New York: Gardner Press.

Landau-Stanton, J. (1982). Therapy with families in cultural transition. In J. Pierce & M. McGoldrick (Eds.), *Ethnicity and family therapy*. New York: Guilford Press.

Landau-Stanton, J., et al. (1993). *AIDS health and mental health: A primary sourcebook*. New York: Brunner/Mazel.

Misbin, R. I. (1994). Ethical issues and guidelines in the care of terminally ill patients. *Directions in Psychiatry, 14*(10), 4–5.

Moynihan, D. P. (1965). *The Negro family: The case for national action*. Washington, DC: Department of Labor.

Reiss, D., Gonzalez, S., & Kramer, N. (1986). Family process, chronic illness, and death: On the weakness of strong bonds. *Archives of General Psychiatry, 43*, 795–804.

Rolland, J. S. (1984). Toward a psychosocial typology of chronic and life-threatening illness. *Family Systems Medicine, 2*, 245–263.

Rolland, J. S. (1987a). Chronic illness and the life cycle: A conceptual framework. *Family Process, 26*, 203–221.

Rolland, J. S. (1987b). Family illness paradigms: Evolution and significance. *Family Systems Medicine, 5*, 482–503.

Rolland, J. S. (1987c). Family systems and chronic illness: A typological model. *Journal of Psychotherapy and the Family, 3*, 143–168.

Shelton, D., et al. (1993). Medical adherence among prenatal HIV seropositive African-American women. *Family Issues, 2*(4), 1–16.

Stanton, M. D. (1985). The family and drug abuse, concepts and rationale. In T. E. Bratter & G. G. Forrest (Eds.), *Alcoholism and substance abuse in New York*. New York: Free Press.

Stanton, M. D., & Todd, T. C. (1979). Structural family therapy with drug addicts. In E. Kaufman & P. Kaufman (Eds.), *Family therapy of drug and alcohol abuse*. New York, NY: Gardner Press.

Stanton, M. D., & Todd, T. (1982). *The family therapy of drug abuse and addiction*. New York: Guilford Press.

Turner, C., Mille, H., & Moses, E. (Eds.). (1989). *AIDS: Sexual behavior and intravenous drug use*. Washington, DC: National Academy Press.

Vaillant, G. E. (1966). A 12-year follow-up of New York narcotic addicts: Some social and psychiatric characteristics. *Archives of General Psychiatry, 15*, 599–609.

Walker, G. (1995). *In the midst of winter: Counseling families, couples and individuals with AIDS infection* (rev. ed.). New York: Norton.

7

The Death of a Child: Implications for Marital and Family Therapy

Paula P. Bernstein, PhD, and Leslie A. Gavin, PhD

Dr. Bernstein is Associate Clinical Professor at the University of Colorado Health Sciences Center and Adjunct Associate Professor at the University of Denver. Dr. Gavin is Assistant Professor at the University of Colorado Health Sciences Center and the National Jewish Center for Immunology and Respiratory Medicine, Denver, CO.

KEY POINTS

- The loss of a child has an impact on every member of the family. For parents, a child's death is threatening to their identity and can result in overwhelming guilt.

- Low appetite, separation anxiety, and extreme reactions to minor illnesses have been reported in surviving siblings; the parents' availability is a key factor in the surviving children's adjustment to the loss.

- Strains on the marital relationship after the loss of a child often are inevitable, primarily because the loss leaves both partners so mentally fatigued that they do not have the energy to provide emotional support for each other.

- Miscarriages are a source of deep emotional trauma; this trauma can be exacerbated when parents' reactions are unrecognized and untreated.

- Resistance is common in all families who have experienced child loss. Therapists must work with the family's resistance, identify the loss and recognize its importance in all therapeutic work with the family, and focus on family members' strengths.

INTRODUCTION

The loss of a child has an impact on every member of the family. Sometimes the family system is altered so profoundly that the effects of the trauma can be observed through generations.

Some parents who suffer from difficulties after the death of a child do not consciously connect them with the loss, even when problems in the family drive them to seek help. Indeed, parents may strongly resist making such connections, assuring therapists they have "gotten over" the death of their child. Reluctance to reopen such a terrible wound may cause the therapist to collude with the parents' resistance to doing the necessary grief work. As we show in a series of case examples, these resistances can decisively undermine the therapeutic process. In many instances, work is interrupted despite the best efforts of the therapist to keep the family in treatment.

The therapist must become attuned to the many ways the loss of child affects a family to understand the best way to engage the family in treatment. Focusing the treatment for the family depends on the therapist's ability to "hear" the communications about the impact of the loss hidden in the family's behaviors.

THE IMPACT OF CHILD LOSS

Child loss is thought to be one of the most traumatic events possible in human experience. The resulting grief appears to be more severe than that associated with the loss of a parent, adult sibling, or spouse (Knapp, 1986; Kübler-Ross, 1983; Rando, 1985; Rosen & Cohen, 1981; Sanders, 1980).

The Parents:

When a child dies, the unique dynamics of the parent-child relationship cause parents to feel they have lost not only a child, but also a part of themselves (Rando, 1985). The child represents a source of future investment, hopes, and dreams that is suddenly destroyed (Zimmerman, 1981). The pain of the loss is continually renewed as the future unfolds without the child.

When parents lose a child, they lose a major functional role that may threaten their sense of identity. Of course, the loss means their daily routines and caretaking roles change radically. More painful still, the loss threatens their sense of being adequate parents, having been unable to fulfill parental duties of protection and nurturance (Rubin, 1985). As a result, many parents experience a tremendous amount of guilt, which may be unrelated to any objective responsibility for the child's death (Miles & Demi, 1984).

Kübler-Ross (1983) argues that guilt is heightened for couples whose child dies suddenly. These parents do not have the benefit of time to prepare for the death. According to Kübler-Ross, without this time for reflection, undoing of things regretted, and concentration of loving energy on the dying child, it may be even more difficult to work through feelings of guilt and shock.

The Marital Relationship:

The loss of a child seems to threaten the marital relationship in a way other losses do not. To begin with, in many life crises, it is only one partner who is significantly in pain and in need of support. When a couple loses a child, both partners may experience tremendous grief, leaving them little energy to provide emotional support for each other (Schiff, 1977; Zimmerman, 1981).

Difficulties also may arise when both spouses are mourning but have incompatible styles of grieving. For example, one parent may be overtly emotional, whereas the other is quietly depressed or withdrawn. The one who displays overt grief may believe that the other was not as attached to the deceased and may displace anger about the death on the "less caring" partner. Conversely, the one who "cannot stop grieving" may feel weaker and less worthy for not recovering as quickly. Some couples may have similar styles of grieving, yet their mood cycles (alternating from sorrow to hopefulness about the future) may occur at different rates. This lack of synchrony may cause estrangement, blocked communication, or aggravation of preexisting problems in the marital relationship (Rando, 1985).

The impact of these and other stressors may be seen in the high divorce rate among grieving couples (Schiff, 1977). The fact that many couples are geographically isolated from their extended families may intensify the strain on the marital relationship. At the same time, support networks often evaporate in the face of tragedy. Friends and even members of the extended family are often so uncomfortable with the loss that they avoid the couple.

The Surviving Siblings:

The loss of a sister or brother has a major effect on the lives of surviving siblings (Applebaum & Burns, 1991; Davies, 1991, 1995; Hutton & Bradley, 1994; McCown & Davies, 1995). Cobb (1956) studied parents' perceptions of their child's functioning after the loss of a sibling and noted appetite loss, fear of separation from parents, and physical realities that ranged from minor to severe illnesses.

The sibling bond includes a narcissistic investment in one's siblings. When a sibling dies, the child loses an important object at a formative period. The complex, ambivalent feelings inherent in the sibling relationship can complicate the child's mourning. The relationship between the surviving child and the deceased sibling must be slowly reworked during the mourning process.

The quality of the surviving child's relationship with each parent before the death influences the child's reaction to the loss. The parents' availability is a key factor in the child's adjustment. The fact that the child simultaneously loses the sibling and the parents' availability appears to be particularly salient. In many cases, parents are never the same (Pollock, 1978).

The loss of a sibling often has an impact on the way parents treat the surviving children. Parents may idealize the lost child and then compare surviving children to the one they have enshrined. Such comparisons almost always leave the surviving children feeling inadequate and further compound feelings of guilt and anger that they may have over the sibling's death (Turkington, 1984). Parents may overprotect surviving children or cast them in the role of a "replacement child," compromising their ability to develop a true self (Winnicott, 1965).

The ways in which children understand and adjust to the loss of a sibling are affected by their level of cognitive and emotional development. For example, Rosen (1986) suggests that children younger than age 5 may react with detached curiosity rather than a strong sense of loss, whereas adolescents may react with great visible distress, experiencing confusion, anger, and disorientation. The therapist must explore each surviving child's conception of death and how each child imagines the cause of death. To understand the child's predicament, the therapist should be sensitive to the degree to which the parents have been available to the child and whether support has been provided by other family members. Although painful marital problems may go untreated indefinitely, it may be the maladjustment of a surviving child that brings the family to treatment.

LOSS OF A CHILD DURING PREGNANCY

Reactions to losing a child during pregnancy often go unrecognized and untreated (Leon, 1990; Pines, 1993) because many health care providers and family members may assume that spontaneous abortion is not accompanied by the same distress as other child loss. Women report being told such things as,

"It's all for the best" and, "You can just try again in a few months." Couples receive little social and emotional support and feel guilty for being depressed.

The few studies that have been conducted in this area, mostly with women, have found that women experience a sense of loss and some limitation of daily functioning after miscarriage (Zaccardi, Abbott, & Koziol-McClain, 1993), with elevated levels of anxiety and severe depression (Lindberg, 1992; Neugebauer et al., 1992; Thapar & Thapar, 1992). They often carry a sense of guilt about the loss and do not believe that people around them understand their feelings (Bansen & Stevens, 1992). Women who experience significant physical pain and bleeding after the event may worry that their own life is in jeopardy. All too often, busy health care practitioners (and even family members) pay far too little attention to the heightened anxiety these women may feel during a subsequent pregnancy.

Persons at higher risk for psychiatric symptoms after miscarriage appear to be those with a past psychiatric history, poor social support, and previous history of miscarriage (Iles, 1989). As Pines (1993) pointed out, much of the woman's reaction to the loss may depend on the conscious and unconscious meanings she has attached to the pregnancy and the subsequent loss. For example, an ambivalent woman may experience miscarriage differently from a woman who is highly invested in parenthood. Parents who are trying to have their first child may experience miscarriage differently from those who already have children. Again, it is important to consider both the internal psychological and external social context in which the loss occurs.

CURRENT FAMILY DIFFICULTIES AND THEIR RELATION TO THE TRAUMA OF CHILD LOSS

We will now use case examples to discuss the various familial complications associated with child loss. The first three cases illustrate the types of problems that can develop in a family after a child dies. The fourth case illustrates how the effects of miscarriage can reverberate in the experience of subsequent children. The first three families were seen at a child psychological clinic (Bernstein et al., 1989), and the fourth child was being treated at a tertiary care hospital for asthmatic children. In all four cases, unresolved grief was continuing to operate as a pathogenic agent, leading to a host of diverse problems. The parents had erected massive defenses against reopening the pain of their loss. In some cases, they brought the surviving child for treatment only on the condition that the subject of the dead child be avoided.

Case #1:

Tommy was born 1 year after the cancer death of a 4-year-old sibling. He was referred to the clinic at age 9 because of behavioral and emotional problems at school although his parents reported no problems at home. From the beginning of treatment, it was clear that Tommy's parents were not interested in addressing the death of their other child. In fact, therapy had been attempted previously and terminated twice when therapists had tried to associate the family's chronic problems with the death of their child. Tommy was strikingly immature, functioning at the level of a 4- or 5-year-old child, with difficulty in regulating affect and impulses. For several years, he had been placed in a special classroom for aggressive children.

On entering treatment, Tommy quickly formed a dependent "wooing" transference with his female therapist, wanting to sit on her lap and bring her gifts. Progress seemed slow, and the therapist felt frustrated. As we discussed this case, it became obvious that Tommy was filling the role of a replacement child for his deceased brother (Krell & Rabkin, 1979; Pollock, 1978). It was as though he were destined, unconsciously, never to grow older than the child who was lost and never to separate or individuate. His parents failed to set age-appropriate limits for him. He was allowed to share his mother's bed when his father was working the night shift and was encouraged to sit on her lap. Such snuggling, which was overstimulating and disorganizing for Tommy, was regarded as perfectly normal by his parents. They hesitated to assert parental demands, unable to bear his anger, which implied the threat of separation and loss. As for Tommy, he was enmeshed with his mother and claimed he would never leave her.

Both parents were initially reluctant to change their relationships with Tommy. Eventually, treatment centered on the establishment of more appropriate boundaries between Tommy and his mother, and his parents focused on the quality of their marital relationship. The therapist realized that unless Tommy's parents could gain insight into the impact of the loss of the child Tommy had replaced, gains were likely to be quite unstable.

Case #2:

Mr. and Mrs. B contacted the clinic under pressure from the school to obtain an evaluation of their 6-year-old son, Peter. Teachers had become alarmed when they learned that Peter had tied a cord around his neck and jumped off a stairway. School officials, social service workers, and an evaluator at a local hospital were concerned about this suicidal gesture and insisted Peter obtain treatment. His parents, however, wanted another opinion.

Peter presented as a sad child with low self-esteem who was desperately seeking closeness and support from the adults in his life. He was on odd-looking child who had visual, motor, and auditory impairments. A second son, Bobby, had died of a congenital heart defect when Peter was 2 years old. Mr. and Mrs. B's failure to deal with Bobby's death was interfering with their ability to be sensitive to their surviving son's needs. They were often emotionally unavailable to him. Eventually, this neglect pushed Peter to resort to extreme measures. He used the most powerful tool he knew to show his parents how miserable he felt and to call attention to what could not be discussed. With his suicide attempt, he tried to confront them by essentially saying, "If I die, will you love me, too?"

When the therapist tried to discuss Bobby's death, Mr. and Mrs. B reacted in a mildly hostile manner, complaining that the significance of that event was being exaggerated. They minimized their sadness and expressed a desire to "not live in the past." They believed the death had neither changed their behavior nor contributed to Peter's problems. They refused to acknowledge Peter's depression and the frightening implication that he might be taken from them by death as well. They became progressively more resistant to treatment, repeatedly canceling sessions and finally refusing to allow Peter to be seen at all. They insisted that their very troubled son was "just a normal kid" (i.e., not "defective" like the child they lost) and not in need of treatment.

Case #3:

Ricky, age 6, and his family initially came to the clinic to address the problem of Ricky's noncompliance. Ricky's parents soon disclosed significant marital difficulties, having separated five times since they were married. It was only Ricky, however, who shared that he had had a brother, John, who had died shortly after birth, when Ricky was 3 years old. When asked to draw his family, Ricky included John, depicting himself and his brother sleeping upstairs. Clearly, in Ricky's inner representational world, John continued to be an important member of the family who lived like a ghost in the house.

Ricky's parents had difficulty in talking about their loss or seeing its relevance to their current problems. Ricky's father was struggling with substance abuse, and his mother was suffering from depression. They coped differently with the loss, which caused some tension between them. Ricky's father was anxious to "move on with life" and leave the loss behind, whereas his wife thought about the death often and felt as though she would always mourn John.

In treatment, Ricky was constricted and his affect flat. He had trouble engaging in playful behavior. He was angry and confused, struggling in a world in which perfect behavior was expected. During the course of therapy, both Ricky and his parents wondered whether his problems might be caused by "not having a little brother to play with." After 8 months, shortly before the anniversary of John's death, the family ended treatment, making it impossible for the therapist to help them deal with the grief that would surely have been reawakened by the combined thrust of the anniversary reaction (Pollock, 1971) and the therapeutic process.

Case #4:

Mary, a 34-year-old woman from a small southern city, brought her 3-year-old daughter, Jennifer, to a tertiary referral hospital in a northern city to be evaluated for allergic reactions and respiratory difficulties. Jennifer's symptoms reportedly occurred when she was exposed to the outdoor environment. These reactions became particularly problematic when Jennifer went to visit her father, Mary's ex-husband.

Mary's divorce from her husband was deeply troubling to her because her religion opposed divorce. Mary resented her husband for being unsupportive and, at times, psychologically abusive toward her during the marriage. Estrangement in the relationship had occurred several years earlier when she had two consecutive miscarriages caused by endometriosis. She suffered deep emotional reactions to both losses, to which her husband was completely unresponsive. When she had become tearful 2 weeks after the second miscarriage, her husband had told her "to quit crying and get on with her life."

When Mary and her daughter were seen in the hospital, Mary presented as an angry, stern woman who was enmeshed with her daughter. Each day, they wore coordinated outfits, and Mary never left her daughter's side. She would use the word "we" when describing her daughter's symptoms and explained that she knew exactly what Jennifer was experiencing because she suffered from the same allergic reactions. She described the lengths she would go to at home to keep her daughter protected from the environment, which included having the child wear a particle mask when going outside and confining her to an elaborate indoor play area. This consisted of an indoor "beach," complete with swings, slide, water, sand, and sunlamp. Mary stated that she resented it when people accused her of keeping her daughter in a "bubble" because she had everything she needed to live at home.

Despite extensive medical evaluation and environmental challenges, Jennifer displayed no allergic reactions in the hospital. She did, however, report numerous somatic complaints, which her mother would interpret as severe symptomatology. It was apparent to the consulting team that Jennifer was being kept forever safe in a warm, all-sufficient shelter that remarkably resembled a womb. The therapist wondered with Mary whether her fears for Jennifer might be related to having lost two babies. Mary acknowledged that she grieved the loss of her babies every day and insisted that Jennifer was a delicate child who could die if proper attention were not paid to her allergic symptoms. Therapeutic work with Mary focused on her over-involvement with her daughter, her tendency to see her daughter as vulnerable, and her extreme distress at seeing her daughter experience any physical discomfort. The therapist's task was to help Mary find ways to explore how unresolved feelings about the miscarriages might be affecting her relationship with her surviving child.

RESISTANCE TO TREATMENT

The problems that finally brought these families into therapy were varied and difficult to treat. It was only in reviewing the lack of progress in the first cases that we discovered, to our surprise, that each family had experienced the death of a child. Eventually, we realized this factor was central to the obstacles encountered in treatment. In each case, the grief over the lost child had not been worked through. The therapists had accepted this defense, not recognizing it as a critical resistance. When first presenting these cases, some therapists had forgotten the exact circumstances of the child's death, indicative of the degree to which they had unknowingly colluded with the parents' defenses against the terrible pain of remembering. Treatment was being focused on the children's presentation of problems and was going nowhere. Treatment planning in the fourth case benefited from the experience gained as a result of the first study.

The parents were remarkably similar in their use of defensive denial, even using similar phrases in their refusal to acknowledge that the death might be contributing to current problems. For example, nearly every family expressed the desire to "move on" and "not live in the past." Denial kept them from perceiving problems in their surviving children. Peter's parents could not recognize his depression, even in the face of his suicidal gesture. Ricky's parents also pulled him out of treatment despite his obvious emotional pain. Tommy's parents cast him in the role of replacement child, oblivious to his real age and developmental needs; they stayed in treatment, but their rigid defenses effectively prevented an entire dimension of the family's problems from being addressed. Mary's difficulty in resolving her miscarriages led her to overprotect her daughter to the point of keeping her in a womb-like environment, turning her into an invalid, and severely inhibiting her social and emotional growth.

Trying to convince the parents of the connection between current problems and the earlier loss only intensified resistance, turning a hoped-for alliance into an adversarial stand-off. Conducting the treatment on the parents' terms led just as surely to a therapeutic stalemate. What can a therapist do in such a situation?

The fundamental first step in working with families who have experienced child loss is two prolonged: (a) identify the loss and (b) recognize its primary importance in any therapeutic work with the family. This requires asking all family members at the time of the initial evaluation whether they have had major losses within their family and how many pregnancies they have experienced.

Therapists must be aware that families are likely to have major resistance to addressing questions related to their loss, even though it may be evident that issues of unresolved loss continue to be active in their lives. The best avenue for understanding a family's need to defend against pain may be the therapist's awareness of his or her own inner trepidation about reopening the wound and sharing the anguish of their tragedy. If the therapist colludes with the family's position that the loss is irrelevant to the present, the therapy will stall. What is necessary is a therapeutic stance balanced between ignoring the loss and continually bombarding the family with how issues of loss are being played out.

The therapist should work with a family's resistance instead of against it, finding ways to explore it from within their own framework. Gentle, supportive statements such as, "It must be very annoying when school authorities keep mentioning the death" may help parents ventilate their anger. Gradually, parents may begin to feel safe enough to let their own concerns surface, almost in spite of themselves, saying something like, "Teachers and therapists ought to realize how sad it makes us feel!" or, "It is incredibly unfair to question our ability to be good parents just because of the tragedy we've been through!" Peter's therapist could have commented on how the authorities seemed extremely insensitive to the anxiety any parent who has lost a child might feel when outsiders suggest something might be wrong with a child who, thank heavens, is "normal."

In therapy with family members, it is also helpful to focus on their strengths and on how they previously used such strengths in times of trouble. Questions such as "How did you move on after such a terrible event?" do not criticize or "pathologize" the experience of family members; furthermore they open the subject while supporting the positive coping strategies of the family.

Normalization of the family's experience is important in

helping them address their lingering grief. Comments such as "Many people don't recognize how devastating miscarriage can be" validate the grieving parents' experience. As the therapeutic alliance strengthens, the therapist may move further using the same approach; for example, "Every parent who has lost a child has a heightened awareness of the fragility of life. This sometimes makes it difficult for them to allow their other children to take risks. What has been your experience?"

Some families outright refuse to discuss the death because family members are afraid of triggering an emotional reaction that will disturb the family's equilibrium, which has been carefully maintained by tiptoeing around any mention of the subject. This is difficult to address in therapy without losing the family's trust. It is important to recognize the desire to protect and label it supportively as arising from their loving concern for each other. It is common for one member, perhaps the father, to insist that discussion can only stir up painful memories. He wants his wife (and the children) protected from such pain. It may be helpful to ask the family member (most often the mother) whether she needs protection. We have found that the protected spouse often will discuss the loss openly.

Once the family has begun to feel safe and understood within the therapeutic setting, the same loving concern may be mobilized on behalf of maximizing the developmental potential of the surviving children. The family may be willing to experience the pain of talking "once more" just to ensure the children are not adversely affected — now or in the future — by a traumatic event over which no one in the family had any control. The therapist may be able to explore with parents and children the ways in which the aftereffects of the tragic experience continue to affect the family in subtle ways.

In the case of prenatal loss, lack of attention to possible psychiatric symptoms manifesting immediately after miscarriage may lead to later difficulties for the mother, the marital relationship, and the family. Although it is important not to create problems where none exist, families should be offered the opportunity to address their grief and to have feelings of sadness and fear normalized. Families may benefit from help in acknowledging the significance of the loss, support in obtaining medical information about the reasons for the loss, and working with the therapist on ways to mourn, including, for example, a memorial service for the lost child-to-be (Stirtzinger & Robinson, 1989).

MEASURING THERAPEUTIC SUCCESS

Therapeutic success may be difficult to gauge. It is commonly thought that grief should last for 1 year and that any continued symptomatology past that point is pathologic. Professionals who work with victims of child loss recognize that families may never stop grieving. Thus, success with these families does not mean they will never feel sad or go through active grieving periods as the future unfolds without the child. Instead, signs of therapeutic success appear to be subtle changes in the family's way of coping with the grief. Helping a family develop ways of talking about the lost member is critically important. For siblings, therapeutic success may hinge on providing a safe place to ask questions they have never felt permitted to ask because of the perceived taboos in the family. It may help to hold sessions in which family members "say good-bye" to the lost child in a way not possible before. Agreeing on appropriate memorial rituals, such as visiting the grave on milestone occasions, can also help.

Signs of successful therapeutic work include an acceptance that the grief will always be there to some degree, a forthright attitude toward issues related to death within the family, and the ability of family members to support each other without criticizing or isolating each other emotionally.

CONCLUSION

Families who have experienced the death of a child are especially in need of therapy and, at the same time, can be especially difficult to diagnose and treat. The symptom picture can be confusing until its underlying dynamics are understood. Wary parents, consciously or unconsciously, perceive therapy as a Pandora's box. The extraordinary pain involved in examining what is happening in the family and reopening the unresolved grief can cause parents to avoid seeking treatment or to abandon it prematurely. Failure to address the death often results in the lingering presence of a "ghost from the past" who works mischief in many ways. The goal of family treatment is to turn the ghost of the lost child into a memory, freeing energies of parents and siblings for loving relationships, further development, and creative living.

REFERENCES

Applebaum, D. R., & Burns, G. L. (1991). Unexpected childhood death: Posttraumatic stress disorder in surviving siblings and parents. *Journal of Clinical Child Psychology, 20,* 114-120.

Bansen, S. S., & Stevens, H. A. (1992). Women's experiences of miscarriage in early pregnancy. *Journal of Nurse-Midwifery, 37,* 84–90.

Bernstein, P. P., Duncan, S. W., Gavin, L. A., Lindahl, K. M., & Ozonoff, S. (1989). Resistance to psychotherapy: The effects of the death on parents and siblings. *Psychotherapy, 26,* 227–232.

Cobb, B. (1956). Psychological impact of long illness and death of a child on the family circle. *Journal of Pediatrics, 49,* 746–751.

Davies, B. (1991). Longterm outcomes of adolescent sibling bereavement. Special issue: Death and adolescent bereavement. *Journal of Adolescent Research, 6,* 83-96.

Davies, B. (1995). Toward siblings' understanding and perspectives of death. In E. A. Grollman (Ed.), *Bereaved children and teens: A support guide for parents and professionals* (pp. 61-74). Boston: Beacon Press.

Hutton, C. J., & Bradley, B. S. (1994). Effects of student infant death on bereaved siblings: A comparative study. *Journal of Child Psychology and Psychiatry and Allied Disciplines, 35,* 723-732.

Iles, S. (1989). The loss of early pregnancy. *Baillieres Clinical Obstetrics and Gynaecology, 3,* 769-790.

Knapp, R. J. (1986). *Beyond endurance: When a child dies.* New York: Schocken Books.

Krell, R., & Rabkin, L. (1979). The effects of sibling death on the surviving child: A family perspective. *Family Process, 18,* 471-477.

Kübler-Ross, E. (1983). *On children and death.* New York: Macmillan.

Leon, I. G. (1990). *When a baby dies: Psychotherapy for pregnancy and newborn loss.* New Haven, CT: Yale University Press.

Lindberg, C. E. (1992). The grief response to mid-trimester fetal loss. *Journal of Perinatology, 12,* 158-163.

McCown, D. E., & Davies, B. (1995). Patterns of grief in young children following the death of a sibling. *Death Studies, 19,* 41-53.

Miles, M. S., & Demi, A. S. (1984). Toward the development of a theory of bereavement guilt: Sources of guilt in bereaved parents. *Omega, 14,* 229-319.

Neugebauer, R., Kline, J., O'Connor, P., Shrout, P., Johnson, J., Skodol, A., Wicks, J., & Susser, M. (1992). Determinants of depressive symptoms in the early weeks after miscarriage. *American Journal of Public Health, 82,* 1332-1339.

Pines, D. (1993). Book review: I. G. Leon, When a baby dies: Psychotherapy for pregnancy and newborn loss. *Psychoanalytic Quarterly, 62,* 467-469.

Pollock, G. H. (1971). On time and anniversaries. In M. Kanzer (Ed.), *The unconscious today.* New York: International Universities Press.

Pollock, G. H. (1978). On siblings, childhood loss, and creativity. *The Annual of Psychoanalysis, 6,* 43-481.

Rando, T. A. (1985). Bereaved parents: Particular difficulties, unique factors, and treatment issues. *Social Work, 30,* 19–23.

Rosen, H. (1986). When a sibling dies. *International Journal of Family Psychiatry, 7,* 389–396.

Rosen, H., & Cohen, H. L. (1981). Children's reactions to sibling loss. *Clinical Social Work Journal, 9,* 211–219.

Rubin, S. S. (1985). Maternal attachment and child death: On adjustment, relationship, and resolution. *Omega, 15,* 347–352.

Sanders, C. (1980). A comparison of adult bereavement in the death of a spouse, child, and parent. *Omega, 10,* 303–322.

Schiff, H. S. (1977). *The bereaved parent.* New York: Penguin Books.

Stirtzinger, R., & Robinson, G. E. (1989). The psychological effects of spontaneous abortion. *Canadian Medical Association Journal, 140,* 799–801.

Thapar, A. K., & Thapar, A. (1992). Psychological sequelae of miscarriage: A controlled study using the general health questionnaire and the hospital anxiety and depression scale. *British Journal of General Practice, 42,* 94–96.

Turkington, C. (1984). Support urged for children in mourning. *APA Monitor, 15,* 16–17.

Winnicott, D. W. (1965). Ego distortion in terms of true and false self. In D. W. Winnicott (Ed.), *The maturational processes and the facilitating environment* (pp. 140-152). New York: International Universities Press.

Zaccardi, R., Abbott, J., & Koziol-McClain, J. (1993). Loss and grief reactions after spontaneous miscarriage in the emergency department. *Annals of Emergency Medicine, 22,* 799–804.

Zimmerman, J. P. (1981). The bereaved parent. In O. S. Margolis, H. C. Raether, A. H. Kutscher, J. B. Powers, I. B. Seeland, R. DeBellis, & J. Cherico (Eds.), *Acute grief: Counseling the bereaved* (pp. 126-132). New York: Columbia University Press.

FOR FURTHER READING

Balk, D. (1983). Adolescents' grief reactions and self-concept perceptions following sibling death: A study of 33 teenagers. *Journal of Youth and Adolescence, 12,* 137–161.

Colonna, A. B., & Newman, L. M. (1983). The psychoanalytic literature on siblings. In A. J. Solnit, R. S. Eissler, & P. B. Neubauer (Eds.), *The psychoanalytic study of the child* (Vol. 38). New Haven, CT: Yale University Press.

Edelstein, L. (1984). *Maternal bereavement.* New York: Praeger Books.

Knapp, R. J. (1986). *Beyond endurance: When a child dies.* New York: Schocken Books.

Neubauer, P. B. (1983). The importance of the sibling experience. In A. J. Solnit, R. S. Eissler, & P. B. Neubauer (Eds.), *The psychoanalytic study of the child* (Vol. 38). New Haven, CT: Yale University Press.

Richter, E. (1986). *Losing someone you love: When a brother or sister dies.* New York: Putnam.

Rosen, H. (1985). Prohibitions against mourning in childhood sibling loss. *Omega, 15,* 307–316.

Rosen, H. (1986). *Unspoken grief: Coping with childhood sibling loss.* New York: D. C. Heath.

8

Family Caregiving of the Elderly

Juanita L. Garcia, EdD, and Jordan I. Kosberg, PhD

Dr. Garcia is Associate Professor, Department of Gerontology, College of Arts and Sciences, University of South Florida, Tampa, FL. Dr. Kosberg is Professor, School of Social Work, Florida International University, North Miami, FL.

KEY POINTS

- Family caregiving is the backbone of elderly care. Throughout history, it has been the normative mechanism for care of the elderly.

- An increase in life expectancy and a decrease in the rate of deaths from heart disease and strokes are but two factors making family caregiving of the elderly increasingly difficult.

- The majority of family caregivers are women. However, this dynamic is changing with an increasing number of women entering the work force.

- Two kinds of elderly care are outlined: formal and informal systems. The formal service system includes community services and agencies. Informal caregiving is provided by family, friends, and neighbors.

- Intervention by the formal system of care can help people better care for their elderly relatives.

- The first step to intervention is determining the motivation of caregivers. It is also important for therapists to use diagnostic tests to assess the mental status and cognitive abilities of family members who are under duress.

- Strategies for intervention include support groups, education, clinical interventions (e.g., case management), and concrete community resources.

INTRODUCTION

Family care has been the normative mechanism for the care of the elderly throughout history and has been supported by both social custom and religious admonitions to "honor thy father and mother." Yet, over time, changing values and economic factors have made family caregiving of the elderly increasingly difficult.

Numerous changes in contemporary society have affected the need for family caregiving and the ability of families to provide such care for older family members (Biegel, Sales, & Schulz, 1991). Such changes include an increase in life expectancy, resulting in an aging population; a decrease in the rate of deaths from heart disease and strokes; and longer survival rates for cancer. Thus, more older persons are living longer with greater impairments and greater need for assistance in performing activities of daily living.

Along with the growth in the elderly population, birth rates have decreased, resulting in both a growing proportion of elderly and a reduction in the proportion of younger family members. Changes in the family structure that affect traditional caregiving responsibilities for elderly relatives result from increases in divorce rates, serial marriages, childless couples, and homosexual relationships. Perhaps the greatest influence on caregiving patterns has been the emancipation of women—the traditional care providers for the elderly—from the home.

Yet, family care continues to be seen as a major mechanism to delay costly institutionalization (American Association of Retired Persons [AARP], 1988) and to relieve government of the expense of caring for the elderly (Kosberg & Garcia, 1991). Changes in health care reimbursement policies and early hospital discharges of geriatric patients (determined by diagnosis-related groups, which set the time for a patient's release under the Medicare program), have resulted in the increased possibility of family care for impaired persons (Coulton, 1988).

Those in the helping professions, especially family therapists and clinical psychologists, increasingly will be involved with family members who face challenges in the provision of care to elderly relatives, as well as with those family members who do not wish (or are unable) to provide such care.

OVERVIEW OF CAREGIVING

Caregiving to the elderly can be divided into formal and informal systems.

Formal Resources:

The *formal service system* includes community services and agencies, which are bureaucratically organized and funded by government or private philanthropy. Such services are delivered by trained professionals and provide medical, legal, financial, nutritional, transportation-related, and mental health support to caregivers.

Formal services are a relatively new addition to caregiving. They have been established and organized by modern communities to compensate for gaps in care — when the family is not available or cannot fulfill its traditional caregiving functions.

Informal Sources:

Informal caregiving of family members has been the traditional method by which the needs of the elderly have been met and is provided by family, friends, and neighbors. This system ostensibly evolves naturally (in response to family needs). Although it appears less organized than the formal system, and therefore may be seen as being less effective, the informal system is a highly effective mechanism; many aging and aged family members take its existence for granted and rely on it as their main source of support.

However, the tradition of family caregiving has been seriously challenged not only by societal changes, but also by the ever-increasing complexities of human relationships. Clinicians, service providers, and researchers are attempting to understand better the changes that occur in the caregiving situation and the varying interpretations by family members and elderly relatives that may lead to familial conflicts.

Clearly, not only do changes occur in the perception of family responsibilities between generations, but also with regard to future relationships between caregivers and the care recipients (Litvin, 1992). For example, caregivers (in contrast to care recipients) tend to be more optimistic in viewing the health conditions and social participation of the elderly; they also underestimate health care needs. Such perceptions tend to "protect" caregivers; that is, they reduce the "need" for care and the "guilt" for not providing more care to an elderly relative (Allan, 1988; Brody, 1990).

A decline in intrafamilial interaction may lead to increases of conflict and stress for the caregiver. Formal support to family caregivers will be most effective when it meets the actual and perceived needs of the caregivers. As discussed later, professional interventions should be flexible, because one set of interventions will not work with all families.

RESEARCH ON CAREGIVERS

Demographics of Caregivers:

Research has found that caregivers for the elderly are generally family members, especially women who are middle-age and married (Brody, 1981; Cantor, 1983; Cicirelli, 1983; Horowitz, 1985; Kosberg & Garcia, 1991; Shanas, 1979; Stoller, 1983; Stone, Cafferata, & Sangl, 1987). Nonetheless, the number of men who care for elderly persons has been increasing (Brubaker & Brubaker, 1992; Horowitz, 1985; Stoller, 1983). Many caregivers are themselves older adults; one third of caregivers are 65 years of age or older. Most caregivers are spouses, one third are adult children, and one fourth are other relatives and nonrelatives (Biegel et al., 1991; Stone et al., 1987).

Many factors in the lives of caregivers of elderly persons make it difficult to provide them with the care they need. Almost one third of caregivers are employed outside the home (AARP, 1988), and one fifth encounter conflicts in combining caregiving and work; one third rearrange work schedules, and one fifth work fewer hours and take off work without pay (Neal, Chapman, Ingersoll-Dayton, & Emlen, 1993). About one tenth of caregivers report quitting work to be available to provide needed care to an elderly relative. Approximately two fifths of employed caregivers report losing time, money, or benefits at work due to caregiving responsibilities. In addition, one fifth of caregivers have children under 18 living at home (Brody, 1990).

Research also indicates that caregivers need information on medicine, general health care, and available social services. One third report a need for emotional support and respite. Studies have shown that families provide significant amounts of assistance while juggling competing demands (Neal et al., 1993).

Caregivers from lower socioeconomic backgrounds report lower levels of health than do the general population. Caregiving responsibilities — coupled with lower income and lower self-reported health — suggest a significant need for supportive services and professional counseling and intervention.

As a result of these and other factors, many elderly persons cannot get the help they need from their families. Thus, they must rely on community services (Thorson, 1995).

Activities of Caregivers:

Activities can range from the provision of total care for an elderly family member to assistance in one or two daily activities (Cantor, 1983; George & Gwyther, 1986). The family (generally the primary caregiver) must perform the following activities for an elderly dependent relative: cook, clean, nurse, wash, transport, supervise mobility, oversee administration of medications, help with toileting (when incontinent), exercise, and feed—among other things (Lubkin, 1986). In addition to such instrumental tasks in caregiving are the affective ones, such as the provision of concern and affection.

While assuming the major responsibility for keeping the relative at home, caregivers face eight main social and psychological challenges: preventing or managing medical crises; controlling symptoms; carrying out the prescribed regimens; dealing with social isolation related to home care; adjusting to changes in the course of a disease or disability; normalizing lifestyles and interactions with others; funding the care (e.g., drugs, treatments, services) despite reduced or complete loss of payment; and confronting psychological, social, and familial problems (Straus et al., 1984).

Efficacy of Caregivers:

Studies attempting to measure the competence of family members providing informal caregiving have reported mixed results (Noelker & Townsend, 1987; Townsend & Noelker, 1987). In one study (Kosberg & Cairl, 1991) measuring competence, differences ranged from low to high, with the majority of 96 family caregivers of patients with Alzheimer's disease demonstrating moderate levels of competency. (Areas of competence pertained to meeting the medical, social, psychological, and safety needs of the demented relatives.)

Caregiver burden affects caregiving effectiveness. Awareness of this burden has emerged from studies on the great demands placed on families caring for mentally retarded, mentally ill, and, more recently, demented relatives (Brubaker & Brubaker, 1989; Zarit, Reever, & Peterson, 1980). However, family burden also results from care given to persons with less dramatic health problems. Indeed, the more healthy and active a care recipient may be, the greater the likelihood of "fighting" a growing vulnerability and dependency (and the caregiver). In addition, the cognitive impairments of a physically healthy person can cause burdens, no less burdensome than the caregiving burdens from physical impairments.

Caregiving research originally focused on the global needs of family caregivers in hopes of increasing the level of care or reducing the burden. Efforts to conceptualize caregiver burden more effectively have led to development of quantitative measures (Kosberg & Cairl, 1986; Zarit & Zarit, 1982). Research has determined that the correlates of caregiving burden are the severity of an illness (thus, the greater the responsibilities), the amount of patient change, and the suddenness of a problem's onset (or the awareness of a problem). Demographic variables associated with caregiving burden include gender (female caregivers have greater stress), role relationship (spouses and others who live with the impaired older person have higher levels), those in poorer health themselves, younger age (such persons display greater distress), socioeconomic status (those with higher income levels initially had greater stress, whereas those with lower income levels had long-term needs with fewer resources and greater stress later on). Life status variables associated with burden include the existence of other stresses, such as poor health, conflicting demands, and economic hardships.

Lower levels of burden are associated with marital cohesiveness and positive marital communications. Social support studies have shown mixed results. Some indicate that the informal support system guards against caregiving burden, whereas others have noted a positive relationship between the extent of the social support system and the sense of perceived burden (Kosberg, Cairl, & Keller, 1990; Brubaker & Brubaker, 1989). The lack of conclusive findings between burden and the participation of family members merely reflects the idiosyncratic nature of the dynamics for each caregiving situation.

MOTIVATIONS

The motivation of caregivers must be determined. Such an awareness should give insight into the reasons for the quality and quantity of care given to an elderly person and provide clues for necessary professional intervention (in cases of adversity to the older person or stress to the caregiving family or family members).

Batson and Coke (1983) have discussed two general types of motivations: negative and positive. Negative motivations might involve an anticipation of reward (e.g., expectations of payment, gaining social approval, or avoiding censure; Reis & Gruzen, 1976), receiving esteem in exchange for helping (Hatfield, Walster, & Piliavin, 1978), complying with social norms (Berkowitz, 1972), seeing oneself as a good person (Bandura, 1977), and avoiding guilt (Brody, Litvin, Hoffman, & Kleban, 1992; Hoffman, 1982).

Positive motivations for providing care result from feelings of love, respect, and loyalty. The desire can be based on genuine empathy and altruism; some caregivers are able to adopt the perspective of another and desire to alleviate the suffering of another person. Although no empirical basis exists, one can assume that an ability to empathize is based on kinship, similarity, prior interaction, and attachment—all of which are pertinent to intrafamilial situations. Yet, such considerations can also lead to higher levels of distress among caregivers (Cantor, 1983; Horowitz, 1985), again underscoring the complexities in family caregiving that make it difficult (if not impossible) to arrive at definitive conclusions.

In a more pragmatic view, family care may be chosen because of a lack of alternatives; the motivation to provide care may result from a belief that if care is not provided to an elderly relative, institutionalization will be necessary. Furthermore, professionals often will try to influence family members to assume caregiving responsibilities because such a solution to the placement problem of an older patient is perceived to be the easiest or the professional's own value system supports filial responsibility.

PROBLEMS WITH FAMILY CAREGIVING

Caregiving responsibilities are not limited to caring for a live-in older relative. The provision of care to the elderly person in his or her separate home may require more time, effort, and cost to the caregiver. To be sure, several potential problems exist for those who wish to assume caregiving responsibilities for any elderly relative.

Economic Issues:

Some families and family members are under economic pressures caused by unemployment or underemployment. Additional real (or imagined) expenses may result from the provision of direct or indirect care to an elderly relative. Intrafamilial problems (including child and spouse abuse) often result from economic pressures within the family.

Gender Roles:

In the past, women were socialized to be the major caregivers of family members, and they generally remained at home to provide such care. As a result of the women's movement, however, they are increasingly seeking careers outside the home. Unfortunately for women, they continue to maintain the major responsibility for caregiving within their families along with their employment outside the home (Robinson, Moen, Dempster-McClain, 1995). Dual pressures from the workplace and the home result, including an increased possibility of having to switch from full-time to part-time employment (or to leave the job market altogether) (Neal et al., 1993).

Social Disruption:

Individuals and families have social lives that can be adversely affected by caregiving responsibilities. The freedom to come and go, to invite friends over to one's home, to leave the home for a weekend outing all may be precluded by the need to care for an especially ill, impaired, or confused elderly relative.

Physical Problems:

The severity of physical or mental problems of an elderly relative may adversely affect the ability of family members to meet the person's needs. The health condition of the caregivers themselves will affect their ability to meet the needs of the dependent elderly person. Further, there is a likelihood that, with time, the caregivers will incur health-related problems resulting from the provision of care.

Family Relationships:

Hooyman and Lustbader (1986) argue that family care of an elderly person may be an extension of reciprocal positive regard between the family and the elderly person over the years. Of course, situations exist in which a history of poor interpersonal relationships is evident. The dependent elderly relative might have been a child or spouse abuser, a neglectful father or husband, or had a long history of poor relationships with those on whom he or she is now dependent. Clearly, caregiving responsibilities for such persons will be given ambivalently, if not grudgingly (and, perhaps, harshly).

Physical Barriers:

The physical structure of the home may be incongruent with the needs of the care recipient. Some elderly use walkers or wheelchairs, some have ambulation problems resulting in an inability to climb stairs. If a home is not located near public transportation or needed public or private conveniences, the care recipient can become more like a "prisoner" within the home and more dependent on family caregivers. Finally, the need to care for an elderly relative within one's home may result in overcrowding or dislocation of family members (i.e., moving children out of their rooms) or the need to share rooms.

Values and Expectations:

Caregivers and care recipients do not share common expectations toward their rights and responsibilities. As opposed to the evident responsibility that parents have for their children, there are no clear-cut policies that dictate the responsibilities of family members (especially adult children) toward elderly relatives. Discord from discrepancies between generations may result in various emotions, ranging from guilt to anger (Garcia & Kosberg, 1992).

Moreover, some elderly relatives have been labeled as provocateurs (Kosberg & Cairl, 1986); they are overly demanding, and unappreciative of the efforts of their caregiver(s). Such persons can make caregiving exceedingly difficult for those caring for them.

CONSEQUENCES OF FAMILY CAREGIVING

As reported in two national surveys (AARP, 1988; Cantor, 1983), consequences for providing care can include *decreased* health, income, free time, and privacy, as well as *increased* pressures and isolation. Moreover, negative emotions (anger leading to depression or hostility) may result from the caregiving experience. In fact, however, there can be both positive and negative consequences for family members who assume caregiving responsibilities for elderly persons.

Positive Features:

Colerick and George (1986) found caregivers can realize positive feelings of accomplishment and self-satisfaction resulting from their efforts in providing care to an elderly loved one. Hooyman and Lustbader (1986) found an increase in life satisfaction. Indeed, for some relatives, providing care to another is the major role that they perform, and when the role ends (i.e., a child growing up or the death or institutionalization of an elderly parent or spouse), they can feel a great sense of loss.

Fitting, Rabins, Lucas, and Eastham (1986) found improvements in some spousal relationships that resulted from the caregiving role. Also, Lewis and Meredith (1988) reported on the reaffirmation of the "feminine identity" that resulted from the provision of care to an elderly relative.

Negative Features:

Family Disharmony

Fiore, Becker, and Koppel (1983) found that the needs of an elderly relative may result in marked family disharmony: members of the family bicker about the sharing of responsibility; the perception arises that family members are shirking their responsibility; or an attempt is made to set a financial *quid pro quo* for a relative who is unable or unavailable to share in the caregiving responsibility (e.g., due to living a great distance away). This disharmony can result in bitter intrafamilial feelings. Worse yet, negative feelings may become focused on the elderly relative.

Ineffective Care

In some instances, caregivers are unable to meet the needs of the elderly person, no matter how hard they try. This may be the result of being unable to afford the necessary health resources (equipment or home health care visitors), or it may be a result of being physically or emotionally unable to meet the daily needs of cleaning, bathing, toileting, feeding, or cooking for the elderly person. Indeed, as Kosberg and Dermody (1985) found, one third of discharged geriatric patients were cared for by a person (generally a spouse) who was as old and frail as the discharged patient. Clearly, caregivers — especially those who care for the most impaired persons — must have some degree of strength and physical dexterity to execute their duties.

Elder Abuse

The ultimate adversity resulting from caregiving problems is elder abuse. Such adversity can include acts of omission (neglect out of ignorance or passive behavior) or acts of commission (physical or psychological abuse or active neglect). Many explanations are offered for why family members would abuse elderly relatives (Kosberg, 1988). But persons do have "breaking points." To paraphrase Garbarino (1947), who wrote about child abuse: given the wrong set of circumstances, we can all be a child abuser (or an elder abuser). And often when one faces personal or family problems, the focus of adverse emotions (anger, frustration, depression) is often turned to the perceived source of the adversity — the elderly person.

INTERVENTIONS

Given the demands and possible strains from caregiving to elderly persons, caregivers often also need attention from those in the helping professions, especially if the cared-for person is frail and dependent on others for the performance of many tasks for daily living. The overwhelming and unrelenting effort of providing care (envisioned in the title of a popular book on caregiving to Alzheimer's disease patients, *The Thirty-Six Hour Day* by Mace and Rabins [1981]) has been recognized through the development of community resources (e.g., respite care, family caregiving support groups, and community day-care centers).

Types of caregiver interventions vary in frequency, duration, and intensity of involvement because the caregiving situations vary significantly. In general, however, these intervention techniques can be described as support group, educational, clinical (direct service), and specific community services. These interventions also vary in the level of involvement of professionals; they can include the direct provision of clinical intervention, the formation and conduct of group efforts, or referrals to concrete community resources. However, before interventions are planned, the caregiving situation must be assessed.

Assessment:

A number of tools have been devised to assess the mental status of elderly persons. One tool measures cognitive abilities: the Short Portable Mental Status Questionnaire (Pfeiffer, 1975), which is brief and requires minimal training.

The assessment of affect is particularly important in working with the elderly because depression is not uncommon in response to social loses or in conjunction with physical decline. The Geriatric Depression Scale (Yesavage & Brink, 1983) is a reliable and valid measure consisting of 30 yes or no questions.

Functional assessments can be made with instruments such as the Katz Index of Activities of Daily Living and the Instrumental Activities of Daily Living, both developed at Duke University Center for the Study of Aging and Human Development (1978). These instruments focus on specific deficits, distinguish levels of needed assistance, and translate readily into required services.

For effective intervention to occur, assessment must be made of family members who are under duress (Kosberg & Cairl, 1986; Kosberg, Cairl, & Keller, 1990), and one must delineate the specific dimensions of caregiving burden (George & Gwyther, 1986; Zarit, 1989). Tools such as Kosberg's Cost of Care Index (Kosberg & Cairl, 1986) help identify potential stressors in such areas as physical health, social functioning, and financial burden.

Social assessments include not only the caregiving family, but also the entire social network from which support may be available. The results of such assessments can help determine what specific aid will be required as well as the division of labor (responsibility) between the family members.

Assessment is not a one-time event. Family members need updates on cognitive and physical levels of functioning of the care recipient to identify any necessary changes in caregiving.

Through ongoing professional contacts, the caregiving family is emotionally reinforced in its efforts. The rewards of family care may be few but can be extremely significant (i.e., family cohesiveness and the expression of love, duty, and pride). The burdens of caregiving can be great; they can result in both objective pressures (time, energy, financial expenses) and emotional pressures (anger, guilt, embarrassment, sense of helplessness, grief, depression, feelings of isolation, loss of control). The identification of such consequences is the first step to intervention.

Support Groups:

The support group is designed to offer emotional support and information, and, hopefully, improve coping skills by using guest lecturers and by sharing coping strategies with group members. These groups can be led by professionals or peers. They emphasize the sharing of feelings and experiences, reinforcing the idea that the caregiving family (or individual) is not alone in its struggle. Professionally led groups tend to be time limited (8–15 sessions), whereas peer-led groups usually are ongoing (as long as the need and energy remain). At times, professional efforts are used to start a group, then are continued by indigenous peer leaders who emerge from within the group. Groups are formed within the structure of formal service settings (from private practice to family service agencies).

Henderson, Gutierrez-Mayka, Garcia, and Boyd (1993) found that middle- or upper-class whites are more likely to use support groups than are nonwhites or minority group members. To attend a support group, caregivers must have someone to relieve them from the care of the elderly relative and have transportation (or access to transportation). Such considerations and preconditions must be addressed.

Educational Interventions:

Educational group interventions use professionals in an

information giving/teaching/training capacity. The aim is to transmit and improve caregiving skills. These interventions can be divided into three types: (a) cognitive information only (i.e., how to bathe a frail patient); (b) cognitive information with self-enhancement (i.e., how to bathe an older person with attention to the caregiver's feelings of competence); and (c) behavioral management skills with or without self-enhancement (i.e., social skills training, such as assertiveness training or building a social network).

Such efforts involve the professional provision of information and training skills. Educational efforts vary greatly in purpose and format. Information is better received in an interpersonal setting than through less direct means (i.e., by mail). The considerations in the use of educational types of group intervention are the same as for support groups.

Clinical Interventions:

Clinical interventions, or direct services, include a variety of intervention modalities such as individual or group counseling/therapy, behavioral/cognitive stimulation, general psychosocial interventions, and specific case management.

- *Counseling* can involve any number of theoretical approaches. It may be lengthy and comprehensive or brief and intensive. It can focus on the dynamics within the caregiving family, conflicts between an elderly couple, or the emotions of the primary caregiver.

- *Cognitive/behavioral stimulation* may focus on specific behavioral changes needed to increase awareness or improve communication skills. Such efforts usually are task orientated and time limited and can be directed at either the caregiver or the care recipient.

- *Psychosocial interventions* include a broad range of services. They can be grouped by approaches that usually involve comprehensive assessments followed by a range of treatment recommendations (from institutionalizing older persons to salvage the family, to securing medications for caregivers, to family counseling or better distribution of caregiving tasks) and follow-up treatment (Biegel et al., 1991).

- *Case management* is a new form of intervention that is frequently misunderstood. Although often undertaken by paraprofessionals, case management can involve a clinical psychologist who performs the in-depth assessment of patient problems, develops a plan of action (which may include therapeutic interventions), monitors the progress of the patient, and determines a time for the intervention to end. The case manager may advise and use appropriate formal services (e.g., community resources) in support of the caregiver or caregiving family.

Use of Community Resources:

Professionals who work with family caregivers may need to use a variety of community resources, which may not always be available. Even when such resources are available, these services may have eligibility criteria or waiting lists — a situation that requires creativity and perseverance. However, some community resources are available: Meals-On-Wheels, Senior Companions, Supplementary Social Insurance (for economic assistance), Medicaid (for medical care). In addition to providing direct aid to eligible elderly persons, these services offer indirect aid to many caregiving families. The following points highlight a few interventions that directly assist the caregiver:

- *Respite intervention* can include in-home or out-of-home care, formal or informal services (friends, relatives, or professional involvement). Respite is by definition short-term — a few hours, a weekend, a week. Such assistance can include day-care centers as well as specific respite programs (ranging from a respite worker coming into one's home to care for an elderly person to a temporary placement of the older person in an institutional setting).

- *Hospice care* is designed to aid, support, and train family members caring for a terminally ill patient. The intervention specifically deals with the last 6 months of the patient's life. Family caregivers often continue their association with a hospice on either a formal (officially working with other families) or informal basis.

- *Day hospitals* offer a more structured respite/medical service and can help working families continue their caregiving functions by assuming responsibility for the elderly patients in need of medical attention, supervision, and so on, during the working hours of the primary caregivers.

Such community resources should be considered to support or to replace family caregiving when family burden is excessive, when family members are not appropriately motivated, and, of course, when family members are unavailable (or the older adult has no living family members).

SUMMARY

Family care has been, and continues to be, the backbone of care to the elderly. Although caregivers are most often the women in the family, men are beginning to assume some of the responsibility. Caregivers do any and all tasks necessary to maintain the frail or ill older family member in the community, avoiding institutionalization, often at great expense and sacrifice.

The motivations for family care can be positive or negative. They include personal/familial expectations, which often are derived from cultural or religious teachings. Although most family members desire to care for their older relatives, problems occur in terms of who cares, where, how, and at what cost. The cost is exacted in terms of economics, personal health, relationships, privacy, employment, and disruption of family order. The consequences of family caregiving have an impact not only on the caregiver, but also on the care recipient, as in cases of ineffective, inadequate care — or even abuse.

Proper intervention by the formal system of care can help family members care for older adults. With appropriate assessments, effective strategies can be implemented. Such strategies include support groups, education, clinical interventions (including case management), and the use of concrete community resources. Such interventions often require highly skilled professionals (physicians, psychologists, social workers, physical therapists, occupational therapists), but can, at times, use paraprofessionals and family members effectively.

REFERENCES

Allan, G. (1988). Kinship, responsibility, and care for elderly people. *Aging and Society, 8*(3), 249–268.

American Association of Retired Persons and The Traveler Companies Foundation (1988). *National survey of caregivers: Summary of findings.* Washington, DC: Author.

Bandura, A. (1977). *Social learning theory.* Englewood Cliffs, NJ: Prentice-Hall.

Batson, C. D., & Coke, J. S. (1983). Empathic motivation of helping behavior. In J. R. Capcioppo & R. E. Petty (Eds.), *Social psychology: A sourcebook*. New York: Guilford Press.

Berkowitz, L. (1972). Social norms, feelings, and other factors effecting helping and altruism. In L. Berkowitz (Ed.), *Advances in experimental social psychology* (Vol. 6). New York: Academic Press.

Biegel, D. E., Sales, E., & Schulz, R. (1991). *Family caregiving in chronic illness*. Newbury Park, CA: Sage.

Brody, E. M. (1981). "Women in the middle" and family help to older people. *Gerontologist, 21,* 471–480.

Brody, E. M. (1990). *Women in the middle: Their parent-care years*. New York: Springer.

Brody, E. M., Litvin, S. J., Hoffman, C., & Kleban, M. H. (1992). Differential effects of daughters' mental status on their parent care experiences. *Gerontologist, 32,* 58–67.

Brubaker, T. H., & Brubaker, E. (1989). Toward a theory of family caregiving: Dependencies, responsibility, and use of service. In J. A. Mancini (Ed.), *Aging parents and adult children* (pp. 245–257). Lexington, MA: Lexington Books.

Brubaker, T. H., & Brubaker, E. (1992). Family care of the elderly in the US: An issue of gender differences. In J. I. Kosberg (Ed.), *Family care of the elderly: Social and cultural changes* (pp. 210–231). Newbury Park, CA: Sage.

Cantor, M. H. (1983). Strain among caregivers: A study of experiences in the United States. *Gerontologist, 23,* 597–604.

Cicirelli, V. G. (1983). Adult children in attachment and helping behavior to elderly parents: A path model. *Journal of Marriage and the Family, 45,* 815–820.

Colerick, E. J., & George, L. K. (1986). Predictors of institutionalization among caregivers of patients with Alzheimer's disease. *Journal of American Geriatric Society, 34,* 493–498.

Coulton, C. (1988). Perspective payment requires increased attention to quality of post-hospital care. *Social Work and Health Care, 13,* 19–31.

Duke University Center for the Study of Aging and Human Development. (1978). *The Older American Resources and Services Methodology: Multidimensional Functional Assessment Questionnaire* (Vol. 2, pp. 169–170). Durham, NC: Author.

Fiore, J., Becker, J., Koppel, D. B. (1983). Social Network interactions: A buffer or a stress? *American Journal of Community Psychology, 11,* 423-439.

Fitting, M., Rabins, P., Lucas, M. J., & Eastham, J. (1986). Caregivers of dementia patients: A comparison of husbands and wives. *Gerontologist, 26,* 248–252.

Garbarino, J. (1947). The human ecology of child maltreatment: A conceptual model for research. *Journal of Marriage and the Family, 39,* 721–735.

Garcia, J. L., & Kosberg, J. I. (1992). Understanding anger: Implications for formal and informal caregivers. *Journal of Elder Abuse and Neglect, 4,* 87–99.

George, L. K., & Gwyther, L. P. (1986). Caregiver well-being: A multidimensional examination of family caregivers of demented adults. *Gerontologist, 26,* 253–259.

Hatfield, E., Walster, G. W., & Piliavin, J. A. (1978). Equity theory and helping relationships. In L. Wispe (Ed.), *Altruism, sympathy, and helping* (pp. 115–139). New York: Academic Press.

Henderson, J. N., Guttierez-Mayka, M., Garcia, J. L., & Boyd, S. (1993). A model for Lazeimer disease support group development in Afro-American and Hispanic populations. *The Gerontologist, 33,* 409-414.

Hoffman, M. L. (1982). Development of prosocial motivation: Empathy and guilt. In N. Eisenberg (Ed.), *The development of prosocial behavior* (pp. 281–313). New York: Academic Press.

Hooyman, N. R., & Lustbader, W. (1986). *Taking care of your aging family members: A practical guide.* New York: The Free Press.

Horowitz, A. (1985). Family caregiving to the frail elderly. In M. P. Lawton & G. Maddox (Eds.), *Annual review of gerontology and geriatrics* (Vol. 5, pp. 194–246). New York: Springer.

Kosberg, J. I. (1988). Preventing elder abuse: Identification of high-risk factors prior to placement decisions. *Gerontologist, 28,* 43–50.

Kosberg, J. I., & Cairl, R. E. (1986). The cost of care index: A case management tool for screening informal care providers. *Gerontologist, 26,* 273–278.

Kosberg, J. I., & Cairl, R. E. (1991). Burden and competence in caregivers of Alzheimer's disease patients: Research and practice implications. *Journal of Gerontologic Social Work, 18,* 85–96.

Kosberg, J. I., & Dermody, E. W. (1985). *A follow-up study of discharged geriatric patients from a nursing home and rehabilitation center.* Unpublished paper presented at the annual meeting of the Southern Gerontological Society, Tampa, FL.

Kosberg, J. I., & Garcia, J. L. (1991). Social changes affecting family care of the elderly. *Journal of the International Institute on Aging (Malta), 2,* 2–5.

Kosberg, J. I., Cairl, R. E., & Keller, D. M. (1990). Components of burden: Interventive implications. *Gerontologist, 30,* 236–242.

Lewis, J., & Meredith, B. (1988). Daughters caring for mothers. *Aging and Society, 8,* 1–21.

Litvin, S. J. (1992). Status transitions and future outlook as determinants of conflict: The caregiver's and care receiver's perspective. *Gerontologist, 32,* 68–75.

Lubkin, I. M. (1986). *Chronic illness: Impact and interventions.* Boston: Jones & Bartlett.

Mace, N. L., & Rabins, P. V. (1981). *The 36-hour day.* Baltimore: Johns Hopkins University Press.

Neal, M. B., Chapman, N. J., Ingersoll-Dayton, B., & Emlen, A. C. (1993). *Balancing work and caregiving for children, adults, and elders.* Newbury Park, CA: Sage.

Noelker, L. S., & Townsend, A. L. (1987). Perceived caregiving effectiveness. In T. H. Brubaker (Ed.), *Aging, health and family: Long-term care* (pp. 58–79). Newbury Park, CA: Sage.

Pfeiffer, E. (1975). A short portable mental status questionnaire for the assessment of organic brain deficit in elderly patients. *Journal of the American Geriatric Society, 23,* 433–441.

Reis, H. T., & Gruzen, J. (1976). On mediating equity, equality, and self-interest: The role of self-presentation in social exchange. *Journal of Experimental Social Psychology, 12,* 487–503.

Robinson, J., Moen, P., & Dempster-McClain, D. (1995). Women's caregiving: Changing profiles and pathways. *Journal of Gerontology, 50B,* s362-s373.

Shanas, E. (1979). The family as a social support system in old age. *Gerontologist, 6,* 169–174.

Stoller, E. P. (1983). Parental caregiving by adult children. *Journal of Marriage and the Family, 45,* 851–858.

Stone, R., Cafferata, G. L., & Sangl, J. (1987). Caregivers of the elderly: A national profile. *Gerontologist, 27,* 616–626.

Strauss, A. L., Corbin, J., Fagerhaugh, S., Glaser, B. G., Mainos, D., Suczek, B., & Weiner, C. L. (1984). *Chronic illness and the quality of life.* St. Louis: C. V. Mosby.

Thorson, J. A. (1995). *Aging in a changing society.* Belmont, CA: Wadsworth.

Townsend, A. L., & Noelker, L. S. (1987). The impact of family relationships on caregiving effectiveness. In T. H. Brubaker (Ed.), *Aging, health, and family: Long-term care* (pp. 80–99). Newbury Park, CA: Sage.

Yesavage, J. A., & Brink, T. L. (1983). Development and validation of a geriatric depression screening scale: A preliminary report. *Journal of Psychiatric Research, 17,* 37–49.

Zarit, S. H. (1989). Issues and directions in family intervention research. In E. Light & B. Lebowitz (Eds.), *Alzheimer's disease, treatment, and family stress: Directions for research* (pp. 458-486). Washington, DC: U.S. Government Printing Office.

Zarit, S. H., Reever, K., & Peterson, J. (1980). Relatives of the impaired elderly: Correlates of feelings of burden. *Gerontologist, 20,* 649–655.

Zarit, S. H., & Zarit, J. M. (1982). Families under stress: Interventions for caregivers of senile dementia patients. *Psychotherapeutic Theory, Research & Practice, 19,* 461.

9

Relational Sexuality: An Understanding of Low Sexual Desire

Lynda Dykes Talmadge, PhD, and William C. Talmadge, PhD

Dr. L. Talmadge is a clinical psychologist in private practice. Dr. W. Talmadge is also in private practice. Both are adjunct faculty members in the Department of Psychology at Georgia State University, Atlanta, GA.

KEY POINTS

- Sex therapy techniques have not devoted sufficient attention to the significance of the emotional relationship of the couple. As a result, sex therapists often are unable to help couples presenting with emotional problems associated with low sexual desire.

- "Three patients" are involved in couples therapy: the two partners and the marriage itself. All three need attention.

- Sexuality is strongly influenced by each individual's family of origin, physical health, social context, and the partner's relationship to these factors.

- Therapists should obtain the sexual history of each partner individually and explore the relationship between the couple's intrapsychic issues and interpersonal issues.

- During sexual interaction, unconscious struggles of the early parent-child relationship are easily awakened. To address current problems involving low sexual desire, it is helpful for therapists to explore such early conflicts.

- The overt sexual behavior of the symptomatic partner should be deemphasized. Emphasis should be placed on how the relationship supports the sexual problem and how both partners play a role in perpetuating it.

INTRODUCTION

Research has documented increasing reports of low sexual desire by both men and women (Frank, Anderson, & Rubinstein, 1978; Leiblum & Rosen, 1988; Lief, 1977; LoPiccolo, 1980, 1982; Schover & LoPiccolo, 1982). Low sexual desire results from a complex set of interacting physiologic, psychological, and cultural variables and is generally a matter of degree. The level of sexual desire can be best conceptualized as a continuum: at one end lie relatively mild problems with desire specific to a partner, a situation, or a type of sexual encounter; at the other end is persistently and pervasively inhibited sexual desire, which, in its most severe presentation, becomes sexual aversion.

In diagnosing low sexual desire, it is important to use an instrument capable of establishing behavioral criteria along multiple dimensions. The Multiaxial Problem-Oriented Diagnostic System for Sexual Dysfunctions (Schover, Friedman, Weiler, Heiman, & LoPiccolo, 1982) is such an instrument; it measures behavioral criteria along several dimensions, including global/situational and duration.

However, before sophisticated diagnostic systems are used, a clearer concept of sexual desire should be attained. Zilbergeld and Ellison's delineation of the sexual response cycle (1980) includes five phases: interest, arousal, physiologic readiness, orgasm, and satisfaction. Kaplan's representation of the cycle (1979) includes desire, excitement, and orgasm. Thus, interest or desire is conceptualized differently from arousal or excitement, both for diagnostic and treatment purposes.

If desire is not arousal, then what is it? Levine (1984) proposes that sexual desire results from an interaction of biologic drive, psychological motivation (willingness to behave sexually), and cognitive aspiration (a wish to behave sexually). He believes that psychological motivation is the most critical clinical factor and concludes that sexual desire is "the ability to integrate biologic, intrapsychic and interpersonal sexual complexity" (Levine, 1984, p. 95). LaPointe and Gillespie (1979) maintain that a biologic drive is present in everyone, but it may be repressed or unexpressed because of learned behaviors.

Historical Perspectives:

Historically, sex therapy has focused primarily on the behavioral and technical levels of treatment (Annon, 1974; Barbach, 1975; Heiman, LoPiccolo, & LoPiccolo, 1976; LoPiccolo, 1978; McCarthy, Ryan, & Johnson, 1975; Zilbergeld, 1978). This focus has been useful in two ways. First, it has openly confronted the taboo of addressing sexual problems directly in American culture, thereby facilitating education and treatment in sexual matters. Second, it has clarified and increased our knowledge of human sexuality, especially in its behavioral and functional aspects.

In the years since sex research, education, and therapy were originally legitimized by the pioneering works of Masters and Johnson (1966, 1970) and other professionals in the field, new information about sexual physiology and functioning has continued to surface (Kaplan, 1983; Wagner & Green, 1981). For example, Wagner's discovery of a new artery in the penis has changed the theory of erection and diagnostic procedures for erectile problems (Wagner, Willis, Bro-Rasmussen, & Nielsen, 1982). These are among the important contributions made by the discipline of sex therapy. However, it is incumbent on any school of psychotherapy to acknowledge its limitations.

Since Kaplan (1977, 1979) first discussed the problem of low sexual desire, the desire phase of the response cycle has been increasingly investigated in terms of etiology and treatment (LaPointe & Gillespie, 1979; McCarthy, 1984). However, too little attention has been devoted to the marital system, especially its emotional relatedness, for both diagnostic and treatment purposes (McCarthy, 1984; Messersmith, 1976). Sex therapists are only beginning to draw from the experience of couple therapists. Kaplan (1979) focused primarily on intrapsychic factors, both in etiology and treatment. LoPiccolo (1980) stressed the complexity of desire phase disorders and offered useful assessment procedures for diagnosis (he emphasizes, however, sexual behaviors and attitudes). Others have also stressed behaviors and attitudes, using short-term behavioral and cognitive approaches in treatment (LaPointe & Gillespie, 1979; McCarthy, 1984). Although they report some degree of success with individuals and couples, their sample sizes were very small, and results must be considered accordingly.

Zilbergeld and Killmann (1984) stated that the efficacy of sex therapists (or any other therapists) in treating low desire is debatable. Others were less generous in their appraisal, maintaining that sex therapy procedures have failed with complaints of low desire (Berg & Synder, 1981; LaPointe & Gillespie, 1979). Berg and Snyder (1981, p. 290) stated, "There has emerged a growing consensus that treatment of sexual dysfunctions using a short-term behaviorally oriented directive approach without carefully examining the role of marital conflict and other dimensions of the relationship is both incomplete and shortsighted."

Sex therapy techniques have a poor record of success in treating low sexual desire largely because of the insufficient attention paid to the emotional relationship of the persons involved (Cookerly & McClaren, 1982; LaPointe & Gillespie, 1979) and to psychodynamics. Friedman (1982) maintained that relationship factors such as fear, vulnerability, passive-aggressive styles, and intimacy problems are important instigators of low sexual desire. Even sex researchers who primarily investigate physiologic phenomena related to arousal and sexual attitudes concur that ". . .further research is needed to determine the importance of emotional involvement and trust as facilitating conditions for good sexual adjustment" (Hoon, 1983). In her study of the behavioral and psychological components related to a woman's experience of sexual response and satisfaction, Hoon (1983, p. 151) concluded that it would be ". . .useful to know the degree to which women value commitment and loving along a number of interpersonal dimensions in the context of erotic responsivity and satisfaction."

Although the purpose, duration, intensity, and quality of

each relationship vary greatly, sexual expression remains primarily relational. Human beings have strong needs to be connected to one another in mutual dependency. This assumption derives from an ethologic tradition of research. Observations of the phylogenetically lower primates as well as human infants and children reveal strong evidence supporting the social nature of humans (Bowlby, 1969, 1973; Harlow, 1958). Berscheid and Peplau (1983, p. 1) stated,

> Relationships with others lie at the very core of human existence. Humans are conceived within relationships, born into relationships and live their lives within relationships with others. Each individual's dependency on other people for the realization of life itself, for survival during one of the longest gestation periods in the animal kingdom, for food and shelter and aid and comfort throughout the life cycle — is a fundamental fact of the human condition.

The physical state of each partner, overt sexual behavior, and intrapsychic issues are all important aspects of low sexual desire (Borneman, 1983; Kaplan, 1983). However, this chapter is primarily concerned with relational aspects of the problem. We focus on the intrapsychic and interpersonal issues that arise in marriages and partnerships suffering from lack of sexual desire.

We believe the most useful way to look at the intersection of the intrapsychic and interpersonal realms is through the conceptualization of object-relations theory and systems theory. Our treatment approach originates in systems theory, gestalt psychotherapy, and experiential psychotherapy. We are primarily interested in intimate relationships; therefore, we focus solely on married couples presenting with the complaint of low sexual desire that is not physiologic in nature.

RELATIONAL SEXUALITY

The sexual relationship is a vital part of the personality of the marriage. The sexual character developed by the relationship emerges from the partners' personalities, sexual values, and behavior as well as the affect that they share concerning sexual issues. This sexual character develops as a result of the partners' interaction, the indirect and direct influence of their families of origin, their physical health, and their social context. The following case example involves a couple who had developed no real sexual character in their relationship as a result of physical health problems and their emotional consequences.

> Mr. and Mrs. A had rarely been sexually active for several years. Mr. A had a life-threatening disorder; however, he denied that this had any significant effect on him or on his relationship with his wife. Over time, through therapy, Mr. A began to sense his rage and loss due to the limitations on his ability to take part in activities such as cutting the grass or playing ball with his children. As Mr. A increased this awareness, his rage manifested in explosive outbursts, sadness, and loss. As Mr. A was able to work through these feelings in his wife's presence and discuss them with her, their sexual expression increased and intensified.

The sexuality of most couples runs the gamut from frustration to delight. In a relationship, the time in which partners confront themselves and each other in the most vulnerable way is when they are engaged in pleasurable sexual relations. This primitive vulnerability is the core of the difficulties so many couples experience in their sexual and marital relating. In a committed relationship, sexuality is a physical expression of primary emotional bonds and is best understood in the context of the relationships that govern it, that is, the family of origin and marriage. The experience of giving and receiving physical pleasure in the marriage is often an unconscious symbolic reawakening of early child-parent interactions (Scharff, 1982).

For a homework assignment, a therapist instructed Mr. B to give Mrs. B a full body massage. During this experience, Mrs. B broke out in hives and tearfully pleaded with her husband to stop. In their next interview, Mrs. B was asked to imagine herself engaged in the homework assignment with her husband. As she did this, she was instructed to be aware of any intense feelings, memories, or images that came to mind. Mrs. B began to have a memory of herself at age 4 or 5 watching her father holding the family dog in the air by its hind legs and spanking it. In subsequent weeks she began recalling other incidents of her father's brutality and abusiveness that she had suppressed. Mrs. B eventually told her mother about these memories and gently confronted her with an intuition that her father had been physically abusive to her mother. Her mother initially denied this, but finally confessed that her husband had been physically abusive on various occasions when Mrs. B was a small child.

Mrs. B, through her homework experience and revelations about her mother's denial of her father's abuse, connected her hives and extreme fear to her experience of vulnerability and lack of protection. She was able to recognize that her frightened vulnerable child-self was being activated through the massage exercise.

Each partner has an enormous effect on the other's experience and expression of his or her own sexuality. Spouses' character structures and internalizations of the family of origin as well as the social context shape the emerging sexuality of the couple. Research indicates that when the disinterested partner's sexual desire increases, the spouse may sometimes develop a sexual symptom (LaPointe & Gillespie, 1979; Marshall & Neill, 1977). If we think of the marriage as a system, we can think of both partners as sharing the problem rather than the low sexual desire simply being a "symptom" exhibited by one of the partners. As the therapeutic work progresses, deeper levels of meaning and involvement in the problem are revealed, and the other partner may even manifest a sexual symptom. This process is an indicator of partners influencing each other as part of their bond. A more positive manifestation of a partner's influence can be seen in couples when the husband becomes more intimate and emotionally expressive with his wife and the wife's sexual desire increases (Framo, 1970; Haley, 1978; Jackson, 1957; Watzlawick, Weakland, & Fisch, 1974). The therapist should educate the couple about this process.

The ability to be affectionate can be a healing force in the sexual and personal relating between the partners. If they openly express nonsexual physical affection, they are likely to have heightened sexual excitement, interest, and pleasure. Affectionate touching is a special force that can reawaken old body sensations from the experience of early child-parent bonding (Bowlby, 1969; Harlow, 1962; Hollender, Luborsky, & Harvey, 1970; Montagu, 1978; Wallace, 1981). This contact of skin between husband and wife is a means of conscious and unconscious emotional feeding that can reach the innermost parts of the self. Physical affection between two marital partners has a positive association in sexual desire and expression (Wallace, 1981).

A final aspect of relational sexuality is the ability of the pair to move from parent-child interactions with each other (wherein one is more dependent and the other is the caretaker) to peer relating. It is an enormous asset for any couple if they can move smoothly between these hierarchical and mutual stances with each other. If a couple is stuck in a relationship where the roles are rigidly defined so that one is consistently the parent and the other is the child, they may experience difficulties with sexual desire because of the unconscious influence of incest conflicts. Indeed, it is difficult to relate sexually with a partner who is persistently parental or child-like.

INTIMACY IN MARRIAGE

Problems of low sexual desire are often indicative of difficulty with marital intimacy. The lack of connection within the relationship supports the lack of sexual contact interest and excitement. At this level, the sexual desire problem can be thought of as acting-out behavior of the lack of intimacy between the two.

The emotional connection of a couple is based on the partners' ability to be intimate with each other. As the couple becomes more intimate, their sexual satisfaction, desire, and activity increase. "Intimacy" is derived from the Latin *intimare*, which means "to put, bring, drive, announce, or make known"; this is derived from *intimus*, the superlative of *intus*, which means "within." The contemporary definition of intimacy is to make known the innermost parts of the self. Trust, interdependence, vulnerability, power, mutuality, and the knowing and seeking of self are implied in this understanding of intimacy. L'Abate (1977) referred to intimacy as the capacity and willingness to share hurt feelings. Douvan asserted two elements essential to intimacy: the capacity and willingness to be dependent and "the ability to bear, accept, absorb, and resolve interpersonal conflict and hostility" (Douvan, 1977, p. 26). Waring, McElrath, Lefcoe, and Weisz (1981) and Waring and Reddon (1983) described intimacy as being composed of affection, expressiveness, compatibility, cohesion, sexuality, conflict resolution, autonomy, and identity. Intimacy within marriage requires ego strength, power, vulnerability, interdependency, trust, mutuality, and the knowing and seeking of self. Shepherd (1979) maintained that

> what is revealed and shared is that which is deeply personal, basic, most important, experienced almost as the core of being or soul, that which may often have had to be defended from others and even hidden from oneself. To risk closeness with one another is to risk remembering old pain from violations of trust and oneness in early development, and evoke the early nonverbal conditionings that do not respond easily to cognitive formulas.

Marriage in American culture is the ultimate attempt to

address the primary need for closeness. Parent-child and marital relationships are the two most intense examples of the social-emotional-physical interdependence of human beings. Marital success requires tolerance for regression in the partners, who must allow their child-like (needy) selves to emerge in mutual dependence (Dicks, 1967). Object-relations theorists speak about marital intimacy in a particularly compelling fashion, by considering interaction of the intrapsychic with the interpersonal (Dicks, 1967; Framo, 1965; Friedman, 1980). Accordingly, they acknowledge the public and reality-oriented aspects of marriage but consider them less important than the unconscious connection between the partners.

Intimacy in marriage is especially difficult to achieve because it requires "an established sense of personal identity and ego strength with a preservation of the capacity for dependence" (Dicks, 1967, p. 29). These attributes are often at odds within the person, the relationship, and the culture, producing conflict and confusion about when to depend and when to be self-sufficient. A person might fear that in being too independent, one will lose connection with the beloved, and in being too dependent, one will lose oneself. A paradox in relating is that we cannot be intimate while completely merged—a true intimacy requires some separation, some delineation of the individuals. Thus, marriage is the arena in which the maturity of the personality is most fully challenged because only the emotionally mature can negotiate closeness without merger.

This ambivalence in achieving marital intimacy is illustrated aptly by our historical and cultural contexts for close relationships. Gadlin (1977) traced the history of intimacy in the United States with considerable insight. Intimacy in colonial times largely consisted of physical proximity. Personal life was not private, nor was it separated from public institutions; marriage was to serve the community, not the individual. As society developed, the industrial revolution dehumanized the public sphere to such an extent that a need to compensate in private life emerged. The family decreased in socioeconomic importance and increased in psychological significance. Thus, society arrived at the opposite end of the continuum from colonial times, with our increased expectation of personal fulfillment in marriage.

In our culture, an emphasis is placed on self-sufficiency; furthermore, there is an implicit assumption that marriage should be an emotionally intimate, personally fulfilling relationship. Achieving this is difficult for several reasons. Americans eschew spreading their dependent needs to the extended family and value confining them to the nuclear family (Hsu, 1981). With the emphasis on the individual's self-sufficiency, the resources and abilities for making effective emotional commitments are to be contained within the person. The extended kinship network is not acceptable as a resource in these processes. The spouse and few children of the modern nuclear family are now the primary, if not exclusive, targets of our intense human needs. With this great burden falling on a few shoulders, it is not surprising that we disappoint one another.

Marriage is an organic *process* rather than a *product* (Barnett, 1981). In the very beginning of this process, partners are often ill-prepared for living in a committed, intimate relationship with a peer. They lack successful experience with intimate relationships with peers, perhaps because the main experiences they have accrued have been in intimate relationships when they are children — a time when their parents take care of them. As children, we are usually not required to be overly sensitive or even aware of the needs of other persons.

When most people begin intimate peer relationships, they negotiate this transition from the "child" position in the intimacy to that of the peer. In the beginning of intimate relationships, each partner tends to regress to an infantile fantasy in which the other spouse is viewed as the omnipresent caretaker. Each partner seems to assume that the other exists only for him or her, with the sole purpose in life of attending to his or her needs. Partners may resolve this transferential component to their relationship as they develop together. However, they may also regress to the transference and fantasy perceptions from former intimate relationships when they are under individual or relational stress.

Eventually, confronted with the reality of the partner and the situation, the marriage falls into disillusionment (Warkentin & Whitaker, 1966). At this point, many couples enter divorce proceedings, preferring to give up their partners rather than relinquish their fantasies. If, however, the partners do success-fully negotiate this difficult stage, the potential exists for a deeper commitment and experience based on a shared con-struction of reality (Berger & Kellner, 1964; Sloan & L'Abate, 1985). From this perspective, intimacy is possible as the part-ners learn to be separate, yet close.

Through this process, marriage may be a curative function for the persons involved (Wile, 1981). Sociologists have long noted that one of the functions of marriage is to stabilize and support the adult personalities of the partners (Parson & Bales, 1955). Dicks (1967) maintained that we unconsciously choose our partners for their curative potential. The fact that old wounds can be healed and scars repaired is supported by both clinical experience and Harlow's research with socially de-prived monkeys. Harlow found that the deprived monkey at the birth of her second offspring bonded somewhat better with that offspring because of the efforts of the first offspring to make contact with her (Harlow, 1962; Harlow & Zimmerman, 1959). This assumption that interpersonal relationships can be restoring, as well as damaging, is an underlying premise for all psychotherapeutic work. The marriage can perform a similar role, supporting the adult personality and fostering its growth by the working through of unfinished interpersonal issues with the partner.

To manage the ambivalence inherent in intimacy, partners often deny negative feelings about each other that can poten-tially threaten their connection. The partners may idealize one another, and, in so doing, may assume they must be every-thing to each other, correct all defects, and offer perfect grati-fication of all needs (Dicks, 1967). If the partner lives up to such perfection, the spouse is both gratified and threatened by that excellence. If the partner does not live up to it, the spouse is both relieved and disappointed by the partner's limitations. Again, ambivalence is pervasive.

Idealization requires exclusion of negative feelings from the relationship, the end result of which is an exclusion of all affect. Gradually, partners turn down the intensity of the feeling between them so that an experience of numbness arises. They create a smooth relationship at the expense of their intensity and passion (Dicks, 1967; Kernberg, 1979). Negative feelings must not be eliminated in intimate relationships; instead, they must be incorporated in such a way that leads to a resolution, not an escalation, of issues (Braiker & Kelley, 1979; Gurman, 1978; Rausch, Barry, Hertel, & Swain, 1974; Wile, 1981).

A great deal of energy is required to keep all of this intensity under control. The expenditure of such energy can drain the life from the marriage. Many couples, however, are able to maintain the smooth facade at the expense of intimacy for the maintenance of their lives together. This bound-up energy also may result in physical, emotional, or psychosomatic symptoms in the partners or in their children (Waring, 1980; Waring, McElrath, Mitchell, & Derry, 1981).

Couples who present with sexual desire problems often have an exaggerated form of this difficulty. They usually will present to the therapist by saying, "Everything is fine in the marriage except the sex. I just don't understand it. We never fight. We love each other. She (or he) just doesn't like sex." Things are smooth between them, but little intimate connection and passionate involvement are apparent. The couple simply has no means for incorporating intense feelings into their relationship. The results are a blunting of feeling and expression and heightened anxiety in the relationship, all of which can lead to emotional distancing as a coping mechanism.

OBTAINING A HISTORY FROM BOTH PARTNERS

The *process* of history taking may be more valuable than the *content* obtained. The therapist forms an impression of how the client relates to sexuality in general, takes the opportunity to teach and give permission, and ascertains important emotional issues for the client. Our general format involves an interview with the couple followed by one individual interview with each partner. Provided that sufficient information is obtained, the fourth interview is for feedback, at which time the relevant issues for each individual and how these may relate to their coupling are discussed along with the marital relationship issues.

> During Mrs. C's individual history-taking interview, she was asked about her first intercourse experience. She explained that she had not had intercourse until age 25. At that point in her life she decided, "I needed to get that behind me." She purchased a book on female sexuality and began to teach herself nonorgasmic masturbation for a 5-week period before to having intercourse with her current boyfriend. She explained that she did this in much the same way as one would when trying to get in shape by doing sit-ups.

> From this question came a discussion about Mrs. C's sheltered and inexperienced sexual life and her fears and guilt related to masturbation. In this short interaction, the therapist was able to see that this woman approached her sexual life in a controlled manner to suppress her fears. Through this discussion of her first intercourse experience, the therapist was able to relate to Mrs. C with concern in a gentle and technical style that allowed her to explore the fear of her sexuality in the controlled presence of an expert on sex.

> In subsequent interviews, Mrs. C sought more information related to specific aspects of her sexuality, such as lubrication, intercourse during masturbation, and orgasms, while continuing to explore her fear and desire.

Another important function of the history taking is to establish a productive therapeutic alliance. During this time, the therapist often can ascertain the couple's basic style of interaction as well as the various associated impasses. In this phase of therapy, the therapist is established as a sexual expert with whom the clients are comfortable and free to discuss sexual issues.

> In a history-taking interview with Mr. and Mrs. D, who had been married 22 years, the couple presented the problem that Mrs. D "doesn't like sex." Mr. D repeatedly answered questions the therapist addressed to Mrs. D. The therapist pointed this out to the couple with the suggestion that Mrs. D would probably like sex more if Mr. D respected her more, protected her less, and allowed her to speak for herself.

The sexual history taking is usually completed in a separate interview with each partner. This procedure assumes that if a couple is already experiencing tension and difficulty in sexual relating, the partners may be threatened by discussing sexual questions, issues, and history openly in front of each other early in the therapeutic process. It is also a time when the power of sexual secrets can be diffused. If a revealed secret can be normalized by the therapist and accepted in an open way, its potential deleterious effect can be neutralized.

"THREE PATIENTS"

Three patients are involved in the therapy: the two married individuals and the marriage itself (Warkentin & Whitaker, 1966). In the structure of the therapy, all three need attention. Spouses are worked with individually as well as in couple interviews. Some marital and family therapists disagree with this approach because secrets are unveiled during the individual interviews. These are dealt with in a similar vein to that mentioned above during the history-taking discussion. The individual focus is particularly useful in helping the person take charge of himself or herself in the interdependence, thereby interrupting the blaming of the partner for one's unfulfilled sexual needs. It broadens the Masters and Johnson (1976) focus on the couple to include the individuals as well. Kaplan supports this approach, stating, "Most frequently both factors play a role and the therapist must be prepared to shift the therapeutic emphasis as resistances arise, sometimes confronting the partners with their destructive interactions and at other times working with the intrinsic anxieties of one or the other" (Kaplan, 1983, p. 60). Furthermore, including work with the individual in the context of the marriage is a way to recognize and support that person's ability to be separate as well as his or her ability to make contact. Both are required if a genuine intimacy is to be established.

REFRAMING

In a marriage in which a sexual problem is present, one partner usually carries the low sexual desire symptom for the relationship. The symptomatic partner often is blamed for the lack of sexual desire. One useful therapeutic technique in such cases is that of *reframing* the presenting problem, that is, shifting the emphasis off the symptomatic partner's behavior and onto the relationship itself, which supports the sexual problem.

In this no-fault approach, the therapist gives examples of how both partners participate in the difficulties presented. The therapist deemphasizes the overt sexual behavior of the symptomatic partner and reframes such behavior as being adaptive. The following case example demonstrates how we implement the reframing technique.

> Mr. and Mrs. E, married 9 years, presented with the complaint that Mrs. E was experiencing low sexual desire and Mr. E was sexually eager. The couple had had no sexual intercourse for 15 months before therapy. The therapist told Mr. E that his lack of sexual and emotional involvement with his wife encouraged and supported her lack of desire. The couple reiterated this

dynamic during the therapy session when they described an incident in which they were beginning the initial phases of foreplay and the husband fell asleep. The therapist responded by emphasizing the husband's participation in the problem, pointing out that the husband may have fallen asleep because of his own difficulties with low sexual desire, and giving the following paradoxical intervention. The therapist said that perhaps the couple was seriously and wisely considering all the repercussions that would occur in their marriage if they were to become consistently sexually active with each other. The therapist suggested the couple consider slowing down their changes. Thus, the therapist framed the husband's falling asleep in a positive way by depicting it as a wise, cautious attempt to avoid upsetting the current balance of the relationship.

REGRESSION

In our view of marriage, which is consistent with object-relations theory, each spouse seeks closure on some unfinished business or unmet needs that were not taken care of in the family of origin. Within this context, each partner is encouraged to "reparent" their spouse. Each is told to view a part of the marital partner as a child who requires care. This approach helps in reworking early parent-child interactions that currently may be troublesome to the person. Consider the case of Mr. and Mrs. F:

In a couple session, the therapist told Mr. F that his wife was a needy little girl who should be reminded constantly how wonderful she is and how important she is to him. By making such statements, the husband could address some of the narcissistic needs that his wife was unable to have fulfilled in her original family. The therapist told Mrs. F that her husband was also a needy little boy and wanted her constant attention and involvement. The therapist encouraged both partners to respond to each other in these positions as much as possible. He

forewarned them that there would be times when both partners would feel needy simultaneously and would be unable to
address each other's needs. The therapist suggested that during the times when their neediness collides, the partners comfort each other as best they can (one suggestion was to simply
lie together and hold each other), and try not to assume any
major tasks.

HOSTILITY AND ANGER

Couples who have been experiencing a sexual desire problem
usually have been facing the problem for a substantial period
of time. They have tried to blunt all feeling to contain their
hostility. When the hostility is uncovered during the course of
therapy, the couple should not be left alone to face this newly
surfaced emotion. Once the feelings are openly acknowledged
and expressed, the therapist can begin to move the partners
through their anger into deeper understanding of each other.
This process can be facilitated by reframing the anger as the
result of a deep hurt, an unmet need, fear, or anxiety. Applying
the reframing technique often helps each individual to own
the underlying reasons for anger with the partner and allows
them to move through the anger into a more productive stage.

Mr. and Mrs. G had been married for 3 years when they
presented for therapy. Both had been previously married. Mrs.
G was extremely belligerent in relating to her passive husband;
she frequently made tirades at him. This degree of intense
anger was seriously damaging any hope for the couple. During
one therapy session, Mrs. G broke into one of her tirades. The
therapist waited until she had finished and, after a few moments of silence, reached out and touched Mrs. G and said,
"There surely is a hurt little girl inside you pleading for help."
Mrs. G began weeping and talking about her father, who
abandoned her family of origin when she was 3 years old. The
therapist instructed Mr. G to respond to Mrs. G's subsequent

tirades by asking her, "What does that little girl want?" This continued to deflate Mrs. G's rage and address her hurt and need.

BALANCING THE RELATIONSHIP

According to systems theory, it is common in a marriage for one partner to exhibit most of the need, express most of the affect, provide most of the support, or display most of the power. When a couple becomes imbalanced in these areas, they fail to give each other perspective, and the relationship no longer has a self-correcting mechanism. The result is collusion. The therapist needs to help the couple identify imbalances and understand their implications. For example, when a husband expresses most of the anger in the marriage, the therapist might suggest to the wife that she switch roles with her husband and take her turn at carrying the anger. Because it is unlikely that she will be able to do so on command, a good way to begin is to have the wife role play her husband's feelings. This may lead her to a genuine realization of her own anger within the relationship.

Another means of dealing with the imbalance is to exaggerate it. For example, if the wife expresses most of the neediness within the relationship, she is encouraged to become more and more needy with her husband. Eventually the two cannot carry out the charade, and the gross exaggeration may lead to his discovering his own need and to her discovering her strength.

Mr. and Mrs. H had been married for 14 years. During that period, they had three children, Mr. H became very successful in his career, and Mrs. H became increasingly anxious. Mrs. H dealt with the anxiety that her husband's pursuit of his career ambitions evoked in her by becoming deeply involved with her children and community. In interviews with the therapist, Mrs. H expressed the anxiety, depression, and unhappiness of the couple, as Mr. H sat quietly. At the next interview, the therapist instructed Mrs. H to stop talking to her husband except for those occasions when it was necessary for the functioning of their lives. In addition, the therapist instructed the couple to come to all future interviews in the same car, eat lunch together after the interview, and take a 15-minute walk every evening. Mrs. H again was cautioned about speaking. In subsequent interviews, with much reinforcement to Mrs. H's silence, Mr. H began to express his feelings of sadness about his marriage and family. The affect in their marriage gradually was redistributed.

AFFECTION AND TOUCHING

Sex therapists have emphasized the importance of touch through their use of sensate focus (i.e., exercises for nongenital touching; Masters & Johnson, 1976). Many couples have completely stopped touching each other and expressing affection because of the pain it reawakens in each of them. Often, their only contact is verbal. At this point, we try to decrease the verbiage in the marriage and replace it with more physical contact. The partners are told to physically act out a communication with each other rather than to express it in words.

> In a couples interview, Mr. I was feeling particularly saddened by a recent sexual encounter with his wife. He attempted to express his sadness to her through physical touch. As he spoke of this encounter, tears came to his eyes and he was instructed to wipe his tears from his cheek and place them on his wife's cheeks. This expression was far more potent between the couple than if he had simply said, "I am feeling sad."

Another way of providing the couple with more affection and touching while they are still trying to work on sexual issues is simply to tell them that they need to spend time holding each other. This should not be a sexual experience, nor should they speak to each other. They should merely find a quiet time and place where they are both comfortable with holding. This kind of physical contact can replenish their emotional systems.

EXPERIENTIAL INTERACTION AND MODELING

The interaction between the couple and the therapist within an experiential psychotherapeutic framework becomes an agent of change. One way the therapist can teach the couple about emotional intimacy is by sharing his or her own feelings with them. The therapist thus offers a model of disclosing and assists them in becoming more intimate with each other. Within the therapeutic relationship, then, the therapist demonstrates basic parental qualities with the couple, such as setting limits, nurturing, and offering protection, affection, support, and guidance. Through the modeling involved in these interactions, the spouses are taught to perform these functions for each other.

Mr. and Mrs. J had been having sexual activity with each other about three times a year over the last 4 years. They had become increasingly alienated. Mr. J was stubbornly passive about his wife's ideas, plans, and desires; Mrs. J's resentment, anger, and hurt was exacerbated as a consequence. These feelings became most pronounced in major decision-making processes; as a result, the partners had a difficult time working as a team. Mr. J had been school phobic in his pubescent years and had dealt with his mother's demands by total withdrawal or symbiotic attachment. Mrs. J's father was a "brilliant and gifted professional" who never followed through or finished professional or personal matters. Mrs. J viewed her father as a promise breaker and felt particularly vulnerable to her mother when her father went away on business trips. Her mother was an unpredictable, sullen woman who would sometimes go many days without speaking to family members.

In one interview, Mr. and Mrs. J discussed an argument they were having over the sale of their house. They had been offered a reasonable contract, but Mr. J was passively resisting and Mrs. J was becoming furious and panicked. She was certain that her husband was not going to respond to the contract offer and they would be unable to move to the house of their dreams, for which they had signed a contingent contract. Mrs. J was pouring her rage and fear onto him. She stated, "You haven't done a damned thing about the house all along, and here we have a good offer on the house and you want to negotiate over a few hundred dollars. You're going to let the whole damn thing fall in!" Mr. J withdrew.

At this point, the therapist intervened and drew Mrs. J's fire. The therapist told her, "I feel overwhelmed by your fear, rage, and hurt. It's hard to respond. . . . [Mrs. J started interrupting] Please listen to me, I'm trying to give you something. It's hard to get a word in edgewise with you, much less respond to your need. . . .[Mrs. J interrupted again, to which the therapist firmly replied. . .] Hush! I'm trying to give you something. I know you're terribly frightened and panicked that your husband isn't going to act on this deal—just like your father failed you." [Mrs. J began weeping]

Then, the therapist suggested that Mr. J tell his wife his thoughts about the deal and the alternatives he foresees. The therapist further instructed Mr. J to not let his wife overwhelm him with her interruptions. Through these brief interactions, Mr. J observed how another person (the therapist) was responding to his wife's need and fear by neither withdrawing nor becoming symbiotically attached, which, in this case, would have been to capitulate to her every demand. Mrs. J became less frightened because she had a therapist who would not fail her by abandoning her in distress.

CONCLUSION

The treatment of married couples with low sexual desire is a complex process. Our focus has been solely on the relationship of the couple. We contend that a certain relationship quality must be maintained for the couple to have a satisfactory sex life. Some components of this quality include intimacy, self-responsibility, power, affection, and communication with limited projections. The goals of the therapy are to have both persons claim responsibility for their own needs and for negotiating them satisfactorily with the spouse, increase their emotional capacities, enable them to perform nurturing functions for each other, and reacquaint the partners with their sexual and personal passions.

REFERENCES

Annon, J. (1974). *The behavioral treatment of sexual problems* (Vol. 12). Honolulu: Enabling Systems.

Barbach, L. G. (1975). *For yourself: The fulfillment of female sexuality*. New York: New American Library.

Barnett, J. E. (1981). The natural history of a marriage. *Pilgrimage, 9*, 5–19.

Berg, P., & Synder, D. K. (1981). Differential diagnosis of marital and sexual distress: A multidimensional approach. *Journal of Sex and Marital Therapy, 7*, 290–295.

Berger, P., & Kellner, H. (1964). Marriage and the construction of reality. *Diogenes, 46*, 1–24.

Berscheid, E., & Peplau, L. A. (1983). The emerging science of relationships. In H. H. Kelley, E. Berscheid, A. Christensen, J. H. Harvey, T. L. Huston, G. Levinger, E. McClintock, L. A. Peplau, & D. R. Peterson (Eds.), *Close relationships*. New York: W. H. Freeman.

Borneman, E. (1983). Progress in empirical research on children's sexuality. *SIECUS Report, 12*, 1–5.

Bowlby, J. (1969). *Attachment and loss, I.* New York: Basic Books.

Bowlby, J. (1973). *Attachment and loss, II.* New York: Basic Books.

Braiker, H. B., & Kelley, H. H. (1979). Conflict in the development of close relationships. In R. Burgess & T. Huston (Eds.), *Social exchange in developing relationships.* New York: Academic Press.

Cookerly, J. R., & McClaren, K. A. (1982). Sex therapy with and without love: An empirical investigation. *Journal of Sex Education and Therapy, 8,* 35–38.

Dicks, H. V. (1967). *Marital tensions.* New York: Basic Books.

Douvan, E. (1977). Interpersonal relationships: Some questions and observations. In G. Levinger & H. Raush (Eds.), *Close relationships: Perspectives on the meaning of intimacy.* Amherst, MA: University of Massachusetts Press.

Framo, J. L. (1965). Systematic research on family dynamics. In I. Boszormenyi-Nagy & J. Framo (Eds.), *Intensive family therapy: Theoretical and practical aspects.* New York: Harper & Row.

Framo, J. L. (1970). Symptoms from a family transactional viewpoint. In N. Ackerman (Ed.), *Family therapy in transition.* Boston: Little, Brown.

Frank, E., Anderson, C., & Rubinstein D. (1978). Frequency of sexual dysfunction in "normal" couples. *New England Journal of Medicine, 299,* 111–115.

Friedman, L. J. (1980). Integrating psychoanalytic object-relations understanding with family systems intervention in couples theory. In J. Pearce & L. Friedman (Eds.), *Family therapy: Combining psychodynamic and family systems approaches.* New York: Grune & Stratton.

Friedman, J. M. (1982). *A treatment program for low sexual desire.* Paper presented at the annual meeting of the Society for Sex Therapy and Research, Charleston, SC.

Gadlin, H. (1977). Private lives and public order: A critical view of intimate relationships in the United States. In G. Levinger & H. Rausch (Eds.), *Close relationships: Perspectives on the meaning of intimacy.* Amherst, MA: University of Massachusetts Press.

Gurman, A. S. (1978). Contemporary marital therapies: A critique and comparative analysis of psychoanalytic, behavioral, and systems theory approaches. In T. J. Paolino & B. S. McCrady (Eds.), *Marriage and marital therapy: Psychoanalytical, behavioral, and systems theory perspectives.* New York: Brunner/Mazel.

Haley, J. (1978). Toward a theory of pathological systems. In P. Watzlawick & J. H. Weakland (Eds.), *The interactional view.* New York: Brunner/Mazel.

Harlow, H. F. (1958). The nature of love. *American Psychologist, 13,* 673–685.

Harlow, H. F. (1962). Social deprivation in monkeys. *Scientific American, 207,* 136.

Harlow, H. F., & Zimmerman, R. R. (1959). Affectional responses in infant monkeys. *Science, 130,* 421–432.

Heiman, J., LoPiccolo, L., & LoPiccolo, J. (1976). *Becoming orgasmic: A sexual growth program for women.* Englewood Cliffs, NJ: Prentice-Hall.

Hollender, M. H., Luborsky, L., & Harvey, R. B. (1970). Correlates of the desire to be held in women. *Journal of Psychosomatic Research, 14,* 387–390.

Hoon, P. (1983). A path analysis model of psychosexuality in young women. *Journal of Research in Personality, 17,* 143–152.

Hsu, F. L. K. (1981). *Americans and Chinese: Passages to differences* (3rd ed.). Honolulu: University Press of Hawaii.

Jackson, D. D. (1957). The question of family homeostasis. *Psychiatric Quarterly Supplement, 31,* 69–70.

Kaplan, H. S. (1977). Hypoactive sexual desire. *Journal of Sex and Marital Therapy, 2,* 3–9.

Kaplan, H. S. (1979). *Disorders of sexual desire: And other new concepts and techniques in sex therapy.* New York: Brunner/Mazel.

Kaplan, H. S. (1983). *The evaluation of sexual disorders: Psychological and medical aspects.* New York: Brunner/Mazel.

Kernberg, O. (1979). *Object relations theory and clinical psychoanalysis.* New York: Jason Aronson.

L'Abate, L. (1977). Intimacy is sharing hurt feelings: A reply to David Mace. *Journal of Marriage and Family Counseling, 3,* 13–16.

LaPointe, C., & Gillespie, H. G. (1979). A short-term cognitive and behavioral treatment approach to sexual desire phase dysfunction. *Journal of Sex Education and Therapy, 1,* 35–38.

Leiblum, S. R., & Rosen, R. C. (Eds.). (1988). *Sexual desire disorders.* New York: Guilford Press.

Levine, S. B. (1984). An essay on the nature of sexual desire. *Journal of Sex and Marital Therapy, 10,* 83–96.

Lief, H. I. (1977). Inhibited sexual desire. *Medical Aspects of Human Sexuality, 11,* 94–95.

LoPiccolo, J. (1978). Direct treatment of sexual dysfunction. In J. LoPiccolo & L. LoPiccolo (Eds.), *Handbook of sex therapy.* New York: Plenum Press.

LoPiccolo, J. (1982). *Research and clinical innovations in sex therapy.* Paper presented at the annual meeting of the Society Sex Therapy and Research, Charleston, SC.

LoPiccolo, L. (1980). Low sexual desire. In S. R. Leiblum & L. A. Pervin (Eds.), *Principles and practice of sex therapy.* New York: Guilford Press.

Marshall, J. R., & Neill, J. (1977). The removal of a psychosomatic symptom: Effects on the marriage. *Family Process, 16,* 273–280.

Masters, W. H., & Johnson, V. (1966). *The human sexual response.* Boston: Little, Brown.

Masters, W. H., & Johnson, V. (1970). *Human sexual inadequacy.* Boston: Little, Brown.

Masters, W. H., & Johnson, V. E. (1976). Principles of the new sex therapy. *American Journal of Psychiatry, 133,* 548–554.

McCarthy, B. W. (1984). Strategies and techniques for the treatment of inhibited sexual desire. *Journal of Sex and Marital Therapy, 10,* 97–104.

McCarthy, B. W., Ryan, M., & Johnson, F. A. (1975). *Sexual awareness: A practical approach.* San Francisco: Boyd & Fraser.

Messersmith, C. E. (1976). Sex therapy and the marital system. In D. Olson (Ed.), *Treating relationships.* Lake Mills, IA: Graphic.

Montagu, A. (1978). *Touching: The human significance of the skin* (2nd ed.). New York: Harper & Row.

Parson, T., & Bales, B. F. (1955). *Family socialization and interaction process.* Glencoe, IL: Free Press.

Rausch, H. L., Barry, W. A., Hertel, R. K., & Swain, M. A. (1974). *Communications, conflict and marriage.* San Francisco: Jossey-Bass.

Scharff, D.E. (1982). *The sexual relationship: An object relations view of sex and the family.* Boston: Routledge Kegan Paul.

Schover, L. R., Friedman, J., Weiler, S. M., Heiman, J. R., & LoPiccolo, J. (1982). The multiaxial problem-oriented diagnostic systems for the sexual dysfunctions: An alternative to DSM-III. *Archives of General Psychiatry, 39,* 614–619.

Schover, L. R., & LoPiccolo, J. (1982). Treatment effectiveness for dysfunctions of sexual desire. *Journal of Sex and Marital Therapy, 8,* 179–197.

Shepherd, I. L. (1979). Intimacy in psychotherapy. *Voices, 15,* 10.

Sloan, S., & L'Abate, L. (1985). Intimacy. In L. L'Abate (Ed.), *Handbook of family psychology and psychotherapy.* Homewood, IL: Dow Jones-Irwin.

Wagner, G., & Green, R. (1981). *Impotence: Physiological, psychological and surgical diagnosis and treatment.* New York: Plenum Press.

Wagner, G., Willis, E. A., Bro-Rasmussen, F., & Nielsen, M. H. (1982). New theory on the mechanism of erection involving hitherto undescribed vessels. *Lancet,* 416–418.

Wallace, D. H. (1981). Affectional climate in the family of origin and the experience of subsequent sexual-affectional behaviors. *Journal of Sex and Marital Therapy, 7,* 296–306.

Waring, E. M. (1980). Marital intimacy, psychosomatic symptoms and cognitive therapy. *Psychosomatics, 21,* 595–601.

Waring, E., McElrath, D., Lefcoe, D., & Weisz, G. (1981). Dimensions of intimacy in marriage. *Psychiatry, 44,* 169–175.

Waring, E., McElrath, D., Mitchell, P., & Derry, M. (1981). Intimacy and emotional illness in the general population. *Canadian Journal of Psychiatry, 26,* 167–172.

Waring, E. M., & Reddon, J. R. (1983). The measurement of intimacy in marriage: The Waring Intimacy Questionnaire. *Journal of Clinical Psychology, 39,* 53–57.

Warkentin, J., & Whitaker, C. (1966). Serial impasses in marriage. *Psychiatric Research Reports, 20.* Washington, DC: American Psychiatric Association.

Watzlawick, P., Weakland, J., & Fisch, R. (1974). *Change: Principles of problem formation and problem resolution.* New York: Norton.

Wile, D. B. (1981). *Couples therapy: A nontraditional approach.* New York: Wiley.

Zilbergeld, B. (1978). *Male sexuality: A guide to sexual fulfillment.* Boston: Little, Brown.

Zilbergeld, B., & Ellison, C. R. (1980). Desire discrepancies and arousal problems in sex therapy. In S. R. Leiblum & L. A. Pervin (Eds.), *Principles and practice of sex therapy.* New York: Guilford Press.

Zilbergeld, B., & Killmann, P. R. (1984). The scope and effectiveness of sex therapy. *Psychotherapy, 21,* 319–326.

10

Hypoactive Sexual Desire Disorders in Couples: A Cognitive-Behavioral Perspective

Gilles Trudel, PhD, Marc Ravart, MA, and Sylvie Aubin, MA

For a list of the authors' affiliations, see page 240.

KEY POINTS

- Sexual desire disorders are one of the most commonly encountered complaints among couples requesting sex therapy. They are associated with other primary sexual complaints and have adverse effects on the overall sexual and psychological functioning of both men and women.

- All diagnostic criteria based solely on frequency measures of sexual activities should be combined with other factors that directly or indirectly affect that natural expression of sexual desire.

- Such factors include sexual fantasies; environmental influences; interpersonal factors; anxiety and depression; and the thinking style clients have about themselves, their partners, their relationships, and sexuality.

- The main objectives of the cognitive-behavioral treatment program are to help couples enhance the quality of their sexual relations and to improve the overall quality of their relationships.

- The cognitive-behavioral approach focuses on encouraging couples to improve the quality of intimacy rather than "pressuring" the symptomatic partner to increase the frequency of sex.

This chapter was supported by a grant from the National Health and Research Development Program of Canada.

INTRODUCTION

Trudel, Matte, Fortin, and Boulos (1990) conceptualized sexual desire as the overall motor and verbal behaviors, cognitions, fantasies, and emotional responses that precede sexual activity. However, compared with the arousal and orgasmic phases of the sexual response cycle, relatively little scientific data are available on sexual desire—its origins and any abnormalities associated with it. Consequently, it is difficult to define and evaluate problems related to sexual desire (Trudel, 1991).

Over the years, the interest in studying sexual desire disorders has increased for three reasons. First, sexual desire disorders are one of the most commonly encountered complaints among couples requesting sex therapy (Segraves & Segraves, 1991). Second, sexual desire disorders typically exert adverse effects on the overall sexual and psychological functioning of men and women. Third, an absence or loss of sexual desire is frequently associated with other primary sexual complaints (e.g., male erectile disorder, female orgasmic disorder, and coital pain). When the latter occurs, treatment of the sexual dysfunction is complicated by the presence of an underlying desire problem. This often lengthens the treatment process and contributes to treatment resistance and noncompliance in the application of therapeutic interventions.

The diagnostic definition of sexual desire disorder, based primarily on the works of Kaplan (1977, 1979, 1984, 1995), has remained relatively the same since its inclusion in the third edition of the *Diagnostic Statistical Manual of Mental Disorders*, (DSM-III) (American Psychiatric Association [APA], 1980), which classified the disorder as "inhibited sexual desire"; in the third revised edition (DSM-III-R), it was changed to "hypoactive sexual desire disorder" (APA, 1987). Finally, DSM-IV (APA, 1994) defines hypoactive sexual desire disorder as: persistently or recurrently deficient (or absent) sexual fantasies and desire for sexual activity; the disturbance causes marked distress or interpersonal difficulty; and the sexual dysfunction both is not better accounted for by another Axis I disorder (except another sexual dysfunction) and is not due exclusively to the direct physiologic effects of a substance (e.g., a drug of abuse or a medication) or a general medical condition.

DSM-IV further classifies hypoactive sexual desire disorder as lifelong (presence of hypoactive sexual desire since the onset of sexual functioning) or acquired (development of hypoactive sexual desire after a period of normal functioning) as well as generalized (loss or absence of sexual desire across all potential situations or partners) or situational (hypoactive sexual desire is limited to certain types of stimulation, situations, or partners). The therapist must further specify whether the disorder is cause by psychological or combined factors (both psychological and biologic.). The therapist should rule out biologic causes of hypoactive sexual desire, especially among lifelong/generalized subtypes.

According to DSM-IV, certain drugs and medications, general medical conditions, and abnormalities in total and bioavailable testosterone and prolactin can account for loss of sexual desire. Other organic syndromes and neurologic and metabolic abnormalities specifically may impair the physiologic substrates of sexual desire.

A major problem in DSM-IV's diagnostic evaluation of hypoactive sexual desire disorder is that it lacks objective, behavioral criteria. Although recent attempts have been made to operationalize criteria of hypoactive sexual desire (Leiblum & Rosen, 1988; Schover, Friedman, Weiler, Heiman, & LoPiccolo, 1982; Trudel, Ravart, & Matte 1993), no widely accepted definition prevails. From a research and clinical standpoint, this promotes individual differences of interpretation by the evaluator and problems in professional communication.

EVALUATION OF HYPOACTIVE SEXUAL DESIRE

At present, no validated diagnostic instruments exist to measure the various dimensions of sexual desire. Although the sexual history form used in the Multiaxial Problem-Oriented System for Sexual Dysfunctions (Schover et al., 1982) is a reportedly reliable measure of hypoactive sexual desire, more validation studies are required.

Data provided from survey studies, such as those based on research by Kinsey, Pomeroy, and Martin (1948, 1953), led some authors to propose the frequency of sexual activities as a valid index of sexual interest and desire. Ever since these earlier studies, sex research has shown that sexual desire normally fluctuates and demonstrates some differences in both men and women. Despite considerable individual and within-group variations, sexual desire changes in intensity with age and takes a gender-specific course of development.

Kinsey and his team found that the sex drive in men peaks at approximately 18 years of age and slowly declines with age; the sex drive in women increases with age and peaks between the ages of 35 and 40. Although the frequency of sex in both genders diminishes with age, surveys (Janus & Janus, 1993) have shown that persons who frequently engage in sex at a relatively early age tend to maintain a similar pattern in late adulthood. Women who maintain a relatively high frequency pattern of sexual activities may experience dramatic decreases in sexual desire and behaviors under certain circumstances and return to the previous pattern after some time; men tend to maintain a more stable frequency pattern over time. Based on their studies, Schover et al. (1982) proposed an actual frequency of sexual activity of less than twice a month as the main behavioral criterion for hypoactive sexual desire. The latest extensive statistical surveys on desired frequency for sexual activity among couples suggest that men and women generally desire sex on a weekly basis, often two to four times each week (Janus & Janus, 1993; Laumann, Michael, Michaels, & Gagnon, 1994).

Frequency of Sexual Behavior:

LoPiccolo and Friedman (1988) presented data on "desired"

versus "actual" frequency of couples' sexual activities. The study was based on 93 married couples (mean age for men, 34; mean age for women, 32) who had been living together for an average of 9 years. The couples had an average of 2.6 children and a mean annual income of $33,000. Considering the limits of sample size, the characteristics of the couples resembled those of average American couples.

A key finding in this study was that desired frequency for sex exceeded the actual frequency of couples' sexual activities, which suggests that actual frequency of sexual behaviors should not be used as the only diagnostic criterion for hypoactive sexual desire. A number of factors may explain the differences between desired and actual frequency of sexual activities, including: loss of sexual attraction and interest for one's partner, the presence of behaviors and psychological states incompatible with one's sexual interest, and problems between the partners that limit spontaneous expression of sexual desire.

Although the measure of frequency of sexual behavior is a useful index of desire, many authors have suggested the need to include a subjective measure of desire. For example, Lief (1988) argued, "One cannot simply count sexual outlets, as Kinsey did. A person could conceivably masturbate 20 or more times a week, but lack desire to have sex with a partner; or a person could have sex 20 times a month with a partner, yet never once truly desire it." Therefore, the elaboration of a diagnostic instrument for assessing hypoactive sexual desire should consider not only the actual frequency of sexual activities (as an objective, behavioral measure), but also the desired frequency for sex (as a subjective measure). The difference between actual versus desired frequency of sex is a useful measure with which to assess disorders of sexual desire. Again, however, no criteria exist to describe this procedure.

Should the clinician consider a significant difference between these two frequency measures as an index of hypoactive sexual desire? If yes, in what direction would this difference manifest itself? Several possible scenarios may exist. For instance, some clients may report a very low frequency of sexual activities; however, if motivated to increase their desire, they would increase their actual frequency of sex. Conversely, other clients presenting with hypoactive sexual desire disorder who are poorly motivated to change may, in fact, engage in frequent sexual activities to satisfy their partner's demands — even though they actually desire a much lower frequency of sex.

All diagnostic criteria based solely on frequency measures of sexual activities should be combined with other factors that directly or indirectly affect the natural expression of sexual desire. For example, a very busy client may report a desired frequency of two to three sexual activities per week but not actually maintain this frequency because of workload. A couple may desire sex one time per month and maintain this frequency in actuality. Comparing this couple with others within the same age distribution may suggest a low frequency of sex; however, from the perspective of the couple, their desired versus actual frequency of sex reflects positive marital adjustment. Yet another couple may present with a similar frequency pattern of sexual activities but become highly dysfunctional because of a partner's lack of sexual interest. Therefore, important differences in the desired frequency for sex between partners may create a serious sexual adjustment problem.

Sexual Fantasies:

Another fundamental dimension of sexual desire that motivates someone to engage in sexual activities involves sexual fantasies. According to Leiblum and Rosen (1988), easy access to sexual fantasies constitutes the "fuel" of sexual desire. Pasini and Crepeault (1987) defined sexual fantasies as a series of conscious mental representations that manifest themselves more or less in imagination, have sexual/erotic value, and are susceptible to being translated in actuality. The clinical literature suggests that sexual fantasies occur more frequently during the early phases of the sexual response cycle and tend to decrease as sexual arousal reaches its peak and approaches the orgasmic response (Davidson & Hoffman, 1986; Kaplan, 1979; Kelly, 1978; Murray, 1978; Pasini & Crepeault, 1987). Sexual fantasies are recognized as being important in initiating sexual activities; however, this dimension of human sexuality lacks scientific inquiry, research conclusions are not unilateral, and the sexual/erotic function of sexual fantasies remains, at most, speculatively understood.

Davidson and Hoffman (1986) did not find a clear relationship between the use of sexual fantasies and sexual satisfaction among women. These women did report, however, that sexual fantasies were helpful in provoking and increasing sexual arousal. Kelly (1978) evaluated 38 couples and found a significant relationship between marital adjustment and the use of sexual fantasies to increase sexual arousal during sexual activities. However, Murray (1978) did not find a relationship between the use of sexual fantasies and sexual satisfaction among sexually satisfied married and single clients. Nutter and Condron (1983) compared a group of women with and without sexual desire problems; their results showed that women with sexual desire problems rarely fantasized, compared with women without desire problems who frequently fantasized about sexual activities.

Cognitions:

Following a cognitive-behavioral approach in determining how sexual/erotic imagery may contribute to sexual desire disorders, therapists should evaluate the thinking style and cognitive distortions clients have about themselves, their partners, their relationships, and sexuality (Beck, 1988; Lazarus, 1988; LoPiccolo & Friedman, 1988; Rosen & Leiblum, 1989; Trudel, 1991). Cognitive distortions related to hypoactive sexual desire can be investigated by identifying rigid, irrational beliefs and unreasonable expectations about sexuality. Negative self-talk as a result of early trauma or the effects of a morally strict religious upbringing also require identification and restructuring. Faulty attributions, as well as all other forms of automatic negative thoughts and beliefs that reinforce anti-sexual attitudes and feelings of guilt and shame, should be examined. This internal form of negative self-talk plays a significant role in reducing sexual interest and desire and affects the quality of overall sexual response.

Environmental and Interpersonal Factors:

Other important variables that directly or indirectly may affect sexual desire include environmental and interpersonal factors. Sexual desire can be negatively affected by one's past (e.g., antisexual family upbringing, sexual trauma, or unresolved past negative intimate relationships) and present environment (e.g., marital conflicts, financial difficulties, occupational stress, or family problems). The quality of the couple's current relationship is one of the most important causal factors of hypoactive sexual desire.

Variables related to dysfunction that may promote and maintain sexual desire problems include disagreements, arguments, and associated negative affects; lack of physical attractiveness; poor sexual skills in a partner; habituation after many years of cohabitation; differences in personality style and sexual interests; and the lack of complicity that results. Numerous instruments are available to assess the quality of couple functioning. These include the Dyadic Adjustment Scale (Spanier, 1976), the Marital Attitude Survey (Baucom & Epstein, 1990), and the Locke Wallace Adjustment Scale (Locke & Wallace, 1959).

The therapist should assess the presence of other sexual dysfunctions because persistent male and female sexual dysfunctions are associated with low sexual desire (Trudel et al., 1990; Trudel, Ravart, & Matte, 1993). The mechanism of action probably is related to an increase in anxiety toward the idea of engaging in sexual activity with one's partner and the establishment of unfavorable conditions for the natural expression of one's sexuality. Such a situation provides evidence in support of the interdependence between the various phases of the sexual response cycle. Within the evaluation process, the therapist should investigate whether the desire problem is secondary to another sexual dysfunction.

A series of interpersonal factors also can contribute to an increase or decrease in sexual desire. Emerging feelings of love, sexual desire, and receptivity are contingent on factors related to one's overall sense of well-being and basic trust in one's partner. LoPiccolo and Friedman (1988) described how fears of intimacy, closeness, commitment, and abandonment; control issues directed toward self or partner; an inability to fuse feelings of love and sexual desire; and unresolved feelings of anger, hatred, and resentment may all play causal roles in creating and maintaining hypoactive sexual desire. Other causes of hypoactive sexual desire include religious orthodoxy, aging-related concerns, obsessive-compulsive/passive-aggressive personalities, sexual orientation and identity issues, sexual aversions and phobias, and masked sexual deviations.

Anxiety and Depression:

Many people who complain of low sexual desire also have concurrent anxiety or mood disorders. A large body of literature describes how dysphoric mood, stress, anxiety, and other negative emotional states (e.g., anger, fear) can adversely affect the emergence and maintenance of sexual desire (Kaplan, 1983, 1984, 1995; Leiblum & Rosen, 1988, 1989; Rosen & Leiblum, 1995; Schreiner-Engel & Schiavi, 1986). Disabling anxiety and depressive states will psychologically and physiologically inhibit the arousal or orgasmic phases of the sexual response cycle, thus becoming negatively associated with a group of events, behaviors, or stimuli that are integral to sexual activity.

Patients and their sexual partners often report feelings of depression or anxiety about their sexual difficulties. For most of these couples, the desire disorder, which is caused mainly by the lack of emotional and sexual intimacy in the relationship, in turn precipitates their negative emotional states. The negative emotions typically will subside as treatment progresses and sexual desire improves. In other cases, an underlying anxiety or mood disorder in the symptomatic partner may, in fact, have created and maintained the hypoactive desire. For these clients, symptom-focused psychotherapy should be initiated; if needed, couple sex therapy should follow. For the latter group of clients, the clinician should also assess the utility of antianxiety or antidepressant medications to help further alleviate the primary anxiety or mood disorder. Kaplan (1995) reported that sexual desire spontaneously returns to normal, soon after the depression or anxiety dissipates. Kaplan (1987) also reported that antipanic medication facilitates treatment of patients who manifest more severe forms of hypoactive sexual desire, as found in cases of sexual avoidance, sexual aversions, and sexual phobias.

Overall, clinicians should rule out underlying depression or anxiety disorders before initiating sex therapy with patients who complain of low sexual desire as well as of other sexual dysfunctions. If a patient's chief complaints concern problems with anxiety or depression, we also believe it prudent to inquire about the effect their problems may have on the quality of their sex life in an attempt to determine whether any problems here are causing or maintaining the anxiety or depression.

TREATMENT OF HYPOACTIVE SEXUAL DESIRE

The knowledge we have gathered on the treatment of sexual desire disorders essentially is based on clinical information. Our cognitive-behavioral treatment program stems primarily from ongoing clinical research on individual and relational characteristics of hypoactive sexual desire (Trudel, 1991; Trudel, Aubin, & Matte, 1995; Trudel, Boulos, & Matte, 1993; Trudel, Fortin, & Matte, in preparation; Trudel, Marchand, Turgeon, Ravart, & Aubin, 1995; Trudel, Ravart, & Matte, 1993). In addition, components are incorporated from various hypoactive sexual desire treatment programs, such as those described by Kaplan (1979), LoPiccolo and Friedman (1988), and McCarthy (1984).

The main objectives of our multimodal treatment program are to help couples enhance the quality of their sexual relationships and improve the overall quality of their marital relationships. We do this by using a combination of techniques directed at breaking the sexual avoidance pattern that is typical among couples presenting with hypoactive sexual desire. Particular focus is placed on encouraging couples to improve the quality of intimacy as opposed to "pressuring" the symptomatic partner to increase the frequency of sex.

Providing Sexual Education and Information on the Dynamics of Desire Disorders:

In this phase, the therapist provides clinical and statistical information on healthy sexual functioning and desire disorders. Various sexual myths about sexuality are explored and disputed. Additional information focuses on ways couples can become more intimate and experience sexual pleasure and satisfaction.

Identifying Immediate and Long-Term Causal Factors of Sexual Desire Disorders:

A number of immediate and long-term factors directly or indirectly may create or maintain hypoactive sexual desire. These factors are reviewed by Kaplan (1979, 1984, 1995), LoPiccolo and Friedman (1988), and Trudel (1991). Immediate factors that may inhibit sexual desire include significant levels of depression, anxiety, and stress (Trudel & Larose, 1991). Other immediate factors, such as marital distress, fatigue, antisexual attitudes, and work overload, also may actively inhibit sexual desire.

Various long-term factors include childhood sexual guilt and shame, unresolved past sexual trauma, and unresolved past negative relationships. After the interfering factors have been identified with the couple, appropriate treatment strategies are initiated to alleviate the negative influence of these factors. As couples progress therapeutically, subsequent phases of the treatment program may be incorporated to further the process of treating the sexual desire disorder.

Increasing the Quality of the Marital Relationship:

After a careful evaluation and identification of the major sources of marital distress, several therapeutic techniques that may be used include basic communication and listening skills, communication of negative thoughts and emotions, problem-solving skills training, and the working through and resolution of past hurts and resentments (Barbach, 1982; Baucom & Epstein, 1990; Beck, 1988; Wright, 1985). Many couples with hypoactive sexual desire disorder initially report having no particular communication problems; however, when their ability to communicate sexual and emotional concerns is assessed, this area of communication often is noticeably lacking. These couples typically avoid intimate topics of conversation because of the symptomatic partner's fear of intimacy. One of the main objectives of communication skills training is to help couples express themselves constructively about intimate issues within their relationship.

Increasing Sexual Intimacy, Receptivity, Arousability, Pleasure, and Satisfaction:

Various therapeutic strategies have been used to help couples overcome their desire problems and improve the quality of their sexual relationship. One strategy focuses on helping couples achieve more reasonable and realistic expectations about their sexual relationship. Couples learn that not all sexual activities lead to a state of optimal sexual satisfaction in both partners.

Other therapeutic exercises focus on genital and nongenital

desensitization techniques, such as those described by Kaplan (1979), Masters and Johnson (1970), and McCarthy (1984). These therapeutic procedures progressively reduce the level of anxiety as well as negative thoughts and emotional reactions associated with sexual activities. They also foster awareness of emerging sexual responses in both partners.

Other therapeutic strategies help couples enhance the quality of their sexual interactions. Couples are encouraged to experiment with various sexual activities in and outside the usual sexual context. Moreover, partners are invited to discover their sexual preferences and to function sexually at a pace that will elicit mutual sexual pleasure.

Still another therapeutic strategy consists of having couples willingly place themselves in a sexual situation that previously has evoked feelings of sexual discomfort. Couples learn to identify the various factors that contribute to their state of mutual discomfort. The couples then engage themselves in a problem-solving process and generate solutions that will help them neutralize and overcome their negative emotional states and inhibitions.

Some strategies help couples explore sexual attraction within their relationship. Rather than viewing sexual attraction as something magical that results from some unexplainable body chemistry, each partner is encouraged to express realistic and constructive suggestions to the other to increase mutual attraction and desire. Another exercise explores various suggestions partners may have regarding sexual activities and scenarios they would like to experience in real life.

A final therapeutic strategy focuses on helping couples understand the impact that the sexual desire problem has had on their overall relationship. Issues related to trust, self-confidence, rejection, and vulnerability are discussed. This phase of treatment is particularly important because many couples may believe the sexual desire problem symbolizes an overall lack of interest or loss of feelings of love on behalf of the symptomatic partner. In these cases, desire problems may even evoke suspiciousness in the asymptomatic partner of an ongoing extramarital affair. Such beliefs between partners inevitably will create tension, and feelings of doubt and uncertainty will arise. This could lead to, or further reinforce, sexual desire problems — thereby adversely affecting the quality of the marital and sexual relationship.

Modifying Negative Thoughts, Beliefs, and Other Cognitive Distortions Related to Desired Disorders:

Clients with hypoactive sexual desire typically develop various negative thoughts before, during, and after sex; such thoughts lead to negative beliefs about their bodies, their genitalia, and sexual functioning. Consequently, when engaged in sexual activities, many of these clients manifest strong negative thoughts and emotional reactions regarding their body image. Some clients with hypoactive sexual desire report constant negative thinking patterns during sexual encounters (e.g., "My partner is not sufficiently sexually excited!" "My partner doesn't have a good enough erection!" "My partner moves and kisses me too much!" "My partner rarely caresses me the right way!").

Culturally induced false messages about sexual relationships often can lead to misconceptions about what constitutes appropriate sexual activities. These messages can reinforce existing anxiety during sexual activities, creating an avoidance pattern. For example, a man with hypoactive sexual desire may pressure himself and avoid sex by consequently believing that the entire sexual relationship rests on his shoulders. Conversely, a woman with hypoactive sexual desire disorder may believe she must depend entirely on her partner for sexual arousal and orgasms; if her sexual relationship is not satisfying, she will lose interest and avoid sex all together.

Other negative thoughts and beliefs may occur after a sexual encounter. For example, partners who have exceedingly high standards about sexual performance may devalue themselves and their partners whenever they have disappointing sexual experiences. These self-defeating thoughts may promote frustration and guilt because the couples believe their sex lives depend entirely on successful sexual performance. They also may resent their partners for being sexually inadequate and blame them for the problem. These negative thinking patterns can be modified by using traditional cognitive restructuration techniques (Baucom & Epstein, 1990; Beck, 1988) and rational-emotive therapy procedures (Ellis, 1977).

Promoting Positive Sexual/ Erotic Thoughts, Images, and Fantasies:

This therapeutic phase varies in its application and ranges from suggestions of erotic literature to the use of therapeutic techniques (Gochros & Fischer, 1980) aimed at increasing the frequency and use of sexual/erotic fantasies. Enhancing a client's ability to experience sexual fantasies constitutes a crucial treatment strategy for hypoactive sexual desire because fantasies are strongly related to the emergence and maintenance of sexual desire (Kaplan, 1979, 1995; LoPiccolo & Friedman, 1988; Rosen & Leiblum, 1989, 1995; Trudel, 1991). Accordingly, the more a person nourishes a healthy sexual/ erotic fantasy life, the more he or she will experience sexual desire.

Our treatment strategy for enhancing sexual fantasies involves several steps. First, information is provided to couples regarding the impact of sexual fantasies on sexual desire. Second, clients are asked whether they have sexual fantasies; if they do, they are asked to list them. If the symptomatic partner reports having sexual fantasies but rarely uses them, we help the client explore the factors that may inhibit the natural expression of these fantasies. Frequently, clients require cognitive restructuring to help neutralize their negative-thinking pattern associated with the use of sexual fantasies. If sexual fantasies are rare or absent, the next step consists of helping clients find ways to increase the frequency of their fantasies. Various types of sexual fantasies are presented; clients are encouraged to read erotic literature to help them discover fantasy material that might elicit sexual desire and help increase arousal during sexual activities. Categorical examples of sexual fantasies include sexual/erotic behaviors (e.g., group sex), sexual/erotic locations (e.g., having sex at an unusual place), sexual/erotic moments (e.g., having sex while watching television), sexual/erotic characters (e.g., having sex with an attractive, well-known actor), sexual/erotic contexts (e.g., being undressed by someone special), and sexual/erotic sensations (e.g., the sound of one's partner's heavy breathing during sex).

As an adjunct to the second step, the third step consists of encouraging partners with hypoactive sexual desire to explore various sexual/erotic materials that they may find particularly sexually arousing. They are invited to "shop" for their sexual fantasies. The final step helps clients imagine as vividly as possible the sexual fantasies they have collected and decide which is the most sexually arousing. They are encouraged to practice this imagery technique daily until they report no difficulties in visualizing and elaborating on their particular sexual fantasies. To fulfill the sexual needs of the couple, the symptomatic partner receives help integrating these sexual fantasies during the couple's sexual activities in a way that will increase pleasure and satisfaction.

CONCLUSION

Sexual desire disorders are serious problems that adversely affect couples' sexual functioning and satisfaction. They reduce the frequency of the couple's sexual activities considerably; in extreme cases, they may completely inhibit such activities. In the recent past, therapists believed that simply by improving the sexual functioning of couples they would also resolve the sexual desire problem. For this reason, clinical research specifically designed to study hypoactive sexual desire was neglected (O'Carroll, 1991). However, it is now becoming more apparent that several individual and relational factors may have a direct or indirect impact on sexual desire. Couples who seek treatment of a sexual desire problem generally present a complex clinical picture, comprised of a series of contributing variables that inhibit the natural emergence and expression of sexual desire.

Despite the lack of controlled treatment studies, two clinical studies have supported the usefulness of a cognitive-behavioral treatment approach to hypoactive sexual desire. McCarthy (1984) reported significant treatment gains in the majority of couples using a multimodal treatment program. Schover and LoPiccolo (1982) examined various problems related to desire disorders (including sexual aversion disorder) and evaluated treatment outcome results on a series of selected dependent variables. Overall, they found that a cognitive-behavioral treatment program produced positive results in many areas of couple sexual functioning, including sexual satisfaction. More clinical, empirical research is needed to increase our understanding of the characteristics of clients with hypoactive sexual desire. By understanding the underlying dynamics of psychosexual disorders, more effective treatment programs may be designed to manage the complexity of sexual desire disorders.

REFERENCES

American Psychiatric Association. (1980). *Diagnostic and statistical manual of mental disorders* (3rd ed.). Washington, DC: Author.

American Psychiatric Association. (1987). *Diagnostic and statistical manual of mental disorders* (3rd ed., rev.). Washington, DC: Author.

American Psychiatric Association. (1994). *Diagnostic and statistical manual of mental disorders* (4th ed.). Washington, DC: Author.

Barbach, L. (1982). *For each other: Sharing sexual intimacy.* New York: Anchor Press.

Baucom, D. H., & Epstein, N. (1990). *Cognitive-behavioral marital therapy.* New York: Brunner/Mazel.

Beck, A. T. (1988). *Love is never enough: How couples can overcome misunderstandings, resolve conflicts, and solve relationship problems through cognitive therapy.* New York: Harper & Row.

Davidson, K. J., & Hoffman, L. E. (1986). Sexual fantasies and sexual satisfaction: An empirical analysis of erotic thought. *Journal of Sex Research, 22,* 185–204.

Ellis, A. (1977). The rational-emotive approach to sex therapy. In A. Ellis & R. Grieger (Eds.), *Handbook of rational-emotive therapy.* New York: Springer.

Gochros, H. L., & Fischer, J. (1980). *Treat yourself to a better sex life.* Englewood Cliffs, NJ: Prentice-Hall.

Janus, S. S., & Janus, C. L. (1993). *The Janus report on sexual behavior.* New York: Wiley.

Kaplan, H. S. (1977). Hypoactive sexual desire. *Journal of Sex and Marital Therapy, 3,* 3–9.

Kaplan, H. S. (1979). *Disorders of sexual desire and other new concepts and techniques in sex therapy.* New York: Brunner/Mazel.

Kaplan, H. S. (1983). *The evaluation of sexual disorders: Psychological and medical aspects.* New York: Brunner/Mazel.

Kaplan, H. S. (Ed.). (1984). *Comprehensive evaluation of disorders of sexual desire.* Washington, DC: American Psychiatric Press.

Kaplan, H. S. (1987). *Sexual aversion, sexual phobias, and panic disorder.* New York: Brunner/Mazel.

Kaplan, H. S. (1995). *The sexual desire disorders: Dysfunctional regulation of sexual motivation.* New York: Brunner/Mazel.

Kelly, L. A. S. (1978). Imaging ability, marital adjustment, and erotic fantasy during sexual relations in married men and women. *Dissertation Abstracts International, 39,* 1457B–1458B.

Kinsey, A. C., Pomeroy, W. B., & Martin, C. E. (1948). *Sexual behavior in the human male.* Philadelphia: Saunders.

Kinsey, A. C., Pomeroy, W. B., & Martin, C. E. (1953). *Sexual behavior in the human female.* Philadelphia: Saunders.

Laumann, E., Michael, R., Michaels, S., & Gagnon, J. (1994). *The social organization of sexuality.* Chicago: University of Chicago Press.

Lazarus, A. A. (1988). A multimodal perspective on problems of sexual desire. In S. R. Leiblum & R. C. Rosen (Eds.), *Sexual desire disorders.* New York: Guilford Press.

Leiblum, S. R., & Rosen, R. C. (Eds.). (1988). *Sexual desire disorders.* New York: Guilford Press.

Leiblum, S. R., & Rosen, R. C. (Eds.). (1989). *Principles and practice of sex therapy: Update for the 1990s.* New York: Guilford Press.

Lief, H. I. (1988). Foreword. In S. R. Leiblum & R. C. Rosen (Eds.), *Sexual desire disorders.* New York: Guilford Press.

Locke, H. J., & Wallace, K. M. (1959). Short-term marital adjustment and prediction tests: Their reliability and validity. *Journal of Marriage and Family Living, 21,* 251–255.

LoPiccolo, J., & Friedman, J. M. (1988). Broad-spectrum treatment of low sexual desire: Integration of cognitive, behavioral and systemic therapy. In S. R. Leiblum & R. C. Rosen (Eds.), *Sexual desire disorders.* New York: Guilford Press.

Masters, W. H., & Johnson, V. E. (1970). *Human sexual inadequacy.* Boston: Little, Brown.

McCarthy, B. (1984). Strategies and techniques for the treatment of inhibited sexual desire. *Journal of Sex and Marital Therapy, 10,* 97–104.

Murray, E. L. (1978). The relationship between sexual fantasy and reported sexual behavior and satisfaction. *Dissertation Abstracts International, 39,* 2512B.

Nutter, D. E., & Condron, M. K. (1983). Sexual fantasy and activity patterns of females with inhibited sexual desire versus normal controls. *Journal of Sex and Marital Therapy, 9,* 276–282.

O'Carroll, R. (1991). Sexual desire disorders: A review of controlled treatment studies. *Journal of Sex Research, 28,* 607–624.

Pasini, W., & Crepeault, C. (1987). *L'imaginaire en sexologie clinique.* Paris: Presses Universitaires de France.

Rosen, R. C., & Leiblum, S. R. (1989). Assessment and treatment of desire disorders. In S. R. Leiblum & R. C. Rosen (Eds.), *Principles and practice of sex therapy: Update for the 1990s.* New York: Guilford Press.

Rosen, R. C., & Leiblum, S. R. (Eds.). (1995). *Case studies in sex therapy.* New York: Guilford Press.

Schover, L. R., Friedman, J. M., Weiler, S. H., Heiman, J. R., & LoPiccolo, J. (1982). Multiaxial Problem-Oriented System for Sexual Dysfunctions: An alternative to DSM-II. *Archives of General Psychiatry, 39,* 614–619.

Schover, L., & LoPiccolo, J. (1982). Treatment effectiveness for dysfunctions of sexual desire. *Journal of Sex and Marital Therapy, 8,* 179–197.

Schreiner-Engel, P., & Schiavi, R. C. (1986). Lifetime psychopathology in individuals with low sexual desire. *Journal of Nervous and Mental Disease, 174,* 646–651.

Segraves, K. B., & Segraves, R. T. (1991). Hypoactive sexual desire disorder: Prevalence and comorbidity in 906 subjects. *Journal of Sex and Marital Therapy, 17,* 55–58.

Spanier, G. B. (1976). Measuring dyadic adjustment: New scales for assessing the quality of marriage and similar dyads. *Journal of Marriage and Family Therapy, 38,* 15–27.

Trudel, G. (1991). Review of psychological factors in low sexual desire. *Sexual and Marital Therapy, 6,* 261–272.

Trudel, G., Aubin, F., & Matte, B. (1995). Sexual behaviors and pleasure in couples with hypoactive sexual desire. *Journal of Sexual Education and Therapy, 21,* 210-216.

Trudel, G., Boulos, L., & Matte, B. (1993). Dyadic adjustment in couples with hypoactive sexual desire. *Journal of Sex Education and Therapy, 19,* 31–36.

Trudel, G., Fortin, C., & Matte, B. (in preparation). Sexual interaction and communication in couples with hypoactive sexual desire.

Trudel, G., & Larose, Y. (1991). Comparaison de couples avec ou sans problemes de desir sexuel hypoactif a l'Inventaire sur la depression de Beck. Presentation a un symposium sur l'approche cognitive de la depression a la XIXieme journee scientifique de l'Association francaise de therapie comportementale et cognitive. Paris.

Trudel, G., Marchand, A., Turgeon, L. Ravart, M., & Aubin, S. (1995). *Cognitive-behavioral treatment of hypoactive sexual desire.* Washington DC: Association for Advancement of Behavior Therapy.

Trudel, G., Matte, B., Fortin, C., & Boulos, L. (1990). Comparaison de couples avec ou sans probleme de desir sexuel. XXieme congres annuel de la European Association of Behaviour Therapy. Paris.

Trudel, G., Ravart, M., & Matte, B. (1993). The use of the Multiaxial Diagnostic System for Sexual Dysfunctions in the assessment of hypoactive sexual desire. *Journal of Sex and Marital Therapy, 19,* 123–130.

Wright, J. (1985). *La survie du couple: Une approche simple, pratique et complete.* Montreal: Les Editions La Presse.

AUTHORS' AFFILIATIONS

Dr. Trudel is Professor in the Department of Psychology at the University of Quebec, Quebec, Canada. He is also a clinical psychologist at the Behavioral Therapy Unit, Louis H. Lafontaine Hospital, Montreal.

Mr. Ravart is a clinical psychologist and sexologist at the Human Sexuality Unit of Montreal General Hospital, and a Ph.D. candidate in Psychology at the University of Quebec.

Ms. Aubin is a clinical psychologist at a marital and family consultation clinic in Montreal, and a Ph.D. candidate in Psychology at the University of Quebec.

11

The Clinical Management of Jealousy

Paul E. Mullen, MBBS, DSc, MPhil, FRCPsych, FRANZCP

Dr. Mullen is Director, Forensic Psychiatry Services, Rosanna, Australia; and Professor of Forensic Psychiatry at Monash University, Melbourne, Australia.

KEY POINTS

- Jealousy can be divided into two broad groups: reactive jealousy and symptomatic jealousy. Reactive jealousies can be further classified as normal versus pathologic ranges of reaction. Symptomatic jealousy arises from mental illness.

- Although jealousy is a common clinical problem, it is often difficult to assess because it is not only a common reaction to infidelity but can also derive from a mental disorder.

- It is extremely difficult to assess jealousy without interviewing the suspected partner, who can often clarify the history of the relationship. Eight key elements to guide the assessment of jeal-

ousy are highlighted, with particular emphasis given to the assessment of the risk of violence.

- Three approaches are outlined for the treatment of normal jealous reactions: individual, situational, and relationship approaches.

- In the treatment of pathologic reactions, treatment should be based on the particular characteristics of the jealous individual.

- Symptomatic jealousies often are left untreated because the primary pathology takes precedence. However, techniques used for controlling reactive jealousies and medications have been successful treatment options for this type of jealousy.

INTRODUCTION

Jealousy is a complex emotion generated by a perceived threat to a valued relationship. Although it can occur in a variety of contexts, jealousy causes the most trouble in romantic or sexual relationships.

In a random community sample, conducted by Mullen and Martin (1994), 351 respondents acknowledged having had some experience of romantic jealousy. Forty percent reported jealousy without good cause on at least one occasion. Nearly 20% said their partner's jealousy had created "a great deal of problems" in their relationship, and 15% of both men and women reported experiences of physical violence motivated by jealousy. Although jealousy significantly distresses both the jealous person and the object of suspicion, it does not do so equally: the suspected partner—not the actual or supposed rival—bears the brunt of the hostility. Given the associated unhappiness and fear, it is not surprising that those involved in a relationship tainted by jealousy seek professional help.

The clinical assessment is complicated because jealousy is a common reaction to infidelity; it is further complicated because it forms the content of delusional preoccupations arising in the context of mental illness. Paranoid illnesses (particularly the schizophrenias) may give rise to delusions of infidelity; such delusions are prominent in 14% of cases (Shepherd, 1961). In a more extensive study of 8,134 inpatients, Soyka, Naber, and Völcher (1991) reported delusions of infidelity to be found in 7% of persons with organic psychosis, 6.7% of those with paranoid disorders, and 2.5% of those with schizophrenia. Depression also can be associated with the emergence of morbid jealousy (Mooney, 1965). In fact, any mental illness (even one with an obvious organic origin) capable of generating delusions or other morbid preoccupations, such as obsessions and overvalued ideas, can engender pathologic jealousy.

The protean and occasionally dramatic manifestations of jealousy in the general population, combined with its complex relationships to a wide range of mental disorders, frustrate attempts to provide a simple, consistent classification. The earliest classification attempt (Mairet, 1908) recognized four types of jealousy: normal jealousy, excessive (hyperesthetic) jealousy, jealous monomania, and jealous insanity (in which the passion forms one part of a more generalized psychotic state). Jaspers (1910, 1963) used the classification of jealousy to illustrate his division of mental disorders into reactions, developments, and processes; however, he recognized that these were not mutually exclusive descriptions of clinical realities. The division of jealousy into two broad groups (White & Mullen, 1989) — jealous reactions and the jealousy arising as a direct symptom of an underlying mental disorder — is used in this chapter.

REACTIVE JEALOUSY

Normal Jealousy:

Jealous reactions occur in response to a provocative event or state of affairs that can be reasonably related to fears about a partner's fidelity. The characteristics of jealous reactions that can be considered within normal limits are listed in Table 11.1.

Parrot (1991) suggested normal jealousy can be divided into *suspicious jealousy* (characterized by apprehension and uncertainty occurring when the threat to the relationship remains unresolved) and *fait accompli jealousy* (arises when the threat becomes an accomplished fact and when sadness, anger, and envy of the former partner come to the fore). The jealous person often vacillates between the suspicion of infidelity and the certainty of betrayal. Even when infidelity is openly acknowledged, the jealous person often remains preoccupied with asking the unanswerable question of whether the unfaithful partner still "really" loves him or her and with attempting to grasp the extent of the physical and emotional betrayal he or she has suffered. Sadness develops until the relationship is accepted as irretrievably compromised; when

Table 11.1
JEALOUS REACTIONS (NORMAL RANGE)

Jealous reactions remain within normal limits when:

- They are a response to events that can reasonably be related to fears about the partner's current or future fidelity

- The suspicions are focused on a plausible rival

- The feelings, desires, and behaviors evoked broadly remain within the limits acceptable to the jealous individual's self-concept and within the wider cultural norms

- They have a course and evolution that can be understandably related to the provoking situation and subsequent developments

- The jealous person seeks (and eventually accepts) reasonable reassurance and a resolution of the conflict—or can accept that the relationship is coming to an end

normal individuals reach this stage, they have gone beyond the realm of jealousy and have entered the realms of regret, resentment, and nostalgia.

Pathologic Jealousy:

Jealous reactions may be considered morbid when they involve an exaggerated psychological and behavioral response beyond the normal limits for the culture. These exaggerated responses are predisposed by aspects of the individual's character, current state of mind, or personal history (Table 11.2).

Paranoid personality disorder is particularly noted in the fourth edition of the *Diagnostic and Statistical Manual of Mental Disorders* (DSM-IV) (American Psychiatric Association, 1994) as predisposing to morbid jealousy. Clients with sensitive, self-referential, or narcissistic characters are also prone to excessive jealousy (Vauhkonen, 1968). A lowered mood or an

---

Table 11.2
PATHOLOGIC JEALOUS REACTIONS

Jealous reactions can be considered morbid when, despite being a reaction to situations that might conceivably lead to apprehension of infidelity, they:

- Involve exaggerated psychological and behavioral responses (with respect to the norms for the individual and the culture)

- Involve a state that sensitizes the subject to respond with excessive jealousy that may be one or more of the following:

    1. A personality deviation, such as a paranoid personality disorder
    2. A mental disorder, most frequently depressive
    3. Past experiences of being deceived or deserted
    4. Substance abuse, notably involving alcohol or cerebral stimulants

- Focus on inherently unlikely rivals or a multiplicity of possible rivals

- Do not respond to reasonable reassurance and seek either prolongation of conflict or complete subjugation of the partners

- Will not accept either a termination of the relationship or an end to their "right" to be jealous (even if one of them leaves)

---

impaired memory may contribute to a grossly exaggerated response or to a misunderstanding conducive to jealousy. In this context, the distinction from symptomatic jealousy is that the mental disorder augments the reaction, rather than the jealousy being itself a direct product of the illness. (This distinction may be impossible, particularly in cases of depression.) Finally, those exposed in the past to desertions and infidelities may be particularly vulnerable to further threats to their relationships; hence, they may respond with inappropriate vehemence.

No clear demarcation between pathologic and normal jealous reactions exists. Even though most examples either clearly fall inside or outside the limits of normality, marginal cases do appear. It is also important to emphasize that the limits of normality are *culturally dependent* and are dependent to a degree on what is normal for the individual. Jealousy within the normal range usually is accompanied by a desire for reassurance that the fears are groundless; if confirmed, the fears are marked by either an attempt to repair the relationship or begin negotiations about its termination. The anger and distress usually give way to relief or sadness, depending on the outcome.

In morbid jealous reactions, suspicions override all attempts to reassure, placate, and seek confirmation; the jealous person remains incapable of accepting refutation — or even modification — in the face of contrary evidence. Normal jealous reactions do contain an element of the unresolvable doubt, but it is not the all-conspicuous feature of the morbid reaction. In morbid reactions, anger, resentment, and self-righteousness, rather than doubt and distress, are often prominent.

The evolution of jealous reactions, inside and outside "acceptable" limits, depends on:

- The actual situation — (Is there infidelity? Is the relationship breaking down?)

- The suspected partner's response — may promote, maintain, or alleviate suspicions

- The changes in the jealous person's own state of mind

- The jealous individual's coping strategies, in addition to his or her behavior around the partner

Vehement accusations, threats, violence, and apparent imperviousness to appeals amplify preexisting rifts and create new uncertainties about the relationship. Morbid jealous reactions can include delusional developments that may be encountered in abnormal, often paranoid personalities who have been exposed to a situation in which their partner's fidelity was seriously doubted. Such disorders find a rather uncomfortable berth in DSM-IV under "brief psychotic disorder."

SYMPTOMATIC JEALOUSY

Symptomatic jealousies owe their genesis to a mental disorder that is the necessary, if not always the sufficient, cause (Table 11.3). In clinical practice, characterological, historical, and relationship issues often make the emergence of jealousy (even in symptomatic cases) appear understandable.

Table 11.3
THE SYMPTOMATIC JEALOUSIES

- Owe their genesis to an underlying mental disorder that emerges contemporaneously with, or prior to, the jealousy

- Have a course and evolution related to the progress of the underlying disorder

- Are accompanied by the clinical features of the underlying disorder

- Are not usually related to a provocation that could reasonably be related to fears about the partner's fidelity

---

The interaction between initiating illness and features that shape the content of the abnormal experiences is illustrated by one of our cases in which a person presented with delusions of infidelity typical of paranoid illness, probably of a schizophrenic type.

The client, whose father had deserted the family for another woman when the client was in his early teens, had always been an oversensitive person prone to possessiveness and given to forming intensely dependent relationships. His first wife ran off with his best (and only) friend, and his second marriage had been tumultuous in the period preceding the onset of his illness. He responded well to treatment with antipsychotic medication and returned to his family and to work, albeit in a less demanding occupation. He remained symptom free on a small but regular dose of an antipsychotic medication for 7 years before presenting with florid delusions of infidelity. On that occasion, he presented with some mild disorientation, memory impairment, and a variety of neurologic signs. His second illness was a neurodegenerative disorder, known as Jacob-Creutzfeldt disease—not a recurrence of the original paranoid illness; however, his jealous preoccupations and delusions were similar. In this case, even though his underlying illnesses were necessary for the emergence of his delusions, the fact that jealousy (rather than persecution, grandeur, or some other delusional preoccupation) manifested seems to reflect the client's personality and life experiences.

Not all symptomatic jealousies are necessarily delusional. Both depression and mania can generate jealous preoccupations without qualifying as delusional. The relationship between alcohol abuse and jealousy is complex although in most cases it probably exacerbates preexisting suspiciousness and possessiveness.

Jealous thoughts may be experienced as intrusive, excessive, and unreasonably persistent. Jealousy is nearly always associated with an urge to check on the partner and to test his or her fidelity. Those who are jealous often describe repeated attempts to dismiss suspicions and resist impulses either to accuse or surreptitiously investigate. Jealousy is, in everyday parlance, often obsessive and obsessing; therefore, it comes as no surprise that attempts have been made to annex nondelusional jealousies of pathologic intensity to obsessive-compulsive disorder (OCD) (Cobb & Marks, 1979; Rasmussen & Eisen, 1992; Stein, Hollander, & Josephson, 1994). Clear examples of suspicions of infidelity that form a dominant content in OCD have been described (Cobb & Marks, 1979; Mairet, 1908; Stein et al., 1994).

The phrase *obsessive jealousy*, as used by Mooney (1965, p.

1024), refers to a far broader concept: "irrational jealousy in which enough reality testing remains for the client to appreciate the inconclusiveness of the evidence and view the jealousy as symptomatic of emotional difficulty." Mooney's patients with obsessive jealousy tended to have marked depressive features, but they did not suffer from OCD. Care should be taken not to mistake unwanted suspicions, resisted urges, and distressingly insistent thoughts for obsessional phenomena in the clinical sense.

The DSM-IV describes jealousy as a specific subtype of delusional disorder in which the delusions of infidelity constitute the core of the disorder. Such disorders have been considered reaction induced in those rendered vulnerable by personality disorders and by situations beyond their coping capacities (Bleuler, 1924). Despite being clinically enlightening, this latter view is so unfashionable that the jealousy of delusional disorders is perforce to be regarded as symptomatic or left as an independent entity analogous to the jealous monomania noted by Mairet (1908).

It is misguided to attempt to distinguish normal from pathologic jealousy on the basis of whether the suspicions are based on actual infidelity or are clearly erroneous. The actual facts are often as opaque to the therapist as they are to the jealous person. In any case, clearly pathologic jealousies may be essentially correct in their central conviction about the partner's infidelity, just as jealousy in the normal range may arise from egregious error.

ASSESSING JEALOUSY

Assessing jealousy is difficult because it occurs in the context of a relationship, thereby virtually necessitating an interview with the suspected partner—not only to clarify the history (particularly with regard to threats and violence that the jealous person typically understates), but also to understand the history of the relationship.

The assessment of jealousy includes eight main elements:

1. A history of *this* episode of jealousy should be compiled, including the precipitating events (if any), the context of the jealousy's emergence, and the chronology of the jealousy's development.

2. The history of the relationship should be determined; the partners may have radically different perspectives. In particular, each partner's perceptions of the following should be established:

    a. Power relationships — jealousy occurs more frequently in the partner who regards himself or herself as more dependent or whose sense of influence and control has been threatened

    b. Equity issues — the partner who has made greater investment in the relationship is usually more sensitive to possible infidelity

    c. Exclusivity norms, especially related to sexual behavior

    d. Benefits — what valued outcomes each partner obtains and expects from the relationship

    e. Gender-role expectations — may have been radically at variance without ever having been openly discussed)

    f. Remedies attempted by the partners to overcome or cope with the jealousy.

3. A history of previous relationships and jealousy issues that have arisen should be obtained. This can raise

interesting questions, particularly when the jealous person has never been so afflicted in previous relationships but the suspected person is always so troubled by accusing partners. A history of previous desertions and infidelities may leave the victim hypersensitive to possible repetitions.

4. A family history, with particular reference to jealousy and domestic violence, should be gathered.

> One client, a man with an apparently unblemished record, began therapy after a serious assault on his wife. He revealed, reluctantly and only on direct questioning, that he had grown up in a household in which both his father and his grandfather repeatedly assaulted their wives; his own mother had been killed by his father in a jealous rage and his paternal grandfather had been imprisoned for repeated assaults on his wife that were also motivated by jealousy. The therapist who had seen this man before the assault might have taken a less sanguine view of the risks and warned the wife about her safety had he obtained this family's history.

5. A personal history, with particular reference to rivalry and envy with siblings as well as reported quality of peer relationships, should be obtained.

6. A detailed account of any alcohol or drug abuse should be obtained. Of particular importance are psycho-stimulants (e.g., cocaine) because these substances are notorious for inducing jealous reactions.

7. The jealous person's state of mind should be determined. The possibility that the jealousy is symptomatic of an underlying mental disorder, such as schizophrenia or an obsessional disorder, must be thoroughly explored. A thorough evaluation of mood is

necessary because depression can generate jealous preoccupations and can supervene because of the distress associated with jealousy.

8. The risk of violence must be established. An ever-present concern in managing the pathologic jealousies is associated with the possibility that aggressive behavior may be imminent (Daly, Wilson, & Weghorst, 1982; Mowat, 1966; Mullen & Maack, 1985). Therefore, it is important to acquire information about the jealous person's violent impulses, desires, and fantasies, as well as past and recent acts of aggression (Table 11.4).

Table 11.4
ASSESSING RISK OF VIOLENCE

Ask directly about:

• Destruction of property (particularly the partner's personal and valued possessions)

• Pushing, shoving, and shaking

• Blows with hands, fists, or feet—how administered

• Throwing of objects at partner

• Throttling

• Attacks with weapons, be they blunt instruments, knives, other sharp objects, or guns

• Any other action that could have inflicted harm (e.g., poisoning, driving at them, interfering with the other's vehicle)

For each act of violence, the context, the damage inflicted, the damage intended, and the frequency of the behavior must be determined.

Inquiries into suicidal impulses and acts should be made, because of the importance of self-damaging acts in jealousy and because of their association with aggression against the partner. Threats, commonly uttered by the jealous person, should always be treated seriously, even though we have painfully little data as to what weight to assign to such threats. In assessing violence, almost more than anywhere else, direct and detailed questions are necessary. Most people will avoid offering accounts of their own aggression and take every opportunity to obfuscate any account they do provide. Oddly, however, many will answer direct questions that offer no legitimate opening for avoidance.

MANAGING JEALOUSY

Although jealousy is a relatively common clinical problem, it has attracted no systematic studies of therapeutic management. The literature consists of single case studies, small series in which a particular treatment modality has been used, and the sharing of clinical impressions by those involved in working with jealous clients. The management of reactive jealousy is currently dominated by a combination of cognitive and couples therapies often developed in other contexts and applied with varying degrees of coherence to jealousy. Well-articulated psychodynamic theories date back to Freud (Freud, 1955; Schmiedenberg, 1953; Seeman, 1979), but today these theoretical structures are in eclipse as guides to treatment—at least in the published papers, if not in consulting rooms and clinics. The pathologic extensions of jealousy tend to be regarded (at least from a treatment perspective) by therapists as special cases either of delusional disorder or OCD. In the symptomatic jealousies, particularly those in which the underlying disorder is schizophrenia or affective psychosis, the jealousy is often virtually ignored. Treatment often proceeds for the primary disorder without adequate attention paid to the client's preoccupations with infidelity and accompanying potential for violence.

Clinicians must be constantly attuned to the risks of violence; the risk assessment with regard to violence often dictates the treatment agenda. With couples whose relationship has already been marred by significant violence, it is often advisable to urge separation, at least until the jealousy has been resolved; in practice, this advice is often rejected by both partners. An ethical dilemma and a potential legal liability are created when violence is possible but the couple refuses to separate. At the very least, detailed notes of your advice and its rejection should be kept; some clinicians may prefer to decline to continue treatment in a context they believe risks serious violence. In symptomatic jealousies with an underlying psychotic condition, the issue of compulsory detention and treatment is raised by violence. My own prejudice in these cases is to err on the side of caution by resorting to early admission, despite the frequent consequence of a short-term exacerbation in symptoms.

The issue of whether the jealous person should be managed individually or with the partner can be resolved by the nature of the jealousy (e.g., symptomatic versus reactive), the imminence of the threat of violence, the clinician's usual practice, and the couple's preference. At the very least, the partner should be seen regularly by the treating clinician or by a colleague with whom free communication has been negotiated in advance. I advise against entering into an agreement with either partner to keep in confidence what is divulged by one partner about the jealousy or immediately relevant matters; this leads to collusion, intensifying the problem rather than resolving it.

Normal Jealous Reactions:

Jealousy that may be within the normal limits for the person and his or her culture may, nevertheless, be sufficiently distressing for that person (or the couple) to seek treatment. In Western societies, wherein jealousy is increasingly viewed not simply as an unwelcome experience but as a state of mind indicative of personal pathology or inadequacy, the search for therapy to relieve and resolve jealousy is relatively common (Mullen, 1991).

The therapeutic goals espoused in the clinical literature for jealous reactions are summarized in Table 11.5. Therapeutic strategies that incorporate such goals can address the personal level at which the characteristics of the jealous person are of prime concern; the situational level, which focuses on what provoked and maintains the jealousy; and the relationship level, which involves the couple's joint responsibility and interactions (Clanton & Smith, 1977).

Table 11.5
THERAPEUTIC GOALS IN MANAGING JEALOUS REACTIONS

- Challenging irrational beliefs and assumptions
- Improving communication skills to facilitate general everyday interactions, particularly with the partner
- Facilitating negotiations over limits on behaviors
- Building self-esteem in the jealous person
- Resolving relationship conflicts conducive to jealousy
- Reformulating the meaning of jealousy to provide less malignant, if not actually positive, connotations
- Developing better coping responses
- Increasing the symmetry of power relationships in the couple
- Clarifying relationship expectations and issues of dependency
- Exploring issues of current and future commitment to the relationship

---

Individual Approaches

The manifestation of jealousy reflects personal vulnerabilities and peculiarities. Improving the self-esteem of the jealous person is both a way of dealing with the current crisis and of offering some bulwark against recurrence. Behavioral approaches focus primarily on the jealous person's actions and responses. Desensitization of the person to the "traumatic scene" that lies at the core of the jealousy is claimed to remove the jealousy (Pines, 1992a). This can be attained by variants of graded imaginal exposure or its opposite, flooding, in which the jealous client is instructed to think repeatedly about the feared event until the distress is reduced.

Some researchers (Mathes, 1991; Tarrier, Beckett, Harwood, & Bishay, 1990; White & Mullen, 1989) have attempted to derive a cognitive theory of jealousy that, from a therapeutic standpoint, focuses on the way the jealous person understands and constructs the supposed infidelity (primary appraisal) and considers responses either to restore the relationship or to punish the unfaithful partner (secondary appraisal). The coping strategies that emerge from the appraisals will determine whether a successful resolution or escalating conflict occurs. Therapy aims at helping the jealous person reappraise the relationship in a more productive manner and engage in more effective coping strategies.

Situational Approaches

The realities underlying the fears of the jealous person need clarification as much as possible. The suspicions of infidelity may be groundless or may not represent an ongoing threat to the relationship.

One technique that may be helpful is to reframe jealousy by teaching the client to use less pejorative language (Teismann, 1979). This strategy accentuates the healthier aspects of jealousy: concern for the relationship, fear of loss, passionate commitment, and disappointment over dashed hopes and dreams can be emphasized. If the partner has been unfaithful, that action can be reframed in terms of regret, error, and desire not to hurt. Indeed, an affair may even be considered a cry for help, with the erring partner struggling to regain contact with the partner (Constantine, 1986). The real deprivations and anxieties associated with infidelity must be acknowledged, just as the exaggerated and mistaken ascriptions must be challenged and corrected.

Relationship Approaches

In cases of reactive jealousies, therapeutic strategies that ignore the relationship rarely succeed — because both partners contribute to jealousy. One partner may inadvertently enhance the insecurity of the other by appearing to value more highly the company or advice of others. Some may even intentionally provoke suspicion to attract attention or pander to their own needs for reassurance about their own attractiveness. As Proust (1980) noted, "A little jealousy is not unpleasant. . . for it enables people who are not inquisitive to take an interest in others, or in one other at any rate." Once jealousy is established, it becomes part of the relationship system, with both partners adapting their behavior and responses. Such adaptations can be counterproductive, in the case of the suspected partner who becomes increasingly cautious about giving any excuse for suspicion. In so doing, the suspected person becomes secretive, thereby drawing attention to the very suspicions that he or she was trying to circumvent.

Systems therapists see jealousy as rooted in destructive, self-reinforcing patterns of interaction; therefore, they focus on correcting responses and behaviors that evoke, reinforce, and maintain jealousy rather than on either the individual's personality and history or on the concrete reality to which the jealousy is a response (Pines, 1992b; White, 1991). This viewpoint supports the notion that whether an affair is a form of communication or a form of escape, the jealousy it triggers is always a relationship issue and always serves a function within the relationship, even in delusional jealousy (Friedman,

1989). Constantine (1986) suggested jealousy is a warning to both partners that their relationship needs to be reexamined and, most likely, renegotiated.

A common initial therapeutic ploy is to decrease the interrogations and checking of the jealous person by negotiating set times for inquiry (Marks & De Silva, 1991). As a result, the time allowed for expressions of jealousy is steadily reduced. Conversely, the suspected partner may be instructed to flood the jealous person with tedious accounts of his or her activity in the hope of extinguishing concerns about infidelity.

Paradox has been developed as a therapeutic strategy in couples therapy: instead of discouraging interrogating behavior, the therapist may suggest that *both* partners assert their respective roles (Im, Wilner, & Breit, 1983). Such paradox may be pushed further by suggestions that "your torturing each other and yourselves shows just how strongly you need each other and gives your relationship a real intensity," (Crow & Ridley, 1990). Instead of attempting to "cure" the jealous partner, this approach (like much therapy based on systems approaches) aims to validate jealousy as a legitimate communication that reflects the behaviors and perceptions of both partners.

Role playing and role reversal also have been advocated for increasing mutual insight, desensitizing, and improving coping strategies (Ard, 1977; Constantine, 1986; De Silva, 1987). An interesting variant of role reversal requires each partner to write defenses of the other's conduct (Pines, 1992a). Exaggerating the conflict to the point of absurdity has been recommended (Im et al., 1983), but is not suitable for many couples.

Conjoint therapy to improve the overall functioning in a relationship is integral to most treatment strategies designed to focus on the relationship. Couples therapy aims to improve communication skills and resolve long-standing relationship conflicts that may induce jealousy. Jealousy often emerges in a context of asymmetrical power relationships. Jealous persons perceive themselves as more vulnerable to desertion or as overly dependent because of limited access to alternative social support or financial resources. Jealousy amplifies the power disparities by placing the jealous person in the role of the discarded supplicant, but provides an element of retribution and an opportunity to express resentment. Couples therapy can expose the power discrepancies and encourage negotiation toward a more equitable relationship and an acknowledgment of the mutuality of dependence. Couples therapy is only productive in resolving jealousy when both partners espouse a commitment to the relationship. Otherwise, the only way forward is to extricate the partners from the relationship while minimizing the damage and distress.

Pathologic Reactions:

The exaggerated behavior and psychological responses in pathologic reactions create greater risks of harm to the partner and, in some cases, generate self-destructive behavior. The morbid nature of pathologic jealousies is largely derived from the characteristics of the jealous individual. Even though relationship approaches are often helpful, they are rarely sufficient. If the excessive response is fostered and sustained by a disorder such as depression, treatment of the concomitant disorder greatly facilitates resolution. Depression should be treated early and vigorously in jealousy; although it is often a response to the distress of jealousy (rather than playing any role in its genesis), it nevertheless prolongs the jealous state and increases the risk of violence.

The presence of marked disorders of personality (particularly those characterized by excessive suspiciousness, oversensitivity, and narcissism) is a major therapeutic challenge. The clinician must attempt to ameliorate the jealousy in the short term, often relying on clarification, reassurance, and support; he or she should abandon attempts to work on the personality difficulties until the crisis has subsided. These individuals, particularly if also impulsive and prone to antisocial behavior, are at high risk of acting violently and are not candidates for the more confrontational and provocative therapeutic strategies.

In clinical practice, what is often striking about pathologic jealous reactions is not just the vehemence of the expressed jealousy but the imperviousness of the sufferer to reassurance or reasoned argument. There is an apparent need to check on the partner, test his or her fidelity, and incessantly review past events, despite the obvious pain it produces in both partners. The obsessive quality of such jealousy been treated by treatment approaches used for OCD, with anecdotal claims of considerable success.

Pathologic reactions may be fueled by previous experiences of desertion and betrayal that have left a legacy of distrust and oversensitivity. Although the continuing influence of the past is usually apparent to the therapist, jealous persons do not realize how their learned expectations have shaped their opinions on infidelity into a self-fulfilling prophecy. Helping the jealous person disentangle present reality from the echoes of the past can ameliorate the jealousy.

Substance abuse, particularly involving alcohol, may precipitate morbid jealousy. This can occur for a variety of reasons:

- Especially suspicious of their partners, substance abusers are never far from operating in a world governed by paranoia.

- Chronic alcohol abusers may seek to blame sexual dysfunction associated with drinking on their partner's disinterest.

- Damaged self-esteem and guilt can leave the addicted person expecting rejection and desertion.

Control of the underlying addiction nearly always ameliorates, if not removes, the pathologic jealous reactions.

The Symptomatic Jealousies:

In theory, symptomatic jealousies should resolve when the

underlying disorder is treated. But in practice, the underlying disorder (e.g., schizophrenia) may be one in which it is difficult to induce full remission. However, the jealousy — though initiated by the illness — may persist despite the abatement of the other symptoms. In such cases, some of the techniques for managing reactive jealousies may be useful. The emergence of jealousy may well have created distress in the partner and may jeopardize the future of the relationship. This should be addressed during the recovery and rehabilitative phase of management (Table 11.6).

Table 11.6
THERAPEUTIC GOALS IN MANAGING SYMPTOMATIC JEALOUSY

- Vigorous treatment of the underlying disorder (where possible)

- If delusions of infidelity are present, administration of antipsychotic medication

- Clarification, and, in suitable cases, confrontation of the misinterpretations that sustain the preoccupations with infidelity

- When appropriate, joint sessions to repair damage to the relationship and, if possible, to modify elements that may have encouraged and sustained the jealousy

- Constant monitoring and response to risks of violence, primarily to partner but also to self

---

Jealous preoccupations, particularly delusions of infidelity, may emerge in organic disorders ranging from thyroid dysfunction to multiple sclerosis. In many cases, the primary pathology is irreversible, but this does not mean the jealousy is untreatable. Delusions of infidelity must be managed independently of the initiating disorder in almost all situations. In depressive illness accompanied by delusions, it is usually not sufficient to rely on antidepressants and other management strategies directed at the mood disorder; for optimal response, treatment should be directed at the delusions, usually in the form of antipsychotic medication.

> A patient presented with delusions of infidelity that emerged in the context of thyrotoxicosis. Effective treatment of her endocrine condition was not sufficient to end her jealous pre-occupations, but she responded to low doses of an antipsychotic agent in the context of regular psychotherapy. She was weaned off psychotropic medication over the subsequent 6 months and discharged. She presented about 4 years later with delusions of infidelity and was again found to be thyrotoxic, on this occasion because of a prescribing error. The thyroid imbalance was rapidly corrected, but it took many months for the delusions to cease.

In disorders where delusions of infidelity form the core of the clinical picture, good results have been claimed for mild to moderate doses of antipsychotics, with pimozide (Orap) appearing to be particularly effective (Hoaken, 1976; Munro, 1984). Regular supportive psychotherapy is necessary to maintain compliance because it is not easy to persuade someone that by taking a pill their partner's supposed flagrant infidelity will improve.

When suspicions of infidelity form the central feature of OCD, treatments developed for OCD (both pharmacologic and psychological) may be applied to remedy morbid jealousy. The interest in the efficacy of antidepressants in OCD, particularly the selective serotonin reuptake inhibitors (SSRIs), has led to their exhibition in morbid jealousy. Some single case studies (Gross, 1991; Lane, 1990; Wright, 1994) and a series of six cases by Stein and et al. (1994) suggest some moderate efficacy both of the SSRIs alone and in combination with antipsychotics. It is likely that over the next few years, we will see the results of applying SSRIs to pathologic jealous reactions as well as those clearly related to OCD pathology, but currently all that can be said is that the published papers suggest a possible efficacy.

CONCLUSION

Jealousy is a common clinical problem for which treatment options remain problematic. In practice, it is wise to draw from a range of therapeutic strategies tailored to the needs and peculiarities of the specific client. Jealousy challenges many of the currently fashionable assumptions about the nature of psychiatric disorders. Only by combining a range of individual and conjoint therapies can we hope to obtain optimal results.

REFERENCES

American Psychiatric Association. (1994). *Diagnostic and statistical manual of mental disorders* (4th ed.). Washington, DC: Author.

Ard, B. N. (1977). Avoiding destructive jealousy. In G. Clanton & L. G. Smith (Eds.), *Jealousy* (pp. 166-169). Englewood Cliffs, NJ: Prentice-Hall.

Bleuler, E. (1924). *Textbook of psychiatry* (A. A. Brill, Trans.). New York: Macmillan.

Clanton, G., & Smith, L. G. (Eds.). (1977). *Jealousy.* Englewood Cliffs, NJ: Prentice-Hall.

Cobb, J. P., & Marks, I. M. (1979). Morbid jealousy featuring as obsessive-compulsive neurosis: Treatment by behavioural psychotherapy. *British Journal of Psychiatry, 134,* 301–305.

Constantine, L. L. (1986). Jealousy and extramarital sexual relationships. In N. S. Jacobson & A. S. Gurman (Eds.), *Clinical handbook of marital therapy* (pp. 407-427). New York: Guilford Press.

Crow, M. J., & Ridley, J. (1990). *Therapy with couples.* Oxford, UK: Basil Blackwell.

Daly, M., Wilson, M., & Weghorst, S. J. (1982). Male sexual jealousy. *Ethology and Sociobiology, 3,* 11–27.

De Silva, P. (1987). An unusual case of morbid jealousy treated with role reversal. *Sexual and Marital Therapy, 2,* 319–326.

Freud, S. (1955). Some neurotic mechanisms in jealousy, paranoia and homosexuality. In J. Strachey (Ed.), *Standard edition of the works of Freud* (Vol. 12, pp. 221-232). London, UK: Hogarth Press.

Friedman, S. (1989). Strategic reframing in a case of delusional jealousy. *Journal of Strategic and Systematic Therapies, 8,* 1–4.

Gross, M. D. (1991). Treatment of pathological jealousy by fluoxetine. *American Journal of Psychiatry, 148,* 683–684.

Hoaken, P. C. A. (1976). Jealousy as a symptom of psychiatric disorder. *Australian and New Zealand Journal of Psychiatry, 10,* 47–51.

Im, W., Wilner, R. S., & Breit, M. (1983). Jealousy interventions in couples therapy. *Family Process, 22,* 211–219.

Jaspers, K. (1910). Eifersuchswahn: Zeitschrift far die gesamte. *Neurologie und Psychiatrie, 1,* 567–637.

Jaspers, K. (1963). *General psychopathology* (7th ed., J. Hoenig & M. W. Hamilton, Trans.). Manchester, England: Manchester University Press.

Lane, R. D. (1990). Successful fluoxetine treatment of pathological jealousy. *Journal of Clinical Psychiatry, 51,* 345–346.

Mairet, A. (1908). *La jalousie: Etude psycho-physiologique, clinique et méico-legale.* Paris, France: Montpellier.

Marks, M., & De Silva, P. (1991). Multifaceted treatment of a case of morbid jealousy. *Sexual and Marital Therapy, 6,* 71–78.

Mathes, E. W. (1991). A cognitive theory of jealousy. In P. Salovey (Ed.), *The psychology of jealousy and envy* (pp. 52-78). New York: Guilford Press.

Mooney, H. (1965). Pathological jealousy and psychochemotherapy. *British Journal of Psychiatry, 111,* 1023–1042.

Mowat, R. R. (1966). *Morbid jealousy and murder*. London, UK: Tavistock Press.

Mullen, P. E. (1991). Jealousy: The pathology of passion. *British Journal of Psychiatry, 158,* 593–601.

Mullen, P. E., & Maack, L. H. (1985). Jealousy, pathological jealousy and aggression. In D. P. Farrington & J. Gunn (Eds.), *Aggression and dangerousness* (pp. 103-126). New York: Wiley.

Mullen, P. E., & Martin, J. (1994). Jealousy: A community study. *British Journal of Psychiatry, 164,* 35–43.

Munro, A. (1984). Excellent response of pathological jealousy to pimozide. *Canadian Medical Association Journal, 131,* 852–853.

Parrot, W. G. (1991). The emotional experience of envy and jealousy. In P. Salovey (Ed.), *The psychology of jealousy and envy* (pp. 3-30). New York: Guilford Press.

Pines, A. M. (1992a). Romantic jealousy: Five perspectives and an integrative approach. *Psychotherapy, 29,* 675–683.

Pines, A. M. (1992b). *Romantic jealousy: Understanding and conquering the shadow of love*. New York: St. Martin's Press.

Proust, M. (1980). *Remembrance of things past* (F. Scott & T. Kilmartin, Trans.). New York: Random House.

Rasmussen, S. A., & Eisen, L. E. (1992). The epidemiology and differential diagnosis of obsessive-compulsive disorder. *Journal of Clinical Psychiatry, 53*(suppl.), 4–10.

Schmiedenberg, M. (1953). Some aspects of jealousy and of feeling hurt. *Psychoanalytic Review, 15,* 1–16.

Seeman, M. V. (1979). Pathological jealousy. *Psychiatry, 42,* 351–361.

Shepherd, M. (1961). Morbid jealousy: Some clinical and social aspects of a psychiatric symptom. *Journal of Mental Science, 107,* 607–653.

Soyka, M., Naber, G., & Völcher, A. (1991). Prevalence of delusional jealousy in different psychiatric disorders. *British Journal of Psychiatry, 158,* 459-553.

Stein, D. J., Hollander, M. D., & Josephson, S. C. (1994). Serotonin reuptake blockers for the treatment of obsessional jealousy. *Journal of Clinical Psychiatry, 55,* 30–33.

Tarrier, N., Beckett, R., Harwood, S., & Bishay, N. (1990). Morbid jealousy: A review and cognitive behavioural formulation. *British Journal of Psychiatry, 157,* 317–326.

Teismann, M. W. (1979). Jealousy: Systematic, problem-solving therapy with couples. *Family Process, 18,* 151–160.

Vauhkonen, K. (1968). On the pathogenesis of morbid jealousy. *Acta Psychiatrica Scandinavica Supplement 202.*

White, G. L. (1991). Self, relationship, friends and family: Some applications of systems theory to romantic jealousy. In P. Salovey (Ed.), *The psychology of jealousy and envy* (pp. 231-251). New York: Guilford Press.

White, G. L., & Mullen, P. E. (1989). *Jealousy, theory, research, and clinical strategies.* New York: Guilford Press.

Wright, S. (1994). Familial obsessive-compulsive disorder presenting as pathological jealousy successfully treated with fluoxetine. *Archives of General Psychiatry, 31,* 430–431.

12

Mutuality in Couples Therapy

Paula Schneider, PhD, MSW

Dr. Schneider is Associate Professor of Social Work at Regis College, Weston, MA, and practices couples therapy in Chestnut Hill, MA.

KEY POINTS

- Recent research indicates that relationship behaviors are, in part, attributable to gender differences.

- Gender identification can significantly influence intimate relationships by imposing rigidly defined social and psychological roles on individuals. This can cause conflict in a marriage if different expectations are brought into the relationship.

- Gender identification can also be a source of sexism. The combination of the two can cause marital problems if the man and woman have different views on intimacy. Dynamics that contribute to self-esteem are gender related.

- A primary goal of nonsexist couples therapy is mutuality: helping a man and woman determine what they wish to do, feel, or represent to one another with a high level of concern and mutual respect.

- Therapists helping couples move toward mutuality need to emphasize mutual empathy that goes beyond the individuals and encompasses goals for the relationship itself.

- Although it is important for couples in therapy to establish reciprocity, this will not suffice for the attainment of a truly mutual relationship. Individuals must learn to balance their own self-interest with interest in nurturing the relationship and be aware that they are doing so.

INTRODUCTION

Joyce and Larry, a dual career couple in their early 30s, presented a list of complaints against each other on entering therapy. Both agreed that communication skills represented a major deficit in their relationship. Joyce described how Larry "puts her down" in front of guests and friends. Larry said that Joyce does not stop badgering him, even after he apologizes, and that she is always asking him to do tasks around the house when he is tired from work. Joyce reported that whenever she attempted to have a discussion about their relationship or suggested that Larry play with their child, he tended to "blow sky high."

Joyce and Larry are typical of those who seek help in dealing with the communicative conflicts that can disrupt new marital relationships. Expressions of anger and hostility, withdrawal, shouting, and tears are frequently concomitants to the disappointment and fear of abandonment they may also experience. At this point, most partners know what kind of relationship they do *not* want, but they are uncertain about what to substitute for the conflict and confusion.

Sexism is defined by *Mirriam Webster's Collegiate Dictionary* (1993, p. 1073) as "prejudice or discrimination based on sex; esp[ecially] discrimination against women." Although it is usually portrayed as a societal and institutional attitude expressed in the workplace and between strangers, couples therapists commonly see this phenomenon manifested in patterns of domination and subordination within marriages. Sexism expressed in intimate relationships results from and reinforces rigidly defined social and psychological roles that reflect each partner's gender identification. Unless couples recognize and deal with gender difference appropriately, it inevitably inhibits the intimacy that most couples anticipate when they marry (Schneider & Schneider, 1991).

Knowledge of men's and women's relational development has expanded in the past few years. Recently, self-psychology theory, which was developed solely by men but assumed to be applicable to both men and women, has been studied and

augmented by increasing knowledge about women's development to include the "self-in-relation" theory (Jordan, 1991).
Based on the idea that women's sense of self becomes organized around their need for affiliation and relationships (Miller,
1986), the self-in-relation theory has emerged from the work of
a group of mental health professionals at the Stone Center for
Developmental Services and Studies of Wellesley College (Jordan, Kaplan, Miller, Stiver, & Surrey, 1991). Bergman and
Surrey (1992) have applied these ideas to their work with
helping men and women struggle toward mutuality. Couples
therapists must educate clients about the nature of men's and
women's conflicts with each other and provide strategies for
understanding and working toward their resolution (Lerner,
1989a, 1989b; Markman, 1991; Weiner-Davis, 1993).

MUTUALITY AS A MAIN GOAL OF COUPLES THERAPY

Therapists can help couples mitigate the results of social and
psychological gender role entrenchment by assisting couples
to develop mutuality in their relationships. The *American
Heritage Dictionary* defines mutual as "having the same relationship each to the other"; the term "is properly applied to
what two persons do, feel, or represent to each other." The goal
of the nonsexist therapist is to help the man and woman
determine what they wish to do, feel, or represent to one
another with a high level of concern and mutual respect.

How Gender Identification Contributes to Marital Conflict:

Feldman (1986, p. 345) described how gender identification
and role conditioning affect the marital relationship:

Male role conditioning inhibits the development of emotional
expressiveness and stimulates intellectualization and passive-
aggressive behavior (e.g., ignoring one's spouse, forgetting

important dates, and physical aggression). Female conditioning inhibits the development of cognitive expressiveness and
mature independence and stimulates the development of excessive emotionality, excessive dependency, and verbal aggression (e.g., nagging, complaining, and criticizing).

Gender discrepancies between men and women are often
manifest in differing—or even conflicting—expectations of
the marital relationship, as illustrated by the following case:

By the time John and Barbara, a couple in their late 40s, sought
therapy, they were each feeling disappointed and angry with
their relationship. John held a professional position but did not
earn a sufficient income for the life-style of upper-middle-class
couples. John had told Barbara that if their relationship did not
improve, he would consider separation and divorce.

John felt estranged from and constantly criticized by Barbara.
She was not interested in having sexual relations with him,
which made him sad and angry. Barbara wanted to go out for
dinner and to the movies, but John rarely agreed. She perceived him as "withholding." He was impatient with her constant complaining about housework and the responsibilities of
being a wife and mother. She said, "My life is going nowhere.
I spend so much of my time doing the work of a maid. John
doesn't spend most of his time doing janitor's work."

Barbara had writing talents, but she would require several
years of training to hold a job in this field. The responsibility of
caring for her children, John, and the house without much
money was a constant source of pressure and anxiety. She was
resentful both that John did not make enough money to allow
her to train for a career in her field of interest and that he was
unsupportive of her interest in writing. On the other hand,
Barbara was ambivalent about giving up some of her dependency and identification as a traditional wife and mother. She
felt that working outside of the home would inappropriately
make her career more important than her children, a mistake
she felt her mother had made. If she remained at home, however, she would not have funds to pursue courses in writing.

She felt that her current situation left her with no chance to enhance her self-esteem or position in the family.

John, too, was experiencing conflict about his role as husband and father. He felt unrewarded by his job, and he thought his provider role was burdensome. Therefore, he was somewhat baffled that Barbara behaved as if he had some kind of privilege and prerogative she did not. Moreover, his gender identification was confused by the fact that his father was a withdrawn alcoholic. His mother was controlling; she imposed her expectations on John rather than acknowledging his inclinations and abilities.

Two variables in John and Barbara's situation, which evolve from sexism and gender identification, led directly to their marital conflict: (a) men and women have differing views of intimacy, and (b) the dynamics that contribute to self-esteem are likely to be gender related.

Women frequently define intimacy in terms of talking about thoughts and feelings, whereas men tend to define it more as sexual closeness. This dynamic was dramatized particularly well in the film *Scenes from a Marriage*. In a moving scene, Liv Ullman appears happy as she talks to her husband, until she realizes that he has dozed off — which leaves her disappointed and angry. In the case of Barbara and John, Barbara wanted John to continue courting her, to *talk* with her, and to take an interest in her thoughts and feelings. John wanted Barbara to show an interest in him by being as eager for sex as he was. John sought physical closeness; Barbara needed verbal foreplay.

The extent to which these respective needs are met affects each person's sense of self. Many men seem to feel satisfied *simply by knowing* that they are "in a relationship"; their self-esteem is more closely associated with concrete achievements than with feeling connected through verbal exchange. Miller (1986), Jordan (1991), and Stiver (1984) explained that women invest more in and anchor more of their identity in relationships than do men.

For many women, conversation seems to be the major

symbol for closeness. Barbara needed a context from which to feel intimate. She was rarely interested in sex unless she and John had felt close after doing a pleasant activity together — a walk, dinner in a restaurant, or having an interesting discussion. John was socialized to value independence and autonomy; as a result, he tended to back away from close relationships.

Several authors (Doyle, 1983; Feldman, 1986; Goldberg, 1976; Gould, 1980) have discussed the difficulties men have in grappling with the conflicting demands of traditional and contemporary gender-related expectations. Goldberg (1976, p. 11) suggested that:

> The male has paid a heavy price for his masculine 'privilege' and power. He is out of touch with his emotions and his body. Only a new way of perceiving himself can unlock him from old destructive patterns and enrich his life.

Doyle (1983, p. 16) described the conflict and the confusion that men experience today as follows:

> Society has neither totally abandoned its traditional view of the male role nor has it adopted a completely new version of what it means to be a male in a society where oppression of women and sexism are on the wane. Consequently, men are pulled from many directions. One side says be strong and dominant and the other says be gentle and warm.

For women, self-esteem is enhanced by feelings of connectedness (Gilligan, 1988). When the need for connectedness exists in an unreciprocated way, the negative behavior (as described above) contributes to conflict and marital distress. Women's need for connectedness leaves them vulnerable to fear of abandonment and feeling less powerful in their relationships. "What is immediately apparent from studying the characteristics of the two groups (men and women) is that mutually enhancing interaction is not probable between unequals. Indeed, conflict is inevitable" (Miller, 1986, p. 12).

GENDER IDENTIFICATION AS A SOURCE OF SEXISM

Chodorow (1978) suggested that male development is more complicated than female development because of the difficult shifts of identification that a boy must make to attain his expected gender identification and gender role assumption. She argued that a girl's gender and gender role identification processes are continuous with her earliest identifications and a boy's are not. The psychodynamic hypothesis is that the resolution of the oedipal triangle is best accomplished through the male child's separation from his mother. This allows him to become an autonomous, mature person who meets a societal definition of the masculine role, which is best accomplished through identification with his father. There is no mention, however, of the costs the boy must suffer in having also given up his primary identification with the mother as a repository and purveyor of affective capacities.

Bergman (1991) stated that the separation and individuation that are expected of men involve more than turning away from mother; they also entail turning away from *the process of connection.* That is, boys may never learn to attend and respond to others' feeling states — or they unlearn it as they have more activity with peers. This hypothesis could account for men's tendency to avoid situations in which they can be connected by discussion of feelings. Men must have different affective characteristics from their mothers to feel masculine. The result is that they are so different from their women partners that they find it difficult to connect.

The female child resolves the triangular conflict through her identification and continuous emotional involvement with her mother. Women thus have the capacity to be connected with others, which is demonstrated in the quality of their affective and emotional ties. The costs of women's great desire for affiliations through the years have involved low expectations relative to work, intellectual, and cultural achievements; the loss to society can be seen in the possibility that decisions may be made without the infusion of a woman's perspective. These low expectations have been supplanted with expectations that women continue to function in the home with the same competence and expertise that they did before they pursued professions and occupations.

Men and women assume different gender roles and relational capacities because, even though women's situations have been changing rapidly, they are still differently situated in society relative to reproduction, economics, and sexual activity. Even this late in the 20th century, women's identification and behavior are still primarily related to their reproductive capacities (Bernard, 1972; Chodorow, 1978; Miller, 1986).

DOMINATION AND SUBORDINATION AS A MANIFESTATION OF SEXISM

Throughout modern Western history, women have been socialized to be subordinate to men in social, economic, and romantic relationships. Miller (1986) discussed the relationship between domination, subordination, power, and conflict, and the way each of these conditions influences the inner experience of individuals, their relationships, and interactions. Those who are in dominant positions have defined acceptable roles for subordinates including passivity, weakness, dependency, lack of initiative, and inability to make decisions. "In general, this cluster includes qualities more characteristic of children than adults — immaturity, weakness, helplessness" (Miller, 1986, p. 7). Subordinates must concentrate on basic survival and therefore are fearful of being open and honest. They know more about the dominant persons because they have become highly attuned to them to be able to predict their pleasure or displeasure. They internalize dominant beliefs more readily if few alternative concepts are available.

The following case of Alice and Roger provides a dramatic example of the way in which sexism contributes to gender differences and is expressed through the domination-subordination theme. Alice, age 30, and Roger, age 34, were referred to therapy by the clergyman who performed their wedding ceremony. Our initial interview notes include the following description of their presenting problem:

> Roger and Alice yell and hit each other frequently. When Alice hits Roger, it is usually in response to his hitting her first. During the session, they described their interaction on a camping trip with his friends. Alice, who is attempting to complete her undergraduate degree, had brought her books on the trip but did not tell Roger that she was going to one of the camp buildings to study because she was afraid that he would be angry and insist that she stay with the group. When he found her, a fight ensued. Alice thought that Roger was treating her like a prized possession and stated that she did not want to be merely an extension of him. He agreed that he was possessive of her but thought that this attitude was appropriate for a husband. He rationalized that he was "proud of her."

During the first stage of therapy, we realized that Alice and Roger's respective attitudes were learned in their families of origin. Roger identified with his father, who yelled at and demeaned his mother to control her. Roger carried the domination further by using physical violence, thereby repeating what he had suffered from his parents as a child. Roger's possessiveness was a common aspect of domination and subordination; that is, he objectified Alice by viewing her as his prized possession.

Women traditionally have identified with the stereotype of the wife's role as subordinate; both Alice and her mother carried out these expectations. As long as Alice maintained her view of herself as inferior and not deserving of any better treatment than what she was receiving, she "walked on egg shells," and could neither change within the marriage nor leave it.

Miller (1986) maintained that the suppression of conflict is destructive because it saps energy and blocks its resolution with a resultant undermining of personal growth and of mutuality in the relationship; she concluded that conflict must be reclaimed as a means toward further growth. Expression of conflict, moreover, provides both persons with an opportunity to learn more about themselves and each other. However, for the woman in the subordinate position, initiating conflict puts her at risk of losing a relationship that most often is a crucial part of her identification as a woman.

Even after extensive therapy, however, Roger could not relinquish his feeling that Alice should remain subordinate to him and make every effort to comply with his desires. In this case, the ultimate effect of therapy (which Roger had, in fact, initiated) enabled each of them to move away from an abusive situation toward areas for their own individual growth, rather than actually bringing them closer to mutuality. Alice became independent, gained confidence in herself, and decided that she no longer had to accept the tension and abuse that was part of her life with Roger.

DEVELOPING MUTUALITY

Reciprocity versus Mutuality:

A reciprocal view of marriage holds that each partner uses the other to increase his or her satisfaction—similar to a trading relationship (Held, 1984). Fish and Fish (1986) suggested that all marital relationships are defined by a reciprocity called the *quid pro quo*.

My experience, on the other hand, indicates that whereas a *quid pro quo* (or "something for something") concept is indeed the basis for much current marital therapy, it is not enough to achieve the degree of respect and intimacy required for a truly mutual relationship. Although a couple and their therapist may initially agree to a relationship characterized primarily by reciprocity, this standard should only hold until the partners can achieve sufficient caring to change behavior on behalf of the relationship.

From Reciprocity to Mutuality:

To help the couple move toward mutuality, therapists should consider emphasizing mutual empathy, which goes beyond each individual in the couple and includes their commonly held goals for the relationship. As Jordan (1991) suggested, mutuality involves each partner appreciating the other person with a special awareness of the other's subjective experience because he or she wants to nurture the relationship as well as the individuals in it. A mutual relationship fosters growth, characterized by mutual empathy, mutual engagement, and mutual empowerment (Bergman & Surrey, 1992).

Mutuality involves balancing each person's self-interest with interest in nurturing the relationship and being aware that one is doing this. A husband might recognize that his relationship with his wife may improve if he is able to encourage her personal development — even when this might require him to relinquish a previous pattern of indifference to her growth. This does not mean, however, that the relationship of mutual concern and respect is contrary to self-interest nor that it requires altruism or charity toward the other person (Held, 1984); to the contrary, each partner experiences a feeling of self-worth in being valued by the other.

The sexual relationship between a man and a woman is an area where the difference between mutuality and reciprocity can be seen most clearly. In a relationship based on mutuality, each partner contributes to the pleasure of the other while his or her own needs are fulfilled. In the ideal situation, there is no *quid pro quo* or self-sacrificing altruism on either partner's part — *both* persons receive pleasure, and the relationship itself is enhanced by such interaction. However, this pattern, although not uncommon in sexual matters, is less prevalent in other areas. "Many men are still unaccustomed to regarding the other-than-sexual needs and satisfactions of the women with whom they make love in terms of the interests and goals of the women themselves" (Held, 1984, p. 209).

In a relation of mutual concern, both partners take pleasure in the self-development and wider satisfactions of the other. This condition can be achieved only through each person having the autonomy necessary to pursue what he or she needs and wants in various areas of his or her life. The respect that one has for the other's autonomy allows him or her to renounce the right to decide what is best for the other.

THERAPEUTIC STRATEGIES FOR MUTUALITY

Larry and Joyce, who were described at the beginning of this chapter, had much to accomplish toward achieving mutuality. Larry felt that his job was more important than Joyce's career. He announced that she could quit her job if she finds housework too much to do when she got home; that is, *his* income is more important to their family. She let him know that she felt her work was as important as his. He told her that she could not dictate the nature of his interaction with their child. His volatility and her attempts at controlling the way he acted in everyday situations had to change if they were to "become friends."

During therapy, we incorporated general ideas and information about gender differences and mutuality among the specific strategies for emotional and communication changes that Larry and Joyce were attempting. To help them perceive the context of gender role development and reduce blaming each other for stereotypical attitudes held in the past, certain behaviors were designated as being related to societal values. The futility of using psychic energy to change one another was discussed, and alternatives for changing their own reactions and behaviors were determined.

The first step was verbally expressing their anger and hostility in a safe, productive manner. Second, they needed to develop constructive ways of handling negative affect. They learned how to express negative feelings about specific behaviors without including insults about the other's personality; they used "I" statements and described the impact on their feelings when they acted in a particular way. We suggested strategies for Larry when he felt overwhelmed with anger. Joyce learned how to contain her anxiety and anger that had previously resulted in her nagging.

To elicit mutual empathy, Joyce and Larry were encouraged to make a specific time to write for 10 minutes, then talk uninterruptedly for 10 minutes, before the other responded. They practiced this strategy in the therapy session first and then implemented it at home. However, the most effective strategy the couple used was not actually structured by the therapy: Joyce went away on business for a week, and Larry had to manage the household — including child care. He greeted her at the plane with comments about his newly acquired understanding of her stress.

Other strategies should, of course, be tailored to the situation of each couple; however, they should be developed deliberately in a context of developing mutuality. Therapists should search for and support strengths in the relationship by discovering with the couple the positive feelings they notice in each other when they are not angry. Each member of the couple should concentrate on his or her own behavior while viewing the relationship as a separate entity.

Relational Impasse:

One of the greatest challenges develops when the couple arrives at what Bergman and Surrey designated as "a relational impasse." This occurs "when a relationship is stuck, static, unmoving, with a sense that it may never move again. It is an interactional situation between the partners and arises more from one relational style meeting the other" (Bergman & Surrey, 1992, p. 5).

In my practice, I have often observed that when a man realizes that he is expected to engage in a discussion about feelings or that he has angered or disappointed his wife, he experiences what Bergman refers to as *dread*. Such men describe it as an unbearable pressure; they subsequently flee physically or withdraw emotionally. Their female partners, meanwhile, become angry, and feel abandoned and misunderstood.

Discussion of the feelings associated with this behavior is the first step toward reducing it. The couple sometimes can trace the content of the problem and the style of discussion to earlier situations, either in their families of origin or earlier in their relationship; this helps them shift from the anger/dread impasse position to a more mutual one.

This kind of behavior is exemplified in the interaction between Anna and Ernest. Anna began the session by saying: "After 20 years, I can no longer tolerate Ernest's distance, lack of communication, and criticism. He stayed away when I needed him to help with my sick parents. He never talks with me about his work or shows any concern about my interests."

Ernest's reaction was a mixture of bewilderment and anger. He responded by saying: "I don't know what she wants from me. Nothing I do is right. She criticizes everything about me. She doesn't appreciate how much pressure I feel from my work."

In the first phase of therapy, Anna did most of the blaming, with a litany of complaints. Ernest responded by defensively expressing frustration and anger. Later on, he withdrew from her for several days.

We were empathic and helped each partner to hear how the other subjectively experienced the same situation. Any expression of annoyance from Anna was transformed in Ernest's mind to a request for action. Anna believed she was entitled to express feelings and was hoping for understanding rather than concrete help. Ernest began asking for clarification about Anna's expectations of him, and Anna consequently became more sensitive in letting Ernest know the difference between simple expressions of feeling and occasions when she wanted something specific from him. He, in turn, began expressing his feelings more directly.

Although Anna said that she wanted Ernest to participate in decision making, he perceived her as being reluctant to negotiate or compromise. He felt that "everything has to be done her way" and that arguing was therefore a waste of time. Anna complained that she was forced to make decisions because Ernest rarely expressed opinions. We helped the couple recognize the futility of this pattern and enabled them to have more complete discussions.

Ernest was baffled about why Anna, a very capable person, needed help with her parents. At first, he was unable to see that efforts to talk with his wife about her feelings at this difficult period could be a demonstration of his caring and concern. We asked Ernest and Anna to tell each other how they would like the other to respond. That is, "Ernest — how would you have liked Anna to ask for your help?" and "Anna — how would you have liked Ernest to respond to your appeal for help?"

After several sessions, Anna began to express herself more calmly and less critically. Her verbal aggression (blaming) was replaced by calm expressiveness. Ernest became more aware of his feelings, could better express them, and began to associate them with particular situations and behaviors from his family of origin and in his relationship with Anna. Although we asked Anna and Ernest to say how they each felt and we encouraged them to respond with clarifying questions and statements, we particularly reinforced expressions of feeling from Ernest and encouraged Anna to do the same.

We also made use of family of origin material to clarify possible reasons for their inability to follow through, which had the effect of removing the feelings of shame or guilt that each partner had incorporated from years of identifying with counterproductive patterns of behavior. It also encouraged the other partner to be empathic. Ernest and Anna were then able to negotiate mutually acceptable alternative behavior.

Because their children had recently grown up and left home, Anna decided to pursue her interest in a women's political group. Ernest was critical of Anna's "wasting her time," an attitude that made Anna feel demeaned. It seemed only fair to her that she could at last devote time to a major personal interest because she had spent the previous 30 years on child rearing. We helped them to see how their behavior was a consequence of traditional sex roles and gender identification, and we continually urged them to understand the feelings that each one's behavior evoked in the other and why.

This approach fostered mutual empathy between Ernest and Anna. Ernest became more respectful of Anna's interest in the political group when he learned how significant it was to value her interests. Anna became more appreciative of Ernest's *attempts* to please her, even if the outcomes were not exactly what she had wanted. Finally, Ernest and Anna expressed their caring and began to function with enough mutual concern and respect to feel that their relationship was more rewarding and to end the therapy.

CONCLUSION AND IMPLICATIONS

In the past few years, therapists and researchers have increasingly acknowledged that relationship behaviors are, to some extent, attributable to gender differences. Political and social changes can reduce the factors that make the gender differences a problem in workplaces and social life; similarly, men and women can recognize, understand, and change the feelings, thoughts, and behaviors that threaten relationships and each partner's psychological well-being. Extensive clinical work and research in this field recently have demonstrated that these differences do not have to create problems if couples can choose constructive ways to work with them. Helping a couple achieve mutuality in their relationship is one way family therapists can help in this endeavor.

Virginia Held, a philosopher and ethical theorist, contributes a philosophical values base to this therapeutic stance. In *Rights and Goods* (1984), she asserted that mutual concern and respect for one another, which ideally have their beginnings in the relationship between a men and women, can ultimately have immense implications for wider social relations. Thus, a couple's mutuality can serve as a paradigm for relationships among people within and outside of their families, among groups, and even among countries.

REFERENCES

Bergman, S. J. & Surrey, J. (1992). *The woman-man relationship: Impasses and possibilities*. Wellesley, MA: The Stone Center, Wellesley College.

Bernard, J. (1972). *The future of marriage*. New York: Bantam Books.

Chodorow, N. (1978). *The reproduction of mothering: Psychoanalysis and the sociology of gender*. Berkeley, CA: University of California Press.

Doyle, J. A. (1983). *The male experience*. Dubuque, IA: William C. Brown.

Feldman, L. B. (1986). Sex-role issues in marital therapy. In N. S. Jacobson & A. S. Gurman (Eds.), *Clinical handbook of marital therapy* (pp. 345–359). New York: Guilford Press.

Fish, R. C., & Fish, L. S. (1986). Quid pro quo revisited. *American Journal of Orthopsychiatry* , 56(3), 371–384.

Gilligan, C. (1988). Speech delivered on the occasion of its convocation, Regis College, Weston, MA.

Goldberg, H. (1976). *The hazards of being male: Surviving the myth of masculine privilege*. New York: Nash Publishing.

Gould, R. E. (1980). Sexual problems: Changes and choices in mid-life. In W. H. Norman, & T. J. Scaramella (Eds.), *Mid-life: Developmental and clinical issues* (pp. 110–127). New York: Bruner/Mazel.

Held, V. (1984). *Rights and goods: Justifying social action*. New York: Free Press.

Jordan, J. V. (1991). The meaning of mutuality. In J. V. Jordan, A. G. Kaplan, J. B. Miller, I. P. Stiver, & J. L. Surrey (Eds.), *Women's growth in connection* (pp. 81-96). New York: Guilford Press.

Jordan, J. V., Kaplan, A. G., Miller, J. B., Stiver, I. P., & Surrey, J. L. (1991). *Women's growth in connection.* New York: Guilford Press.

Lerner, H. G. (1989a). *The dance of anger.* New York: Harper & Row.

Lerner, H. G. (1989b). *The dance of intimacy.* New York: Harper & Row.

Markman, H. J. (1991). Backwards into the future of couples therapy and couples therapy research: A comment on Jacobson. *Journal of Family Psychology, 4*(4), 416–425.

Miller, J. B. (1986). *Toward a new psychology of women.* Boston: Beacon Press.

Mirriam-Webster's collegiate dictionary (10th ed.). (1993). Springfield, MA: Merriam-Webster.

Schneider, P., & Schneider, H. (1991). Mutuality in couples therapy: Addressing sexism in the marital relationship. *American Journal of Family Therapy, 19,* 119–128.

Stiver, I. P. (1984). *The meanings of "dependency" in female-male relationships.* Wellesley, MA: The Stone Center, Wellesley College.

Weiner-Davis, M. (1993). *Divorce busting.* New York: Simon & Schuster.

FOR FURTHER READING

Bergman, S. J. (1991). *Men's psychological development: A relational perspective.* Wellesley, MA: The Stone Center, Wellesley College.

Markman, H. J. (1990). Constructive marital conflict is not an oxymoron. *Behavioral Assessment, 13,* 83–96.

Name Index

Subject Index

A

Abilities tests, 23
Abuse
  physical, 122
  sexual, 121, 122
Acceptance, and divorce, 39
Ackerman Institute for Family
    Therapy, 122
Acquired immunodeficiency syn-
    drome
  See AIDS
Acting out
  by children with AIDS, 134
  example of, 14, 18
Addiction
  See also Substance abuse
  high levels of in children of
    immigrants, 122
  stigma of, 122
Addicts, former, 124
Adolescents, 17
  death of sibling and, 151
  involved in planning postdivorce
    future, 41
  raised by single fathers, 64
  sexuality in stepfamily of, 87
  Socratic view of, 100
  substance abuse in, 99-113
Affection, 210-211
  needed for relationship quality,
    213
  physical, 198
African-Americans, 119
  AIDS and, 133
Aged
  See Elderly
AIDS
  case study, 136-137, 138-140
  course of
    chronic phase, 128-129
    crisis phase, 127-128
    terminal phase, 129-130
  and discrimination, 134
  family therapy interventions for,
    117-144

  mental impairment and, 129
  prevention, 143
  seen as death sentence, 124
Alcohol, 100, 101, 251, 260
Alcoholics, children of, 109
Alcoholism, 12, 14, 18, 100
Alimony, 77, 85
  maintenance, defined, 40
Altruism, self-sacrificing, 277
Alzheimer's disease, 172, 179
Ambivalence, 203
  in intimacy, 202
Anger, 5, 49, 129, 151, 208-209, 227,
    268, 278, 280
  case study, 45
  as consequence of family
    caregiving, 177
  and death of child, 149
  and divorce, 39, 44-46
Antidepressants, 228, 261, 262
Antipsychotics, 262
Anxiety, 227, 228, 229, 257
Arousal, sexual, 192, 225, 232
Assertiveness training, 182
Assessing Risk of Violence *(table)*, 252
Autonomy, 199
  adolescent, 103
  in chronic phase of AIDS, 129
Azidothymidine (AZT), 133
AZT
  See Azidothymidine

B

Babies, born with HIV, 133
Baggage, emotional, 86, 94
Barriers
  physical, 176
  relationship, 6-7
Beavers-Timberlawn Family Evalua-
    tion Scales (BTFES), 19-22, 32
  clarity of expression, 20
  closeness, 20
  empathy, 21-22

Contributors

Sylvie Aubin, MA
Clinical Psychologist at a marital and family consultation clinic in Montreal, and a Ph.D. candidate in Psychology at the University of Quebec.

Dennis A. Bagarozzi, PhD
Director, Human Resource Consultants; Licensed Psychologist and Marriage and Family Therapist who holds a private practice in Altanta, GA and Athens, GA.

Paula P. Bernstein, PhD
Associate Clinical Professor, The University of Colorado Health Sciences Center; and Adjunct Associate Professor, The University of Denver, Denver, CO.

Paul J. Ciborowski, PhD
Associate Professor of Counseling, Long Island University, C. W. Post Campus, Brookville, NY, and Chair of the Brookhaven [NY] Youth Board.

Juanita L. Garcia, EdD
Associate Professor, Department of Gerontology, College of Arts and Sciences, University of South Florida, Tampa, FL.

Leslie A. Gavin, PhD
Assistant Professor, the University of Colorado Health Sciences Center and the National Jewish Center for Immunology and Respiratory Medicine, Denver, CO.

Geoffrey L. Greif, DSW
Professor, School of Social Work, University of Maryland at Baltimore.

Florence W. Kaslow, PhD
Director, Florida Couples and Family Institute, West Palm Beach, FL; Visiting Professor of Medical Psychology in Psychiatry, Duke University Medical Center, Durham, NC; and Visiting Professor of Psychology, Florida Institute of Technology, Melbourne, FL. She was the first president of the International Family Therapy Association.

Jordan I. Kosberg, PhD
Professor, School of Social Work, Florida International University,
North Miami, FL.

Paul E. Mullen, MBBS, DSc, MPhil, FRCPsych, FRANZCP
Director, Forensic Psychiatry Services, Rosanna, Australia; and Professor of Forensic Psychiatry, Monash University, Melbourne, Australia.

William H. Quinn, PhD
Associate Professor, Marriage and Family Program, Department of
Child and Family Development, University of Georgia, Athens, GA.

Marc Ravart, MA
Clinical Psychologist and Sexologist, the Human Sexuality Unit of
Montreal General Hospital, and Ph.D. candidate in Psychology at the
University of Quebec.

Paula Schneider, PhD, MSW
Associate Professor of Social Work, Regis College, Weston, MA, and
practices couples therapy in Chestnut Hill, MA.

Lynda Dykes Talmadge, PhD
Adjunct faculty member, Department of Psychology, Georgia State
University, Atlanta, GA, and Clinical Psychologist in private practice.

William C. Talmadge, PhD
Adjunct faculty member, Department of Psychology, Georgia State
University, Atlanta, GA, and in private practice.

Gilles Trudel, PhD
Professor, Department of Psychology, The University of Quebec,
Quebec, Canada; and Clinical Psychologist, The Behavioral Therapy
Unit, Louis H. Lafontaine Hospital, Montreal, Canada.

Gillian Walker, MSW
Senior faculty member, The Ackerman Institute for Family Therapy,
New York, NY.

For information on other books in
The Hatherleigh Guides series, call the
Marketing Department at Hatherleigh
Press, 1-800-367-2550, or write:
Hatherleigh Press
Marketing Department
420 E. 51st St.
New York, NY 10022